Brushing

Back

Jim Crow

Brushing

Back

Jim Crow

Bruce Adelson

The Integration

of Minor-League

Baseball in the

American South

University Press of Virginia

Charlottesville & London

The University Press of Virginia

© 1999 by Bruce Adelson

All rights reserved

Printed in the United States of America by Thomson-Shore, Inc.

Design and production by Running Feet Books.

First published 1999

∞ The paper used in this publication meets the minimum requirements
of the American National Standard for Information Sciences—Perma-
nence of Paper for Printed Library Materials, ANSI Z39.48-1984.

Permission to use selected letters from the Papers of James W. Morgan,
Mayor Arthur J. Hanes, and Commissioner T. Eugene "Bull" Connor
has been graciously provided by the Department of Archives and
Manuscripts, Linn-Henley Research Library, Birmingham Public Library,
Birmingham, Alabama.

Photograph on title page is from the collections of the Texas/Dallas
History and Archives Division, Dallas Public Library.

Library of Congress Cataloging-in-Publication Data

Adelson, Bruce.

    Brushing back Jim Crow : the integration of minor-league
baseball in the American South / Bruce Adelson.

       p.   cm.

    Includes bibliographical references (p.).

    ISBN 0-8139-1884-7 (cloth : alk. paper)

     1. Minor league baseball—Southern States—History.

2. Afro-American baseball players—Southern States—History.

3. Discrimination in sports—Southern States—History. I. Title.

GV875.A1A34 1999

796.357'64'0975—dc21   98-45122

                                                   CIP

This book is dedicated to my favorite author, my late mother, Sandra Adelson, whose talent and verve inspired me to follow in her footsteps; my wife, Valerie, my father, Melvin, and my sister Marcia, whose enthusiasm, advice, patience, support, and understanding are immeasurably vital to me; and all the men who crossed the white lines.

I'm positive you'll never see any Negro players on teams in Organized Baseball in the South, as long as the Jim Crow laws are in force.

—J. ALVIN GARDNER, TEXAS LEAGUE PRESIDENT, 1946

I think all the black guys who played in the minor leagues at the time were like Jackie Robinson. We didn't eat right, but when we played, we had to have endurance, stamina. There weren't any places for us to eat at certain times at night. You had to eat sometimes when you shouldn't eat. I guess God took care of us. I guess he kept us from doing things that probably could have gotten us killed or hurt. I couldn't have done what Jackie did, because I thought, I shouldn't have to. A guy could come over here from Italy and play, from Mexico and play, from any-where in the world and play. I was born here, and I couldn't play. What the hell was going on?

—WILLIE TASBY, 1997

Contents

Photos follow page 22

Brushing

Back

Jim Crow

Introduction

1951

With one month to go in the baseball season, Virginia's Danville Leafs were finishing a disappointing campaign, mired in the Carolina League's second division. The team's attendance, among the worst in the circuit, mirrored the Leafs' lackluster performance on the field. Consequently, many white fans stayed away from the ballpark, and African Americans, already alienated by the league's color line, invariably numbered no more than a handful in League Park's "colored grandstand."

As August began, several of Danville's wealthiest white citizens, including Leafs owner Jim Peters, decided to shake the town and the surrounding tobacco country out of their summer torpor. To spark greater interest in their team and increase revenues by attracting more fans, particularly African Americans, to League Park, they decided on a stunning course of action—hiring the Carolina League's first African American ballplayer. Jackie Robinson and Larry Doby may have integrated major-league baseball in 1947, but that was up north. This was Dixie, where Jim Crow and segregation still held sway.

Mindful of the era's social constraints, these Danvillians were conscious of their decision's magnitude. Barely a handful of African Americans had played minor-league baseball in the South, and only one had lasted more than a game or two. Hoping to soften segregationists' expected reaction, Danville's leading white citizens selected a known quantity as their line breaker. Nineteen-year-old Percy Miller, a local high school sports star, was someone whom local whites knew and were relatively comfortable with. He came highly recommended by leaders of Danville's black community.

Percy Miller had been a three-sport standout at the city's John B. Langston High School. After barnstorming through the South with a black semiprofessional baseball team, Miller returned home to visit his family, play ball with a local squad, and prepare for college in the fall. But Miller's plans took an unexpected turn one evening when his father approached him with an offer he could not believe—a Leafs contract. Percy listened carefully to what his father had to say. This was the man who had taught him baseball's fine points over many years and many games. Percy could tell this was something his father wanted badly. Nearly fifty years later, Miller still feels the emotion of the moment. "I told him I couldn't do it. I said, 'I'm supposed to be at spring football practice at West Virginia State College on the fifteenth of August.' He was upset. He came back again the next day with a contract. I wanted to go to college . . . But my father didn't want me to go . . . He never got the chance to play pro baseball. He told me what a great opportunity playing for the Leafs was. He just broke down and cried. So I signed."

1953

Nineteen-year-old Hank Aaron had an advantage over Percy Miller: He was not alone when he helped integrate the half-century-old South Atlantic (or Sally) League. The future big-league home run king had two black teammates on the Milwaukee Braves' Jacksonville, Florida, farm team as well as two African American opponents with league rival Savannah, Georgia.

But these numbers did not make Aaron's Sally League season easy. Racial invective regularly rained down from the stands, and white and black fans yelled at one another from their segregated seats. In Augusta, Georgia, hostile spectators hurled rocks at one of Aaron's African American teammates, Horace Garner. When the umpire used the loudspeaker to admonish people not to throw things onto the field, the crowd became even more inflamed. Aaron recalls whites yelling, "Nigger, we're gonna kill you next time. Ain't no nigger gonna squawk on no white folks down here."

Aaron and his compatriots took their revenge that day at the plate. Jacksonville's second baseman stroked five hits, and between the three of them, the team's black trailblazers reached base thirteen out of fourteen times at bat.

For Hank Aaron, the 1953 campaign was an exercise in perseverence, a crusade to prove the naysayers wrong: "I'm sure that the Braves knew we were going to have some problems . . . If we had failed, if we had come south and started arguing, fighting, and not having a good year, there would have been something for the press to talk about . . . It would certainly have been something for everyone to say, 'I told you so.'"

1956

Three years after Hank Aaron's Sally League debut, Felipe Alou left the Dominican Republic to begin his professional baseball career in the United States. A New York Giants minor leaguer, he was slated to open the season in Danville, Virginia. But this plan was dashed when visa difficulties delayed his departure for the United States. When Alou finally arrived at spring training, the Danville squad had already broken camp and was headed north. The only team remaining at the Giants' Florida spring training base was the Evangeline League's Lake Charles Giants. Alou donned a Lake Charles uniform and prepared to begin the season in Louisiana. When Alou and his team left Florida for the Pelican State, he had no idea what awaited him during his rookie baseball campaign.

Unaccustomed to segregation while growing up in the Dominican Republic, Alou learned quickly once in Dixie. Although he spoke no English, he understood that he was not welcome. In 1956, the spread of integration in southern minor-league baseball had not lessened racists' passions for preserving their separate-but-unequal traditions. Against the backdrop of the United States Supreme Court's *Brown v. Board of Education* ruling, which declared school segregation unconstitutional, reactionaries were vigorously fighting inroads into Jim Crow in Louisiana. "When they told me I had to leave Louisiana," Alou recalls, "it took me three days on a Greyhound bus to travel from Lake Charles to Cocoa, Florida. The bus stopped everywhere. When we stopped, I had to find the lines that said Colored People. By the time I found that line and got on the line, the bus was ready to depart. I never had a chance to eat. They gave me twelve dollars, meal money for three days. I arrived in Cocoa with ten-something dollars in my pocket. They used to have machines you could put ten cents or whatever in and you'd get some peanuts. That was my food for three days."

1962

In 1962, the South was still caught in the maelstrom. Racial beatings and lynchings were reported in Birmingham, Alabama; Jackson, Mississippi; and many other cities and towns. Police brutality toward African Americans was public policy in several locales. School integration had been forcibly resisted in Little Rock, Arkansas. While the South still faced its final paroxysm of violence before pleading no contest to further racial integration, there were nonetheless positive developments by 1962. Many hotels and restaurants now catered to both whites and blacks. Several school systems had voluntarily dropped their segregated classrooms. Change had come south, albeit at a heavy price.

In 1962, nine years after Hank Aaron had helped break open the South Atlantic League, Don Buford was in his second Sally campaign. The league and its racial mores had been quite an eye-opener to this native Californian when he played for Columbia, South Carolina, in 1961. But Buford noticed a difference after joining Savannah the following season. In 1962, he stayed in the same hotels as his teammates during road trips. He also perceived a more nuanced shift in racial attitudes. While there was still hostility and racism, Buford detected something else. By achieving on the field and interacting with white fans, African American ballplayers had helped break down ignorance and timeworn stereotypes. "In Savannah, Georgia, I'd take time for kids. We'd sign autographs, give them balls. I'll never forget, there was this one youngster that came in and asked for an autograph. I wrote his name out, said best wishes, signed my name. A few nights later, I found out the kid's the son of a police officer. The officer came up to me and said, 'You know, I'll never forget you for what you did for my kid. You're human. You're nice people.' To me, that was a tremendous feeling. I think that was an influence that was happening a lot, not only with myself but with other players."

Brushing Back Jim Crow explores the lives and times of these men. The sporting and social achievements of Percy Miller, Hank Aaron, Felipe Alou, Don Buford, and their compatriots played a largely unrecognized part in the civil rights struggle that gripped the nation during the 1950s and 1960s. Through the vehicle of America's pastime, African Americans shattered Jim Crow restrictions while simultaneously challenging long-held stereotypes of racial inadequacy. The mere act of hitting, fielding, and pitching alongside white teammates and opponents, often equaling or besting their feats, not only belied notions of black inferiority but also signaled the eventual demise of Jim Crow.

The battle began in the North. In 1947, Jackie Robinson became the first African American to play in the big leagues since the advent of baseball's modern era in the early years of the twentieth century. Robinson's debut sent shock waves across the nation and destroyed major-league baseball's exclusionary racial policy. However, his impact was not as immediate in the South as it was in the cities of the National League, where the Brooklyn Dodgers played baseball. By contrast, in the South of 1947, segregation still held firm in the 175 southern cities and towns hosting minor-league baseball teams in twenty-four leagues spanning the old Confederacy from El Paso, Texas, to Radford, Virginia.

Although the National and American Leagues had grudgingly ended their discriminatory policies by permitting Robinson and the Cleveland Indians' Larry Doby to play in the major leagues, the situation was quite different in the South Atlantic League and Southern Association. In these and other southern minor leagues, African American ballplayers remained unwelcome, Jackie Robinson notwithstanding.

Indeed, the Brooklyn Dodgers were quite conscious of southern racial attitudes when they signed Robinson to his first organized baseball con-tract. In 1946, to further Robinson's baseball training, the Dodgers opted to send him to their Class AAA minor-league affiliate in Montreal rather than to the franchise's AA farm club in Mobile, Alabama. The Dodgers' man-agement believed that Canadians harbored more tolerant racial sensibilities compared to those of white southerners in the United States. The Dodgers simply did not wish to inflame whites in the South of 1946 with the sight of an African American ballplayer playing and living among them.

With Robinson's place in the major leagues secured and the Dodgers enjoying the attention, large crowds, and associated economic benefits resulting from his presence on their roster, team president Branch Rickey cast his attention toward the South in search of additional challenges and financial opportunities. It was at this time that Rickey devised yet another bold stroke, a barnstorming trip by the Dodgers through various southern cities as the team ambled north from spring training in Florida. When Brooklyn took the field in these Dixie locales, local fans would be wit-nessing history—the first interracial, professional team athletic competi-tions ever played there.

In the spring of 1948, the Dodgers played exhibition games in Dallas, Fort Worth, Oklahoma City, Tulsa, and Asheville. At each venue, local officials urged Rickey to include Robinson in the lineup when the Dodgers came to town.

In Fort Worth, more than 15,000 fans filled the local minor-league ball-park. In Dallas, African Americans were permitted to sit in the grandstand for the first time. Black fans there were so excited about catching a glimpse of Robinson, they forced the team to rope off a section of the outfield to accommodate the crush of spectators overflowing the grandstand. African Americans stood six deep behind this barrier for a chance to see whites and blacks playing baseball together on the same field. The Dodgers' Asheville experience dramatically demonstrated that there was a place in southern minor-league baseball for African American ballplayers. On 8 and 9 April, drawn by the alluring prospect of seeing Jackie Robinson, more than 9,000 spectators passed through the turnstiles of Asheville's McCormick Field, which had a seating capacity of under 3,000 to watch two games between the hometown Tourists and the Dodgers. These fans, black and white alike, showed their appreciation for Robinson by welcoming him warmly at the start of the two-game series. Three years later, a record crowd of 6,579 watched Roy Campanella, the African American catcher who followed Robinson to the Dodgers, drive in the winning run in Brooklyn's 9 – 8 victory over Asheville.

The integrated and frequently record-setting crowds that turned out to see Jackie Robinson during the tour convinced Brooklyn president Branch Rickey and others of the potential for integrated professional baseball in the South. America's national pastime was about to begin its confrontation with Jim Crow.

The following season, Rickey and his Dodgers ventured deeper into Dixie by visiting cities in Florida and Georgia. Nineteen forty-nine proved to be even more eventful and profitable than the barnstorming trip of the previous season. Record crowds greeted the Dodgers in West Palm Beach and Miami. This success continued as the team traveled north into Georgia, where, despite Ku Klux Klan threats and other resistance, the Dodgers played to large, appreciative, interracial crowds. In Macon, sixty-four hundred fans filled the four-thousand-seat Luther Williams Field for a chance to catch a glimpse of Jackie Robinson and be a part of history.

Although the Dodgers had generated enthusiastic responses through-out their barnstorming tour, nothing could have prepared the team for what awaited them in Atlanta, the biggest southern city on the spring 1949 agenda. The Dodgers drew nearly fifty thousand fans to a three-game series against the Atlanta Crackers, a Southern Association franchise. They attracted a record-setting twenty-five thousand, nearly double the seating capacity of the local ballpark, for the final game of the set.

Joe B. King, a sportswriter for the *New York World Telegram*, wrote an article for the *Sporting News* in which he aptly summarized the historic nature of the Dodgers' Dixie extravaganza during the team's stopover in Atlanta's Ponce de Leon Park.

The crowd, which was to total 17,794, was about two-thirds Negro. The colored people arrived early and swarmed up the picturesque tree-studded hill in deep center in this unique park, and festooned themselves on the four terraced-tiers of signboards in right field. They also presented a ground rule problem when they bulged the restraining ropes around the outfield, and Earl Mann, Atlanta president, gave the word they might occupy the small bleachers on the third base side, adjoining the grandstand. Then came mob action which even Cecil B. DeMille could only dream of. There must have been a half-dozen unknown sprinters of Jesse Owens caliber leading the charge from right field to left. Negroes thudded from the signboards to join the speeding horde . . . Oh, there was a charge, no doubt, for many went down, . . . from overeagerness to gain a position in the bleachers where no Negro had ever been permitted to sit . . . There was the spot for the spark, if there were to be an incident between whites and blacks, but it passed jovially, in laughter rather than resentment. Mann personally thanked all the white fans as they fled from the bleachers into the grandstand—and he received only one complaint.

The excitement generated in the South by the Dodgers, and later by other touring major-league teams featuring African American ballplayers, such as the Cleveland Indians with Larry Doby and the New York Giants with Willie Mays, led many baseball officials to question the policy of segregation in Dixie's minor leagues. Altruism was often not the driving force behind this inquiry. Indeed, the catalyst for integration of most minor-league franchises was economic.

While many whites had come out to watch the Dodgers in 1948–49, large numbers of black fans, most of whom were not regular attendees of local minor-league games, did so as well. This presented visionary owners with a largely untapped market of potential regular season customers. African Americans were now viewed as sources of substantial new revenues for suddenly cash strapped minor-league teams, and economic woes impelled many franchise owners to take dramatic racial steps forward.

They were now prepared to use the African American entertainment dollar to help halt a minor-league attendance decline from the record-setting levels of the late '40s. This drop-off coincided with two innovations that were changing life in the nation's sunbaked southern region and arguably keeping many fans home—television and air-conditioning.

By 1950, the social and political climate had also changed. Integration was beginning to take hold in many select institutions. The process of desegregating the armed forces had started the previous summer by order of President Harry S. Truman. African Americans began enrolling in more historically all-white colleges and universities and voting in larger numbers. Some southern towns and cities made efforts to limit the activities of the Ku Klux Klan with the passage of antimask laws. In 1950, United States Supreme Court decisions mandated openings in interstate railroad cars and other public accommodations. Baseball integration in the South was also influenced by events in the major leagues. After Jackie Robinson broke the color line, several teams sought to follow the Dodgers' lead by signing their own black ballplayers. With more blacks coming into baseball, either from the Negro leagues or the amateur ranks, teams needed to find room for them. Blacks were playing on minor-league teams in the East, Midwest, Northeast, Far West, and Canada. But virtually all major-league organizations had minor-league affiliates in the South, and it became clear they were handicapped by their inability to send prospects to southern destinations.

Hank Peters, minor-league director for the American League's Kansas City Athletics in the 1950s, recalls the new imperative major-league teams felt to send black ballplayers south:

Integration had taken place primarily at the major-league level and some at AAA, where some of the stars from the Negro leagues went to get a little experience and then were brought up to the major-league level. You were getting pretty much finished products out of the Negro leagues. That as a source began to dry up somewhat. People in baseball recognized the talents of the black athlete and realized you'd have to start paying attention to signing and developing these players. Naturally, the tough places to get into this were in the South. For years, training minor-league teams was done as cheaply as possible, wherever you could find a place to play, where the weather was halfway decent. When I first broke into baseball with the Browns, we trained our players in Pine Bluff, Arkansas. It was pretty goddamned cold in the spring, but it was a place where you could do it on the cheap. Over the years, conditions changed, and the philosophy in how you train players changed, so everybody migrated farther south.

During the American Association's 1949 season, Jim Pendleton (St. Paul) and Ray Dandridge (Minneapolis) became the first African American minor leaguers to play in Louisville, when their teams visited the Bluegrass State. This trend continued in 1950 as black ballplayers appeared for the first time with their white counterparts in several locales throughout the South and Southwest. George Nicholson, for example, played briefly for Phoenix of the Arizona-Texas League in the spring of 1950 before being released. Chico Randolph, a catcher for the Paris (Ill.) Lakers of the eight-team Mississippi–Ohio Valley League, joined his teammates when they played in Paducah, Kentucky. Willie Mays shattered the Interstate League's color barrier on 24 June when his Trenton Giants faced the Hagerstown (Md.) Braves.

By the following season, color lines were briefly shattered in Virginia, Tennessee, and North Carolina. But with the advent of the 1951 baseball season, southerners were witnessing something remarkable: blacks and whites interacting as equals on a regular basis in a common endeavor. This very public display of equality represented a first push against the steel door of racism and segregation that permeated the South at that time. However, it was not until 1952 and 1953 that African Americans enjoyed more than passing stints with southern teams. Those years represented the biggest breakthroughs in obliterating color lines, with many ballplayers spending entire seasons and experiencing great success with teams throughout the South. Several of the largest southern cities were also home to integrated professional baseball teams for the first time.

Baseball integration started as the South found itself on the cusp of change. By 1954, the United States Supreme Court's seminal ruling in *Brown v. Board of Education* had ordered the integration of public schools. A year later, the Montgomery, Alabama, bus boycott helped prompt the rise of the Reverend Dr. Martin Luther King Jr. to prominence. When the civil rights movement was just gathering steam in the early and middle 1950s, baseball helped lead the way, integrating segregated ballparks and teams years before Rosa Parks refused the orders of a Montgomery bus driver to vacate her seat for a white passenger. But while Dr. King and other civil rights leaders set out to integrate southern society, the black men who broke the baseball color lines in Jacksonville, Florida; Danville, Virginia; Tulsa, Oklahoma; Lake Charles, Louisiana; and Savannah, Georgia, had less lofty notions of their tasks. They were just ballplayers, playing in the South with the hope of moving up to the major leagues someday. They were not civil rights activists per se, but they were doing the same type of work as marchers, demonstrators, and ministers—opening up previously closed portions of society and changing the attitudes and perceptions of those who watched them play or heard about their accomplishments. As Jackie Robinson was an actor on the national stage, so these southern ballplayers were actors in smaller dramas played out on the local level.

The success of these baseball pioneers played a role in the broader opening of southern society that began in the 1950s and continued through the following decade. Baseball integration did not transform those recalcitrant southern whites into integrationists, but it did help soften dated perceptions of race and help prepare whites and blacks for the broader integration of southern society that was to come. Ironically, this consequence had been predicted by many segregationists the first time Jackie Robinson stepped onto a southern baseball diamond in the late 1940s. They saw baseball integration for what it was—a first break in Jim Crow barriers. While not as well known and goal oriented as, for example, the march from Selma, Alabama, to Montgomery, the integration of southern minor-league baseball played an important role in demolishing the walls of segregation by showing whites and blacks alike that integration could be achieved peacefully, without the apocalyptic consequences predicted by southern segregationists.

Integration helped heighten southern blacks' interest in baseball while also leading many to demand an end to conditions they had long endured: segregated ballpark seating, separate stadium entrances for whites and blacks, and the absence of African American ballplayers on the remaining holdout clubs. The collective action—boycotts and protests—by local African Americans forced changes and opened doors in places where blacks' concerns had long been ignored or suppressed by team management and the white political structure. Integrated minor-league baseball proved to be an effective catalyst for many black southerners seeking to reform their own communities.

But the battle was not easy, either for local activists or, especially, for the ballplayers themselves. While their teams may have been integrated, not much else in their communities was. Local laws and customs forced them to eat and sleep apart from their white teammates. Most of the ballparks they played in were segregated, with black fans being allotted seating in cramped outfield bleachers. Some whites—fans, teammates, and opponents—greeted their presence with racial epithets and slander. Many white fans tolerated black major leaguers playing integrated spring training games in their communities only because the players were there for a very short time, not long enough to disrupt the social order. But African American minor leaguers were another matter. They could be in Natchez, Mississippi, or Macon, Georgia, or Winston-Salem, North Carolina, all summer long. For some, the prospect of watching blacks and whites interacting together as equals for up to six months was too much to bear. Racists took their anger, fear, frustration, and ignorance out on local black minor leaguers, hurling the vilest of taunts their way.

Their targets were hundreds of young ballplayers, most of them in their late teens or early twenties. While learning to hit a curveball or to catch a line drive, African American ballplayers of the 1950s and 1960s also had to endure crude insults and degrading living conditions. Yet they were still expected to perform at a high level on the field. While some ended their careers in the South, unable to bear up under the strain of racism and segregation, many persevered and battled their way to the major leagues. The racial invective motivated these ballplayers to excel and to demonstrate to whites that they were tough enough to compete against white ballplayers and outplay them much of the time.

Throughout the book, you will note the appellations Class AAA, B, C, and so forth. These are used to describe various constituent minor leagues. The minor leagues are divided into several classifications designated with letters—from the highest level, Class AAA, to the lowest, Class D—and Rookie. The labels Class B, C, and D were used to describe various minor leagues until 1962, when the system was reorganized and the current designations—Class AAA, AA, A, and Rookie—were adopted.

The term *organized baseball* is used to describe the minor-league baseball system that began in 1902, following the establishment of the National Association of Professional Baseball Leagues in 1901. The NAPBL was founded and still serves as the minor leagues' governing body. Historically, organized baseball has not encompassed the Negro leagues.

This book draws on back issues of over fifty newspapers. The information discovered in African American newspapers proved to be incomparably valuable. The papers frequently contained material found nowhere else. These newspapers include the *Atlanta Daily World, Baltimore Afro-American, Birmingham World, Dallas Express, Louisiana Weekly, Norfolk Journal and Guide,* and *Pittsburgh Courier.*

The assistance and cooperation of many people helped make *Brushing Back Jim Crow* possible. Grateful appreciation and acknowledgment are extended to all the men whose interviews appear in this book—I will always deeply appreciate the time we spent together and the insights and experiences we shared; Mike Hudson of the *Roanoke Times*; Tommy Cannon; Harley Bowers, former sports editor of the *Macon Telegraph*; Harriet Comer of the *Macon Telegraph*; Willard Rucker of the Washington Memorial Library in Macon; Bob Brown; Chuck Wasserstrom, media relations coordinator for the Chicago Cubs; P. J. Loyello, media relations director for the Montreal Expos; Howie Starkman and Jay Stenhouse, director and assistant director of public relations for the Toronto Blue Jays; Tom Smith of the Texas Rangers' Legends of the Game Museum; Jimm Foster of the Dallas Public Library; Ray Doswell, curator of the Negro Leagues Baseball Museum; Jules Tygiel of San Francisco State University; and especially Dick Holway, my editor, and Mary Kathryn Hassett of the University Press of Virginia, whose enthusiasm for and belief in *Brushing Back Jim Crow* brought us together.

Ed Charles: Parables

Ed Charles was an eighth-grade dropout. In the late 1940s, he left his boyhood home in Daytona Beach to live with his older brother in Miami. But a year later, he was restless, looking for another change, so he relocated to Florida's Gulf Coast to live in St. Petersburg, where his sisters were. He took a dishwashing job in a local restaurant and worked his way up to assistant baker. Charles and his neighbors enjoyed the perquisites of his new position each night when he returned home with freshly baked pies. It was in this neighborhood that the sixteen-year-old Charles began to receive notice for the talents he displayed with a local softball team, the Harlem Hawks. As spring melted into summer, Charles met a neighborhood girl who quickly became the love of his life. But when summer faded and the school year was about to begin, his new love issued an ultimatum—return to school or their relationship would be over. With little deliberation, Charles listened to his heart and enrolled in high school.

But when Charles met with the registrar, he faced a quandary. Not wishing to enroll in ninth grade, two grades behind his girlfriend, he applied for tenth, informing the registrar that his records had been destroyed when his Daytona Beach school burned down the previous year. Accepting him at his word, the school permitted Charles to begin his St. Petersburg education as a tenth-grader, thus preserving his nascent romance. It was a fateful move. Ed Charles became a scholastic athletic star at Gibbs High School, excelling in baseball and football. By his senior year, Charles was the starting third baseman and captain for the baseball team and first-string quarterback for the football squad. Soon he was being courted by baseball scouts. In 1952, at age nineteen, Charles signed with the Boston Braves and was sent to Quebec City, of the Class C Provincial League.

That began Ed Charles's nine-year minor-league odyssey. After Quebec City, his career turned south and became part of a larger drama in America's racial history. He played for eight years for teams in Corpus Christi, Louisville, Jacksonville, and Fort Lauderdale, a southern tenure noteworthy for both its length and its geographic diversity. His experiences in southern locales serve as parables for the difficulties faced by African American baseball players throughout 1950s Dixie, where these men endured the effects of Jim Crow segregation—separate hotels, restaurants, rest rooms. These are the times and tribulations detailed in *Brushing Back Jim Crow*.

> Baseball integration was something I had hoped and dreamed for since I was a little kid in Daytona Beach, Florida. We used to get the Dodgers game on the radio. I liked the Dodgers nickname, the Bums. It symbolized the downtrodden, the less fortunate. That's the way we felt coming up under the Jim Crowism, America's version of apartheid we had to endure in the South. There were all type of restrictions and limitations on what we could do as a race.
>
> My dreams were limited. I couldn't dream the type of dream that a white could dream and really work toward realizing it. I could dream, but everything was saying this would be denied you. It was against the law to work out these dreams. There were signs saying Colored Only here, Whites Only there. You could be put in jail or beaten up if you disobeyed. It was like someone always

saying, "You've got to know your place." You had to accept what had been set aside for blacks.

This was very frustrating to me. You're in school, reading about the Constitution, reciting the Pledge of Allegiance, reading the noble language of these documents. You want to feel pride in your country. But in reality, they didn't apply to you if you were African American. You couldn't help growing up feeling something was wrong with you. Everything was projecting that you were subhuman. Laws said you couldn't do certain things.

Even when Jackie integrated baseball in Daytona Beach [during spring training with the Brooklyn Dodgers in 1946], the problems were still there. After he reached the major leagues, the problems were still there in the South. We comprehended that nothing had really changed in the South in terms of social conditions.

When I saw Jackie Robinson come into Daytona Beach, I was twelve years old. It was a big deal. Everyone was excited, especially people in the black community. This was going to be a first. It represented a hope that it might begin to open the door to mainstream society. We wanted to be accepted like human beings, to have opportunities, to be able to aspire to greatness just like anyone else, without restriction or limitation. If Jackie were successful, it was going to open doors. We were being portrayed as unproductive, that we couldn't do this and that. Jackie could soften attitudes. Everyone in the black community knew the significance of this, the impact on attitudes, where it might lead in terms of providing more opportunities. I referred to him as a messiah. This was a monumental event in the South. He became my hero, my idol.

I tend to refer to us [black players breaking the color lines in the South during the 1950s] as Jackie's disciples. God knows, Jackie endured a hell of a lot. When we came along, we experienced the same thing, perhaps a little more because we spent most of our apprenticeship in the South as opposed to Jackie just touching down in spring training. We spent years and years trying to make breakthroughs down in the South. We were carrying his torch a little further. We were going to show the world that we could keep our self-control, take all the slings and slurs and still reach our goal.

Some of the things we had to endure down there were horrific. Just maintaining our focus on the field to make it to the major leagues was a lot. Many of the guys had the ability to advance to the major leagues, but because of the social conditions we had to endure, they just fell by the wayside.

Jackie helped us by the manner in which he kept himself in control. He knew what the price was going to be. We all tried to emulate Jackie, his demeanor, taking and enduring this to reach our goal, the major leagues. We had to take abuse, turn the other cheek. All the guys patterned themselves after Jackie. They may have gotten to the point where they wanted to quit and they just thought about Jackie. I know I did. That would give me some sort of lift. We were the early crusaders through the South, and Jackie was with us.

We took long bus trips. Sometimes, we'd make stops along the highway to eat in a diner. The other players would bring us sandwiches on the bus. Not only couldn't we eat in the place, we couldn't use the rest room. We had to relieve ourselves in the bushes. All these things were demeaning. But we had to endure them.

We, the black players, talked about this a lot. They expected us to be productive on the field, but we're not treated like our white counterparts. They can lay up in the fine hotels, in air-conditioning, eat the best foods. We're here in the black community with no air-conditioning. We were very conscious of that, and it did bother us. But we knew we had to do what we had to do. It was something we had to accept.

The thing that bothered us the most was occasionally our white counterparts—teammates and opposing players—might express in subtle ways, sometimes openly, their racism. This disturbed us more than anything else. We dealt with it individually, and sometimes, if it got out of hand, we'd bring it to the attention of management, and see if they'd deal with it. Some of them did, some of them didn't. We might say, "One of us has got to go." That's how things were dealt with in those days. Management might get rid of that player, but it depended on your value to the team. If you're a utility-type player and your white counterpart was the star, that person wasn't going anywhere. If you were carrying your load, that guy was out of there.

I can recall 1956 when I was at Wichita. We had a Puerto Rican kid named Juan Pizarro. He had mentioned that something was wrong with his leg. He couldn't run too well. Pizarro told one of the coaches that he couldn't run. The coach thought that he was jaking [feigning injury], that he just didn't want to run. He insisted that Pizarro join the other pitchers in the outfield to get his running in. Pizarro reluctantly went out there. He was pissed off about it because he felt had he been white, he would not have been forced to go out there to run. While he's out there, he's not running at full gallop. A remark was made that if he didn't feel like running, why didn't he go back to Africa. Pizarro became quite angry, naturally, and he went to confront this coach physically.

He told me what happened, and I was quite disturbed about it. It's not something a coach, management, should be into. We could deal with players individually, but now you've got a coach involved. I called the farm director in Milwaukee. I told him about the incident and said none of the black players wanted to play under these conditions. They immediately got Pizarro out of there. He went up to the major leagues the next year, and the rest of us had to stay down there.

Shortly after this incident with Pizarro, I had reached a point where I thought I wanted to leave baseball. Enough was enough. I was very upset. It was too much, having to deal with racism coming from management. You dealt with it coming from players, fans, and the overall climate of the community, where you can't eat here, you can't stay there. It was beginning to take its toll. The Braves weren't doing anything with me, so I was just stuck in the South.

I called my granddad and told him I wanted to give it up. He was a Baptist minister in Daytona Beach. He recognized immediately that I was very upset. He told me, "Son, what I want you to do is get a good night's sleep. If you feel the same way in the morning, I want you to give me a call and then come on home." I didn't sleep well that night. All I could think of was that I didn't want to be a quitter. Jackie wasn't a quitter. I'm not going to be a quitter. That's not what I thought Jackie would do. I'm not going back home a failure. I couldn't deal with the taunts from the guys on my block who'd say, "I told you, you weren't good enough." I had gotten myself back in control the next morning. I could focus again. I knew I could overcome this and somehow realize my goal. That was the only time in my years in the minor leagues that I had reached such a low point that had my granddad said, "Come on home," I'd have jumped.

One of the most disturbing things I experienced was the fact that there were a lot of black players who had comparable skills to their white counterparts, sometimes better, who were let go. This, the quota system, really shook up people. They just were going to have so many blacks. The practice was—it wasn't written in black and white—that there were only going to be so many blacks. We talked about how unfair it was. We knew from all the messages of management what was allowed and what wasn't going to be allowed. There was nothing you could do about it except try to be one of those guys.

Until the South showed an easing of attitudes, it was going to be quite difficult for the major-league clubs to stock their teams in the northern cities, to give black players the proper apprenticeships that they needed to elevate to the major leagues. Most of those teams available to black players in the minors had been of a higher caliber, AAA teams. Most of the guys had to start at lower levels, B, C, and progress up the ladder. They needed teams in the South because almost all of the lower minor-league teams were in that area. Things had to open up, or there wouldn't have been as many black players signed. They needed someplace to develop.

The times that I really experienced the intense racial put-downs were when I ventured into other states [from Florida], like Georgia, Tennessee. In certain cities, the hostility, the racial put-downs, were more obvious, especially during the time I was in the Sally [South Atlantic] League, '56 and '57. I took more in the Sally League than in any of the other leagues I played in. There was nothing in Jacksonville that bothered me. It was only when I traveled, to places like Knoxville, Macon, that you'd hear the name-calling, the put-downs. Some cities were better, like Corpus Christi, very tolerant, like St. Petersburg and Daytona Beach.

But anyplace we played, we had to be careful about what we did and what we said. My first year of professional ball, in 1952, I was assigned to Quebec City, Canada. There were three black players on the team, myself, Bob Smith from someplace in Jersey, and Stanley Glenn from Philadelphia, and I'm coming out of the Deep South. Our experiences in terms of relationships with whites were totally different. I'm used to having whites refer to me as "nigger" and everything derogatory. All of a sudden, I'm out of Florida for the first time.

I find myself in the liberal climate of Canada. Lo and behold, I found out that the team had a designated white family of school-teachers to be our landlords. We were going to live in their home. This was a first for me. I soon found out that there were no blacks living there and that their attitude toward me was not like what it was in the South. I felt a little uneasy with this family. I always thought I'd hear this magic word and they'd start referring to me as a "nigger." I was tense waiting for this. It never did come. I saw they were very decent, genuine human beings. They were not prejudiced. We developed a heck of a relationship. It was an eye-opening experience for me.

We used to walk down to the ballpark from where we lived. We lived up on a hill, in the English-speaking portion of Quebec. We'd leave the house, walk to the ballpark, and little kids used to follow behind. They had never seen anything like it. They'd look weird and strange, like, "We've never seen this before." One day,

Smitty got a little teed off. The kids were behind us, and they were just walking. All of a sudden, Smitty turned around and said, "Boo!" They ran, they scattered. I said, "Smitty, you probably just confirmed what the kids already thought, that we were animals or something." People had the perception that you had tails and all this kind of stuff. You were from some other world, especially if you were in certain areas.

In the early days, you were always mindful of these things. You tried to present your best image to the public. This was what Jackie had to do. We had to do the same thing. Most of the guys coming along in those days were conscious of this. They had to present this type of image. Management expected this too. A lot of times, if you didn't project that image, they'd call you a troublemaker. The next thing you knew, you were out of there, released or sent to a lower league. We were on pins and needles in the minor leagues. We didn't speak out on issues because we felt that if we did, management would label us as troublemakers and the word would get around baseball. These things happened.

You had [black] baseball fans prior to integration. They identified with their local professional teams. You had segregated seating, where black fans would be put out in the bleachers somewhere and not be allowed to go into the main grandstand. You still had some blacks who would go out to see the all-white teams because they were into sports. That was a limited amount of blacks.

When integration came, all blacks wanted to identify with the local team. They now felt it was their team, too, because they've got some of us now. Black attendance increased, and baseball garnered the attention of more blacks. You had that type of ripple effect. You didn't have to talk to anybody about this. They expressed it. They were so happy. "We've finally got some black ballplayers here. We didn't want to root for them before because we knew they were prejudiced. We knew we had blacks who could play with the whites. We're glad you're showing them." They were very supportive. Their numbers at the ballparks increased because we were there. They gave us a lot of support, which we really needed. We needed to see blacks in those stands. They went out of their way to try to make things comfortable for us. Naturally, we were very appreciative. They were aware of the things we had to endure, but they were glad we were out there.

I feel sorry for some of my colleagues, the black players I knew who fell by the wayside because they were labeled as troublemakers or because of a quota system, guys like Nat Peeples, who was in the Braves organization with me, and I know how things affected him. There were other players in the Braves system, like Horace Garner, who were also affected. It just hurts. Let's thank God the experiment was successful. It brought us all to another level, closer to the democracy I read about in school.

Ed Charles was twenty-eight, old by baseball standards, when he reached the majors in 1961 with the Kansas City Athletics. The highlight of his career came in 1969, when as a thirty-five-year-old long shot, he forced his way onto the roster of the New York Mets with an inspired performance in spring training. By October, he and his teammates were celebrating their improbable victory over the Baltimore Orioles in the World Series.

Since 1987, Ed Charles has worked as a teacher, providing education and guidance to at-risk children detained by New York City's juvenile justice system.

Chuck Harmon with the Cincinnati Reds, 1954. (Courtesy of Chuck Harmon)

Three Macon Peaches in the inaugural season of the newly integrated Southern League. Lee May is at left. (Courtesy of Middle Georgia Archives, Washington Memorial Library, Macon, Georgia)

Felipe Alou of the San Francisco Giants, 1963. (Courtesy of the National Baseball Hall of Fame Library, Cooperstown, New York)

Leaving the Texas League behind, Ruben Amaro makes it to AAA— Rochester Red Wings, 1958. (Courtesy of the National Baseball Hall of Fame Library, Cooperstown, New York)

Billy Williams of the Chicago Cubs. (Courtesy of the Chicago Cubs)

Dave Hoskins signs an autograph for a fan in an early season game at Burnett Field, Dallas, 1952. (From the collections of the Texas/Dallas History and Archives Division, Dallas Public Library)

The San Antonio Missions' Joe Durham, 1954. (Courtesy of the Institute of Texan Cultures, The San Antonio Light *Collection)*

Three San Antonio Missions, 1955. Willie Tasby is in the middle. (Courtesy of the Institute of Texan Cultures, The San Antonio Light *Collection)*

The Milwaukee Braves' Hank Aaron returns to the South Atlantic League in 1954 and crosses home plate after hitting a home run in a spring exhibition game at Macon's Luther Williams Field. (Courtesy of Middle Georgia Archives, Washington Memorial Library, Macon, Georgia)

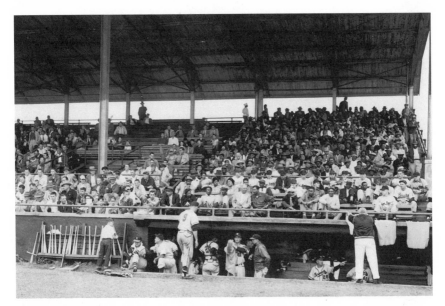

Segregated grandstands behind third base at Luther Williams Field. (Courtesy of Middle Georgia Archives, Washington Memorial Library, Macon, Georgia)

Danville's League Park, 1956. Segregated grandstand for African Americans is at right. (Courtesy of Tommy Cannon)

Percy Miller of the Danville Leafs, 1951. The Carolina League's first African American player. (Courtesy of Tommy Cannon)

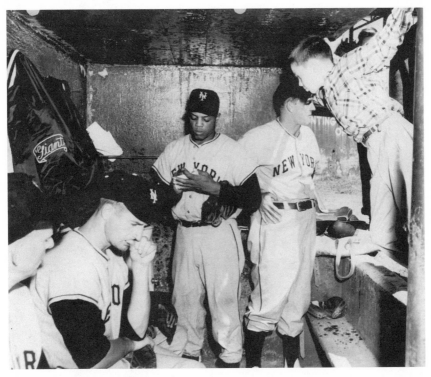

The New York Giants' Willie Mays signing an autograph before an exhibition game in Danville, Virginia, 1955. (Courtesy of Tommy Cannon)

The Danville Giants' team photo, 1958. Manny Mota is in the second row, second from left. (Courtesy of Tommy Cannon)

Three Danville Leafs, 1953. Bill White is on the left. (Courtesy of Tommy Cannon)

Danville team photo, 1953. Bill White is in the third row, on the right. (Courtesy of Tommy Cannon)

Danville's League Park, 1955, before an exhibition game featuring the New York Giants. (Courtesy of Tommy Cannon)

Danville team photo, 1956. Future Baseball Hall of Famer Willie McCovey is on the far right in the top row. (Courtesy of Tommy Cannon)

Future big leaguers in Danville, 1956. From left to right are Tony Taylor, Willie McCovey, Jose Pagan. (Courtesy of Tommy Cannon)

1 | Color Lines Start to Fall: 1951

I think it is all right to play Negroes. I played with them in professional football and once the game is underway you don't realize that you have them on the team—Just another ball player as far as I am concerned.

—ACE PARKER, MANAGER, DURHAM (N.C.) BULLS, 1951

Nineteen fifty-one marked the first time minor-league color barriers in Texas (J. W. Wingate), Tennessee (Bob Bowman), and Virginia and North Carolina (Percy Miller) collapsed. The achievements of these men began the slow process of southern baseball integration. However, their organized-baseball tenures were quite brief, ranging from a handful of games to three weeks. In the early days of integration, teams had difficulty locating players with sufficient experience to last beyond more than the briefest time in organized baseball. Some teams were also clearly more interested in the African American ballplayer for his novelty, his entertainment value, and his ability to attract fans to the ballpark than in his baseball skills. Nevertheless, these men played a crucial role in baseball integration. Their presence, however brief, opened the door, setting the stage for the large influx of players to come.

J. W. Wingate's experience illustrates what African American ballplayers faced in the early days of minor-league integration. Before spring training began, the Lamesa (Tex.) Lobos of the Class C West Texas–New Mexico League announced plans to integrate their circuit. Owner Cy Fausett committed himself to finding a nonwhite athlete capable of playing at the Class

C level and enduring the expected adverse reaction of those resistant to integration. Lobos manager Jay Haney, whose previous opposition to employing African Americans evaporated after he had the chance to play baseball and associate with minority teammates while in the armed forces, actively sought out qualified ballplayers locally and as far away as California. Eventually, Wingate and Connie Heard were invited to join the Lobos for a tryout.

However, a few weeks after practice began, Haney announced the players' release, noting that they "fell short of the rigid standards he had set for the first Negro players in Organized Ball in Texas only on ability." Wingate, the more promising athlete of the two, was the victim of a numbers crunch as Lamesa prepared to open the 1951 season: He was the seventeenth player on a team with only sixteen roster slots.

But just as Wingate prepared to join an all-black team in Tennessee, Haney called him back, adding him to the Lobos' squad. Once he began to play, Wingate's performance quickly dissipated some of the racially motivated criticism of his signing. Hitting safely in his first six games and collecting three doubles, Wingate silenced those who doubted his ability to play professional baseball for an all-white team.

Unfortunately, this success was short-lived as Wingate's performance quickly fell off. His slump eventually prompted Lamesa to release the twenty-three-year-old shortstop before the end of May. Although he batted a respectable .250 for the Lobos, Wingate (who left Lamesa to play for the Negro American League's Kansas City Monarchs) did not instantly manifest the star qualities expected of African American ballplayers who crossed southern minor-league color lines. Many believed, with some justification, that white fans, already discomfited by the prospect of watching blacks and whites playing interracial baseball, would have their angst salved only by the opportunity to watch the best African American athletes available, making the act of purchasing tickets to integrated games easier to swallow. Countless black ballplayers in the 1950s faced this same reality. If they did not produce immediately, they would find themselves released from the team or banished to the end of the team's bench. As Lamesa and other franchises discovered, employing African American ballplayers with staying power would be more difficult than baseball executives first anticipated.

As baseball took its first tentative steps toward integration, the rest of the South was also approaching an important intersection. Jim Crow remained firmly rooted throughout Dixie. Communities maintained the status quo of separate-but-unequal facilities for whites and blacks. Racially motivated violence occurred in different locations. Crosses were burned in Goochland County, Virginia, in front of the homes of three African American business owners. Two soldiers were arrested in Macon, Georgia, for objecting to being called "niggers" by a white bus driver.

Despite such incidents, plans for effecting drastic change were afoot. The National Association for the Advancement of Colored People and like-minded groups and individuals pursued a strategy of attacking segregation in the federal courts. Lawsuits pushing the integration of interstate transportation and graduate education had already won favorable rulings and prompted a wave of similar constitutional challenges to the southern way of life. In cases where lower federal courts or state courts ratified Jim Crow restrictions, most of the decisions were immediately appealed to the United States Supreme Court in the hope that the high court would eventually right the wrongs of Jim Crow.

In a ruling by a three-judge panel of the United States Court of Appeals for the Fourth Circuit in June, Judges Timmerman and Parker opined that the school segregation law before them was valid, resulting in their upholding segregation in a South Carolina school district. Their decision was quickly appealed to the Supreme Court. Although this lawsuit did not garner nationwide attention at the time, just three years later it would. As part of a consolidated appeal that also involved the Topeka, Kansas, Board of Education, the decision of Judges Timmerman and Parker was overturned by the high court in what would become known as *Brown v. Board of Education*, the monumental decision that rocked the South by declaring segregated schools to be unconstitutional.

19 MAY

BIRMINGHAM, Ala.—A campaign to focus national attention on racial violence in Birmingham was launched this week by the Birmingham branch of the NAACP following the May deliberate burnings of two Negro homes [in an area once zoned as white-only] in this city's nine unsolved racial bombings . . . Four days before last Christmas, less than 48 hours after the U.S. Circuit Court of Appeals decision striking down Birmingham's racial zoning laws, the home of Monroe Monk was bombed. — *Norfolk Journal and Guide*

26 MAY

CINCINNATI — FBI agents and Cincinnati police still are trying to track down the letter writers who threatened to kill [Jackie Robinson]. Scores of federal and city officials were assigned to Sunday's Brooklyn-Cincinnati doubleheader in response to two letters which said Robinson would be killed while he was playing. Robinson dismissed the threat on his life. [He] proceeded to drive in four runs in the first game . . . and went one for two in the second game. — *Norfolk Journal and Guide*

2 JUNE

GREENSBORO, N.C. — Applications by five Negroes for admittance to University of North Carolina graduate schools have spurred the university trustees to prevent an influx of Negro graduate students. The trustees have approved the formation of a special committee to map plans for expansion of the North Carolina College for Negroes at Durham. Enlarging the graduate school at the all-Negro college would make fewer Negroes eligible for graduate work at U.N.C. — *Norfolk Journal and Guide*

4 AUGUST

Discrimination at Friendship International Airport [Baltimore] will be put to a legal test by attorneys Donald G. Murray and Mrs. Juanita J. Mitchell who are representing several citizens who have been refused service in the airport's restaurant and other facilities. — *Baltimore Afro-American*

4 AUGUST

Another frontier was crossed in Organized Baseball last week with the signing of the game's first colored umpire. He is Emmett Ashford, 35, a postal worker who has 15 years of softball umpiring behind him. Ashford was signed for work in the Class C Southwest International League. The league president, Les Powers, in announcing the move, stated emphatically that it was not an attempt to exploit Ashford. "This experiment," President Powers asserted, "is not based on anything pertaining to race. Ashford will be given a permanent job if his work merits it . . ." Powers told reporters five cities had already requested Ashford's services. He declined to identify them but did say that the umpire would not be assigned in El Paso, the only team located in what is generally known as the "deep South." Said Powers, "I think he should be given a chance to prove himself before being sent there."—*Baltimore Afro-American*

After a lengthy apprenticeship, Ashford made it to the major leagues in 1966, becoming the first African American umpire in big-league history. He served as an American League arbiter for five seasons, until 1970.

In August of 1951, Percy Miller Jr. stepped uncomfortably into the role of racial trailblazer when his hometown Danville Leafs signed him as the Carolina League's first black ballplayer. He did not think of himself as a pioneer. He just wanted to make his father happy by playing ball.

Miller was only nineteen and barely out of high school, but he seemed to be a perfect candidate to break barriers in the Carolina League. He had enjoyed excellent baseball training from his father. Miller had been a sports star at John B. Langston High, Danville's all-black school, serving as captain on its football and basketball teams and as a starter for its baseball squad. He was named All-State in basketball and was one of the heroes of an undefeated football team. He had two scholarship offers waiting for him more than a year before his graduation in the spring of 1951.

Miller also had experience in interracial competition. Prior to signing with the Leafs that summer, Miller batted .375 for the Danville All-Stars, a local black semiprofessional team that featured three white players. As a youngster, he had played baseball and other games with white friends in Danville. Often, they would play in a pasture outside of town that was surrounded with plum trees. After a long game on steamy summer days, they would clamber up those trees, then pick and eat the juicy fruit in the leafy shade.

Billy Miles's father was a doctor. Nate Colsby, I think his family was in real estate. After we'd stop playing ball in the fields, I'd go home with Billy, and we'd play Ping-Pong, shoot pool, because he had everything in his basement. Once I was waiting tables at the golf course, and Billy was there for a tuxedo affair. He tried to get me to sit down with him. That's how close we were.

When I was coming up, thirteen, fourteen years old, I could do it all, pitch, catch, play any position. My father used to tease me about not hitting many home runs. I hit one, one day, that hit the top of a brick wall and bounced back. He said, "See, if you'd have put a little ummph under it, it would have went over." He used to say that all the time. He was saying that to keep my drive, keep me interested.

I was the batboy for the local sandlot team when my father was the manager. I was always begging them to let me play. They always said I wasn't good enough. But I finally got to play. When I was fifteen, we were playing a team from Florida, the Jacksonville Eagles, that was barnstorming all over, and I was playing right field. Every time a fly ball was hit to my father in center field, he'd yell, "Come on, Junior!" During the game one time, my father was on second base and the score was 1–1. The older players asked him, "Is Junior going to hit ?" He said, "We win with him or we lose with him." Then I doubled off the wall, and we beat them. The manager of the Eagles came up to me and said, "I'm going to take you with me." I said, "My father won't let me go." He said, "When I talk to him, he'll let you go." He told my father, "If you let this kid go with me, I'll make a heck of a ballplayer out of him. You won't have to worry about him. When I eat, he'll eat. When I sleep, he'll sleep. From the first to the fifteenth, I'll give him some money." He talked to my mother about it. She didn't want me to go. She thought I was too young. My father said, "Go pack your clothes. I'll straighten it out with her after you're gone." I was sitting down on the curb on Patton Street, waiting for the team bus to leave at twelve o'clock that night. The rest of the players were inside, playing cards or whatever. I didn't play no cards, so I was just sitting on the curb, waiting until the time to go. The police came by and said, "What are you doing sitting here?" I said, "I'm a ballplayer and I'm going to Florida." He said, "You're a ballplayer? What's your father's name?" I said, "Percy Miller." They knew my father, and they called him. He told them I was waiting on the team bus to go to Florida. That's how I got my start in baseball. I played the whole season with Jacksonville. That was '50.

When I got home, I played with a local black team in Danville. We would travel around to Greensboro, Winston-Salem, Reidsville. They used to pay in those days 60–40, 60 percent of the gate if you win, 40 percent if you lose. Sometimes, you'd do pretty good.

They had a man here named Jim Peters who'd built his own ballpark. My father used to book a lot of games with him. They were very close. There used to be a guy here, Walt Miles, who ran the local paper, the *Commercial Appeal*. He contacted Mr. Peters and discussed the fact that they wanted to get some colored ballplayers to play for the Leafs. He asked for a recommendation, who he thought would be the best player. Mr. Peters told him I was.

My father told me about it. I told him I couldn't do it. I said, "I'm supposed to be at spring football practice at West Virginia State College on the fifteenth of August." He was upset. He came back again the next day with a contract. I wanted to go to college. I played baseball, basketball, and football in high school. There weren't any specialists neither. You played offense and defense. But my father didn't want me to go.

He was a small guy, only about 150 pounds, but he could hit a ball a ton. He never saw me play football until one Saturday morning when people walking by his job would say, "Did you see in the paper what your son did?" I got knocked out in a game where he saw me play. They were giving me smelling salts, and he came down and told me, "You've got to be the dumbest son of a gun I know." He didn't like football. He wanted me to play baseball. He never got the chance to play pro baseball. He told me what a great opportunity playing for the Leafs was. He just broke down and cried. So I signed.

I wasn't aware I was going to be the first black ballplayer in the Carolina League. After I found out, I felt pretty lucky. I knew I was going to be a ballplayer someday for somebody. Playing in my hometown was an extra-special treat. My father had gotten me prepared for playing with whites. Believe it or not, we used to play mixed football in the afternoon against the white boys over at G. W. High School. We'd play pickup games, with six or seven guys we'd go over there and play them. This wasn't something that wasn't done. It was just something that wasn't publicized.

Not surprisingly, reaction to Miller's signing was not uniformly favorable. In 1950, segregation was firmly entrenched in Virginia's laws and customs. Rumors of boycotts against the team in other cities surfaced before Miller played his first game. But whatever potential problems existed, they were resolved, and Miller joined the Leafs and accompanied his teammates for Danville's remaining away games that August. After Miller's signing, several white fans protested the integration of local minor-league baseball, informing the Leafs that they would not attend any games while Miller was on Danville's roster. Team officials reported more favorable reactions from local residents than negative ones, although the local newspaper recorded a number of adverse "man on the street" comments.

The *Danville Bee* polled Miller's teammates and pronounced reaction as "mixed—but generally favorable. No player spoke out against the Negro in interviews. Several polished off questions with a 'no comment' answer. The observation of Danville's Roy Peterson was typical, 'I never played with a Negro before but as far as I feel now I see nothing wrong with it, especially if this boy Miller can help us win ball games.'"

Although he took amateur interracial athletic competitions in stride as having no overwhelming importance, Miller's boyhood and adolescent experiences in this regard did not prepare him for the racial difficulties he encountered in the three weeks he spent on baseball diamonds in Danville, Winston-Salem, and Raleigh, North Carolina.

Miller played his first game in Danville on 10 August before 1,763 fans, of whom 300 to 600 were estimated to be African American, filling half of the segregated bleacher seats near third base. Before 10 August, the Leafs had attracted approximately 50 black patrons per home game. The nineteen-year-old Miller did not disappoint the hometown African American fans, who gave him rousing receptions—often accompanied by white patrons—seemingly each time he appeared from the dugout. He drove in Danville's first two runs with a fourth-inning single.

James Slade, Miller's high school baseball coach and a lifelong Danville resident, recalls his protégé's barrier-shattering debut:

> I was one of the most enthused and excited of anyone other than his daddy. I was thrilled. He was my product. I had to be selfish. I knew he had the talent. It made me proud.
>
> The first game he played, they gave him an old uniform so big it would have fit Shaquille O'Neal. I saw him get his first hit. From third base to left field, there was a rope. Blacks sat past third base to as far as the stands would go. The rest of the ballpark was white. The bathrooms were segregated. If you had to go, you had to go out of the ballpark. Blacks in the city really responded to him. They also knew he wasn't getting a fair shot. Everyplace that he would go, they'd segregate him from the team. The local whites accepted him on the field. But when the game was over, he went right back to the way it was. Don't forget that Danville was the last capital of the Confederacy.

Some hometown fans booed or made nasty remarks as Miller walked by the grandstand. But Miller never remembered it "getting out of hand," and he kept quiet rather than say something that might lead to a confrontation. He thought that was the best way to fight prejudice. ·

> When I got to the ballpark for the first game, I couldn't change in the clubhouse. I had to change clothes at home or in my car. I'd drive to the ballpark in my uniform. Sometimes, I changed in the hallway outside the clubhouse. The uniform they first gave me was too big. It was like a 48, but I had a 31 waist. It was all they had for me.
>
> The most outstanding thing that summer was when it got so the players would play catch with me. At first, they'd be throwing the ball to each other, and I'd be standing on the side. I started rolling the ball up on the wire behind home plate and catching it when it

came off. Then one day, they said, "Get a bat. We'll play some pepper." I grabbed the bat and started to pepper them. I was good at that. I hit it to each individual. After that, they seemed to warm up to me. But I only felt accepted by a few. When you're on a team and you're brushing shoulders with another fella and he doesn't speak to you, it's kind of odd. There were a few guys who said a little, to let me know they were friendly. They would say, "Don't worry, kid. Hang in there. You'll get 'em next time," if I hit a fly ball.

The night that I made my first appearance with the Leafs, they had roped off a section of the ballpark for black people. There must have been two hundred black people on that side. There's a story that I always tell. We had a pitcher named Al Ronay. He was sitting beside me in the dugout. One of our batters fouled a ball off into the black section. The fans went scrambling for the ball. He hit me on the leg and started laughing. He said, "Boy, look at them niggers scramble." He looked right in my face. I got up, stretched. I was going to get some water. I came back and sat down. He wouldn't look at me. But that changed matters, too. Somebody else that had said nothing to me spoke. He was the first player on the team to talk to me. He was used to only playing with whites, but now he treated me like one of the other players. Nobody came up to me and said I wasn't welcome. But ignoring people is sometimes worse than words.

Before the game, my father told me, "They're going to throw you fastballs. Just be ready. If the first pitch gets in there, you hit it." That's what I did. I drove in two runs. The black fans went wild. People were calling my house all night. They said, "Congratulations! We don't want to hold you up because it's getting late, but we're just glad to see it [a black player in the Carolina League] finally happened." That made me feel good.

My father was proud of me. One thing that stands out in my mind was when we went to Raleigh. Everybody was getting off the bus at the Sir Walter Raleigh Hotel. They were just running right in. I was going to run in, too. My manager grabbed me by the arm and said, "Wait a minute. Go to this address. There's a cab waiting for you right there." He gave me eight dollars and an address. I had no idea where I would be going, and I had no idea it was going to take place. That was a shock to me. If they had told me before we left Danville, I would have been more prepared.

At the ballpark in Raleigh, Joe Medwick [former member of the St. Louis Cardinals and future Baseball Hall of Famer] was coaching, and he was playing the outfield. During the game, he ran by me, smiled, and said, "Keep plugging away. You'll be all right." I thought that was pretty nice. Raleigh was okay to play in. People just went about their business.

It was a funny thing. I never got too many catcalls from the dugout. But there were a lot from the stands. They let you know how they felt. One guy looked like he was about forty years old. He said, "If my daddy were living, he'd run you off the field." I just looked at him. Winston-Salem was the worst place in that league. I came into one game there as a pinch hitter. They really booed me. I tried to think I was in my own backyard in Danville. I thought, "If I could take it there, I could take it here."

By 16 August, Miller found himself in such a deep slump that the Leafs left him in Danville for two days of intensive batting and fielding practice when they left on a road trip. Although his on-field performance improved after returning to the lineup, Miller continued to struggle intermittently with Carolina League baseball.

By 3 September, he completed what would turn out to be his only organized-baseball campaign, batting .184 over nineteen games and thirty-nine at-bats. Five months later, the Leafs released Miller, announcing that he "is not ready for Class B ball."

The Leafs released me after the season, and I went back to the Jacksonville Eagles. The Pittsburgh Pirates wanted to sign me as a bonus player. But the Eagles wanted $25,000 for me, so the Pirates didn't take me. Then I got a phone call that I got drafted into the service. They put me into a group learning how to shoot the M 1 rifle to go to Korea. One of the guys got me and said the CO wanted to see me. He said, "I saw a black fella named Miller playing in the Carolina League in Raleigh. Could that have been you?" I said, "Yes, sir." He gave me a shot to make the team there, and I did. I made the team. That's where I got hurt. I busted my knee in the service. That ended my playing career.

I don't like to be referred to as Jackie Robinson because I consider him the greatest. I'm not in his class. But I feel pretty good about what I did. When a guy said something derogatory toward me, I just looked at him. If I would have said something, it would have been blown out of proportion. As long as you don't say anything, nothing happens, even though you have to take something you don't appreciate taking. I think what I did may have put something in people's heads in Danville about being together.

Percy Miller, the first African American to play interracial organized baseball in Virginia and North Carolina and the first to play in more than a handful of games for a southern minor-league team outside of Texas, was a trailblazer. Although he never returned to the Leafs, his three weeks in the Carolina League nevertheless helped set the stage for other African American ballplayers to follow his lead with teams throughout the South over the next several years.

In 1997, forty-six years after his debut with Danville, Percy Miller's role in integrating southern minor-league baseball was recognized by the Carolina League, which honored him at the Carolina League–California League All-Star game in Durham, North Carolina. To a standing ovation, Percy Miller Jr. took the field in the Carolina League again to throw out the game's ceremonial first pitch.

2 | Dramatic Developments: 1952

Negro players are now spread throughout organized baseball, from the most insignificant Class D league to the majors. Only three big league teams do not have at least one Negro player some place in their far-flung farm systems, Detroit, the Boston Red Sox and the St. Louis Cards.

—Pittsburgh Courier, 24 MAY 1952

This was the first year of widespread integration throughout base-ball. By the end of May, 104 nonwhite players were scattered across the minor leagues, from California to Florida. One franchise, Porterville, Cali-fornia, of the Southwest International League, at one time even featured an entire roster of African Americans.

While black players were making an impact all over the nation, no-where was their presence felt more keenly than in the South. In the Florida International League, for example, some owners were concerned about the potential repercussions of a black pitcher's hitting a white batter with a pitch during a game. But this did not stop the league's integration. Attempting to ease black players' transition into the league, team owners ensured that nonwhite athletes were paired on each integrating team so that these pioneers would not have to face Jim Crow alone. Napoleon "Nap" Daniels, a nineteen-year-old pitcher and alumnus of the Negro American League, helped boost the fortunes of Sherman, Oklahoma, in the Class D Sooner State League. In his debut as the circuit's first African American, Daniels helped attract 2,000 fans to Sherman's Twin Park, one of the team's best attendance marks to date. Rufus Hatten (Bluefield, West Virginia) and Ray Mitchell (Longview, Texas) also garnered much positive attention in their history-making appearances in the Appalachian and Big State Leagues, respectively. Indeed, the 3,025 who watched Mitchell pitch on 10 August in Texarkana, Texas, were the most people to watch a game in this northeast Texas border city since 1949, when the Cleveland Indians and the New York Giants played an exhibition game there.

Most significantly, 1952 was the first year African American minor leaguers spent entire seasons with their teams. But while many southern franchises secured quality black ballplayers, other teams remained unable or unwilling to sign the best athletes available. Instead, they remained content to bring in any black player willing and able to put on a uniform for a few games so team owners could reap the short-term financial benefit of drawing African American spectators and curious whites to their games while causing only passing discomfort to segregationists.

In the Class D Coastal Plain League, New Bern's Charlie Roach played only three games before leaving this North Carolina town. Charlie England, a pitcher for Raleigh's Shaw University, signed with Rocky Mount, North Carolina, and was released less than two weeks later after yielding twelve hits and nine runs in eight innings over two starts.

At the same time, Dallas, Miami, St. Petersburg, Houston, and Tampa became the first large cities in Dixie to host integrated minor-league baseball. African Americans were now playing in front of larger crowds than ever before. This increased the possibility of influencing greater numbers of whites and blacks than ever before, when games were played in such small venues as Danville, Rocky Mount, and Texarkana. Reactions in these and other populous cities were closely watched by southern communities that were contemplating integrating their teams.

Baseball was not alone in moving the cause of integration forward in 1952. Small gains were being won across Dixie. In Miami, Aubrey W. Henry was hired as the first African American physician at a southern whites-only hospital. Presidential candidate Dwight D. Eisenhower fostered cautious optimism among many blacks when he suggested during the election campaign that he would consider naming an African American to his cabinet if elected. This was something of a reversal for Eisenhower, who had testified before the Senate Armed Services Committee in 1948 in favor of the segregation of troops in the armed forces.

A poll by the *Pittsburgh Courier* further confirmed the notion that change was coming. In a survey about southern race relations, the paper discovered that 78.5 percent of its readers believed southern whites "are at least getting rid of some of their hidebound prejudices on the color line." While the poll was suggestive of progress, it also revealed how difficult such reform was proving to be. One reader from Columbia, South Carolina, stated that "the old die-hards are contesting every inch of the ground," while a Louisiana farmer's prescient comment hinted at the struggles to come: "The white South is consolidating itself more and more against the colored race."

The fight for racial justice was still in its infancy. Nineteen fifty-two, a gubernatorial election year in Florida, brought an upsurge of violence against African Americans who wanted to exercise their right to vote. A large number of Florida's black voters also lobbied the gubernatorial candidates for the integration of the State Board of Control to aid in opening up the state's schools. The board set policy for, among other institutions, three universities, including one for African Americans. But politicians greeted such advocacy with empty platitudes, while racists responded with cross burnings and other violent acts.

On 27 May, a bomb was thrown onto the roof of an African American business college, and another, onto the porch of the house belonging to David H. Dwight, president of the Democratic Alliance, a group concerned with African American political rights in Florida. But the state's black voters showed they would not surrender to racism or abandon their right to vote. They went to the polls in record numbers to cast their ballots in the primary election on 6 May.

Efforts to pry open southern society continued through judicial intervention. Thurgood Marshall, head of the NAACP's legal department, announced the group's 1952 strategy in a speech in Oklahoma City, promising that the NAACP would, while awaiting the results of school desegregation appeals to the United States Supreme Court, step up its judicial challenges to segregation in public recreation facilities and transportation.

The judicial results were uneven. The Interstate Commerce Commission rejected a complaint against the separation of the races in southern railroad cars. In turning down Elmer W. Henderson's petition, the ICC chose to ignore the import of a 1950 Supreme Court ruling in a lawsuit filed by Henderson in which the Court outlawed a railroad's policy of reserving only one table in each dining car for African Americans. The federal commission, like many courts and semijudicial bodies, was unwilling to go beyond the exact letter of a high court ruling to strike out further against Jim Crow. Certain judges and commissioners were uninterested in upsetting the status quo, either because of segregationist sympathies or because of judicial caution.

A three-judge panel of the United States Court of Appeals for the Fourth Circuit affirmed segregation in South Carolina's schools for the second time in two years. This time, the panel was unanimous in denying a request for an injunction abolishing school segregation, although the court did direct the equalization (i.e., of resources and finances) of the racially separate educational facilities in rural Clarendon County rather than outlawing the district's separate schools for white and black children.

The panel's unanimity reflected a change in its composition. Judge J. Waties Waring, known for opening South Carolina's primaries to African Americans and who had dissented from the 1951 majority opinion, retired from the bench after ten years of service. His replacement sided with Judges Parker and Timmerman in upholding school segregation. Sometime after the appellate tribunal released its ruling, Thurgood Marshall enthusiastically announced that the Supreme Court had added the case to its docket for decision.

2 APRIL

BARTOW, Fla.—A local city ordinance barring Negroes from using the clubhouse at Municipal Stadium served to prove how popular Jim (Buster) Clarkson, veteran Negro infielder, is with his Milwaukee teammates. When the Brewers arrived here for an exhibition with the Buffalo Bisons, Jack Tighe, manager of the International League club, explained apologetically that there was a sign, "White Only," on the clubhouse door, but that Clarkson could dress—alone—in the National Guard armory across the street. The other Brewers, however, chorused in unison: "We dress where he [Jim] dresses," and followed Clarkson to the armory.—*Sporting News*

2 APRIL

The 1952 spring training junket was the worst the tan Dodgers have experienced since the Brooklyn club became integrated in 1947 . . . The itinerary of the Dodgers called for stops in Tampa and St. Petersburg, Fla.; Mobile and Montgomery, Ala.; Nashville and Chattanooga, Tenn.; and Lynchburg and Richmond, Va. Four special cars were provided for the entourage [for the players to live in]. Except for St. Petersburg and Richmond, hotel accommodations were relatively nil. And only because one or more members of the tan contingent had friends in Nashville and Lynchburg, were they able to obtain decent meals . . . In one Alabama city, "the best place in town" was a linen-less marble counter with flies and roaches meeting customers at the door.—*Baltimore Afro-American*

21 JUNE

WASHINGTON, D.C.—America's beloved Stars and Stripes is now being used for a macabre purpose, according to a group of mothers in the area around the Rosedale playground, where Negro children are not allowed—by law—to play. When the American flag is flying it is a notice to the Negroes that they are not allowed in the playground, according to the parents. Attempts had been made by several white persons to prevent the colored children from entering. Rosedale has been a bone of contention recently, for it has a swimming pool, which only whites can use. —*Pittsburgh Courier*

Two months later, the situation at Rosedale changed dramatically. One hundred African American children integrated the park by climbing over and under a wire fence. Nearby police officers did not intervene. "I can't arrest these children," one officer said. "They're having such a good time."

Mickey Stubblefield, a twenty-four-year-old pitcher from Mayfield,

Kentucky, became the Class D Kitty League's first black player when he signed with Paducah. President Shelby Peace polled all eight Kitty League clubs in Kentucky and Tennessee to determine their reactions to Stubblefield's presence. Peace relayed the results of his poll to the *Pittsburgh Courier*.

12 JULY

Jackson, Fulton, and Union City tell me they don't want Negroes playing in their parks but they do not plan to take any action to prevent it. Madisonville is a municipally owned [park], and they have a city ordinance that will prevent Negroes from playing there. Hopkinsville is afraid Stubblefield's appearance will hurt attendance. Negroes played in the Paducah Park when Paducah was a member of the [Mississippi—Ohio Valley] League, and there should not be any objection to his presence there. Actually, none of the club owners are in favor of Negroes in the league, but there is no law that would prevent it, except in parks that are municipally owned.

This initial, grudging assent to Stubblefield's presence in the circuit did not last. Subsequent protests by Kitty League teams forced Mayfield to release their pitcher before the end of the season.

6 SEPTEMBER

CHARLOTTE, N.C.—Old man jim crow received a dramatic last-minute stay of execution here last week when the Rock Hill (S.C.) Chiefs fielded a Negro player over the protest of the Tri-State League president, Bobby Hipps. David Mobley, 22-year-old native of Lancaster, S.C., made an unheralded appearance in the sixth inning of a game between the Chiefs and Knoxville. His appearance in left field resulted in an emergency meeting of the Chief's board of directors who defied Hipps request not to sign the Negro player. Frantic moves during the night to prevent Mobley from further participation paid off and the next day, Eral Shirer, president of the Chiefs, phoned Hipps that Mobley's name was withdrawn from the roster to keep harmony in the eight-team league. Mr. Shirer told the Courier that his office was deluged with phone calls from officials of the other teams in the league who expressed the fear that if Mobley was played "it would break up the league."—*Pittsburgh Courier*

Earlier in the season, the Tri-State's Asheville and Charlotte clubs had sought to add black players to their rosters. However, the players selected were released following unsuccessful tryouts. African Americans were barred from playing in Anderson and Greenville, South Carolina, Tri-State cities, because of city ordinances or court rulings.

Texas League

Beaumont	Oklahoma City
Dallas	San Antonio
Fort Worth	Shreveport
Houston	Tulsa

During the winter following the 1951 baseball season, Dallas oil baron Dick Burnett decided to search for an African American to include on the roster of his all-white Dallas Eagles in 1952. A major impetus behind Burnett's decision was the arrival of integrated professional football in the South, which happened when the New York Yankees National Football League franchise relocated to Texas with its three black players, Buddy Young, George Taliaferro, and Sherman Howard, and changed its name to the Dallas Texans. Burnett believed that the Texans and Eagles competed in Dallas for local sports fans' attention. With the Texans' integration of professional sports in the Lone Star State, Burnett feared his team would be left behind if the Eagles remained all-white.

But unlike many southern minor-league team owners, Burnett was not interested in bringing in black players merely as drawing cards to attract African Americans to the ballpark. He wanted to improve his club by finding a player talented enough to help him win. If that player was African American, so much the better. Indeed, he felt that bringing integration to the circuit would be his contribution to the cause of equal rights for African Americans. He recalled the black friends who had sacrificed for him when he began his career in the oil business. "I am indebted to the colored race," Burnett told the *Dallas Express*.

For Burnett's line breaker, there would be no quick flameouts. Burnett wanted a quality ballplayer with staying power. He also recognized that only an individual of a certain demeanor and talent would be able to cope with the stresses of being the first black ballplayer in a previously all-white southern league, one with the highest minor-league classification (AA) and the largest cities of any to integrate so far. In his quest for a groundbreaker, Burnett enlisted the assistance of Hank Greenberg, general manager of the Cleveland Indians, the Eagles' major league affiliate since 1951. At this time, Cleveland had more African American minor leaguers than any other major-league organization.

Following a preseason tryout where none of over two hundred black ballplayers was considered talented enough to earn a Dallas contract, Burnett finally found two men skilled enough to merit spring training invitations. They were Othello Renfroe, a twenty-seven-year-old shortstop who batted .322 in the Cuban League the previous season, and Ray Neil, twenty-six, a second baseman and veteran of several campaigns in the Negro leagues who had batted .346 for the Indianapolis Clowns in 1951.

Renfroe quickly eliminated himself from consideration by mysteriously never showing up at training camp in Daytona Beach although Burnett sent transportation money to his home in Atlanta. This left Neil as the only remaining African American on a Texas League team, a fact that did not go unnoticed by the second baseman and media members covering the Eagles in Florida. The first question from reporters was simple: "How do you feel about this?" Neil's answer was quiet but just as direct: "I've thought about it, and I'm not afraid."

Days after this interview, the Eagles released Neil, stating that he did not have enough skill to compete in the Texas League. However, the *Pittsburgh Courier,* citing sources, opined that Neil was cut loose because "he didn't have the flash expected of a Negro player." Neil later denied this, claiming he had been treated fairly. With his departure from Daytona Beach, the prospect of integrating this AA circuit in 1952 seemed virtually nil. No other Texas League club planned to add black players. Even Fort

Worth, which was affiliated with the groundbreaking Brooklyn Dodgers, stuck with the status quo.

Again, Burnett sought the advice of Hank Greenberg. Cleveland's general manager suggested a right-handed pitcher who batted left-handed and could also play the outfield. Dave Hoskins, twenty-six, who was in his first year as a full-time pitcher, had already faced Dallas in an exhibition game that spring, impressing Burnett by retiring all six men he pitched against. Hoskins, a veteran of six seasons in the Negro leagues, where he learned about pitching from the great Satchel Paige, had been a pioneer in race relations even before being considered for a similar role with the Eagles. He understood the significance of his past achievements and, more important, what would be in store for him if he played for the Eagles.

In 1944, when Hoskins was exclusively an outfielder, he, Jackie Robinson, and Sam Jethroe were invited to try out for the Boston Red Sox and Boston Braves. This trial was arranged by Wendell Smith, sports editor of the *Pittsburgh Courier,* who capitalized on building political pressure in Boston for these teams to employ African American ballplayers. But Hoskins's team, the Negro National League's Homestead Grays, refused to give him permission to take part in this seminal event. Another player, Marvin Williams, journeyed to Boston instead.

Four years later, Hoskins batted .393 for Grand Rapids as the first African American ballplayer in the Class B Central League, a six-team circuit with franchises in Ohio, Indiana, and Michigan. He so impressed the Cleveland Indians that they signed him to a contract after the 1949 campaign, when he won five of his six decisions for Grand Rapids while posting a 3.60 earned run average. While playing for the Central League's Dayton squad in 1950, Hoskins was struck in the head with a fastball, causing a concussion that left him in critical condition. This was the second time he had suffered a head injury; in 1943, while playing high school football in Flint, Michigan, he had fractured his skull, an injury severe enough to keep him away from athletics until he signed with the Grays in 1945. After recovering from his second close call, Hoskins experienced a baseball epiphany, deciding to devote himself more to pitching to reduce the number of times he came to bat, minimizing his chances of another beaning.

A brief spring tryout placed Hoskins with the Eagles in 1952. Departing Florida for Texas, the Eagles played a series of exhibition games against all-white teams from the avowedly segregationist Class AA Southern Association. Faced with playing against the Eagles and their new African American pitcher, the association's president revealed much about his racial sentiments as well as those of many whites in the Deep South when he commented, "There are folks down here who just don't want their kids growing up to admire a Negro ballplayer even if he is Willie Mays or Hank Aaron."

On 13 April, Hoskins won his Texas League regular season debut, beating Tulsa 4 – 2 and getting a warm reception from a racially mixed home crowd of nearly four thousand. Burnett's integration effort was off to an auspicious start. His decision to integrate his team caused some initial disquiet around the Texas League, but this did not stop the Eagles' iconoclastic owner.

Don Mossi, who pitched for Dallas in 1952 and knew Dave Hoskins from the season before in Wilkes-Barre, Pennsylvania, says Dick Burnett had the moxie to ensure that his plan succeeded: "Burnett was a very flamboyant owner. He had a lot of oil wells and was very wealthy. The ball club was like his toy. He was forceful about things. He was forceful about Dave. He wanted him on the team and that was it. He didn't want to hear any complaints."

In June, Burnett fought against a bill introduced in Louisiana's legislature that would outlaw interracial athletics in that state. In a pointed challenge to Burnett, the bill's sponsor, state senator B. H. Rogers, stated that his legislation was specifically directed at the newly integrated Texas League. Angry that his plans were being interfered with, Burnett prepared to ask George Trautman, president of the National Association of Professional Baseball Leagues, the minor leagues' governing body, to shift all Dallas games scheduled for Shreveport (a Texas League city) to sites outside Louisiana should this bill become law. He also pointedly addressed the legislation, stating that "Negroes and whites fight side by side in Korea and I can see no reason why they shouldn't compete together in athletic events." Rogers's bill eventually died in the Louisiana Senate, eliminating the most serious obstacle to Burnett's integration of the circuit.

As the season progressed, it became obvious that Dallas had a true phenomenon on its hands. Not only was Hoskins quickly becoming the star of the Texas League, but he was also attracting African Americans to ballparks in unprecedented numbers. Black fans occasionally outnumbered white patrons in some early season games where Hoskins pitched. In his third straight victory, a 9–2 win over the Houston Buffaloes, 5,954 of the 11,031 fans were black. The crowd, one of the largest in Houston sports history at that time, overflowed into the outfield, where African Americans cheered every move made by the Eagles' star hurler. The average attendance for the two games of the series when Hoskins was not on the mound was 2,935.

In Beaumont, a record crowd of 5,430 (3,402 were African Americans) watched Hoskins lose his first game of the year. The average attendance for the remaining three games of the Beaumont series was 1,570. Days later, a crowd of 5,466 watched Hoskins defeat the Shreveport Sports at Dallas. Half of the fans that night were black. By the end of May, Hoskins was credited with attracting half of the 50,580 fans who came to various ballparks when he pitched.

The enthusiastic reaction to Hoskins caught even Dick Burnett by surprise. During one early season game in Dallas, where half of the 5,721 patrons in attendance were black, 300 of these fans, with no place to sit, stood in the outfield against the left field fence. The portion of the stands set aside for African Americans was full, while "hundreds of seats" remained available in the white section. Following this game, Burnett apologized for his lack of foresight and integrated the grandstand at his eponymous ballpark, making seats available to black fans for each game from then on.

While many whites greeted Hoskins warmly, blacks were doubly enthusiastic about the young pitcher. Not only was he a groundbreaker in this southern circuit, but Hoskins was also the star of the Texas League. He won his first five games and batted .400 while ignoring whatever racial slurs were tossed at him. Fans often helped the Eagles hurler, sometimes drowning out the insults with applause and cheers. Hoskins's on-field achievements and quiet demeanor, along with the overwhelming fan response, prompted other Texas League owners to consider signing African Americans for their teams.

In fact, Hoskins's performance was exactly what Branch Rickey predicted would be needed for this venture to succeed. Upon being told of Hoskins's addition to the Eagles roster just before the start of the regular season, Rickey, recalling Jackie Robinson's inaugural campaign, opined that for Texas League integration to triumph, "[Hoskins] should be a good ballplayer. He should be a valuable player. Otherwise, such a move would be unnecessarily daring."

Hoskins's exalted status, however, did not alter the realities of southern life. On road trips, he roomed with John Hobbs, the Eagles' African American trainer. They stayed in private homes or black hotels and were restricted to eating in segregated restaurants. Hoskins was given a new roommate on 17 May, when the Eagles added their second black player, pitcher Jose Santiago, who quickly matched his teammate's success, drawing fans (3,140 African Americans out of a total crowd of 6,580 in Houston on 3 June) and winning games. Two months later, Oklahoma City made it three black pitchers in the league by signing twenty-six-year-old Bill Greason, who won the first game he pitched before the largest home crowd (5,751) of the season. On 3 August, Greason and Hoskins faced each other in what was billed as a historic first-time duel between black pitchers. This event drew Dallas's biggest crowd of the season, 11,007, to Burnett Field, including 5,841 African American fans. They watched Greason top the hometown star 3 – 2 in the opener of a doubleheader. That night, after the ball game, Dick Burnett was recognized for his line-breaking efforts by the Dallas YMCA. He was presented with a plaque that read "The One Who Has Done Most to Improve Race Relations in 1952."

As the 1952 season drew to a close, Hoskins was still attracting people to Texas League ballparks and winning, notching his twentieth victory on 28 August, Dave Hoskins Night at Fort Worth's LaGrave Field. Fort Worth's African American fans, more than one-third of the 9,671 fans present at the ballpark, gave several gifts to the Dallas pitcher before the game. Dallas held a night of its own for Hoskins on 3 September, when local black fans showed their appreciation for Hoskins by similarly showering their hometown hero with various presents. While his popularity had its roots in his trailblazing status and playing ability, Hoskins also endeared himself to African Americans throughout the league in 1952 by giving much of himself through appearances at numerous community group functions. Throughout the summer, Hoskins signed countless autographs for children and adults alike.

The 28 August attendance in Fort Worth brought the total number of fans who had watched Hoskins pitch in thirty-two games throughout the Texas League to 183,643, a per-game average of 5,739. If Dave Hoskins had been his own ball club, the number of fans who paid to see him pitch in 1952 would have ranked the pitcher third in total season attendance among actual Texas League franchises.

Paced by Hoskins's league-leading 22 wins, as well as his 280 innings pitched, 26 complete games, 2.12 ERA, .328 batting average, and league All-Star selection, Dallas captured the regular season pennant but lost in the first round of the play-offs to Oklahoma City. The Eagles' two wins in this series were fittingly credited to Dave Hoskins. Not surprisingly, Dallas, with its all-star pitcher and the Texas League's prime gate attraction, also led the circuit in total attendance, with 266,523 — 39,269 more than in 1951. The Eagles were the only franchise to top 200,000 fans in 1952, a year when league-wide attendance dropped more than 36,000 from the previous year's total.

Dave Hoskins, who reached the major leagues with Cleveland in 1953, was the most significant figure up to this point in the early integration of southern minor-league baseball. Through his spectacular performance and stoic endurance of segregation and racism, he defied stereotypes and calmed anxieties. Hoskins, together with Jose Santiago (14–7) and Bill Greason (9–1), showed southern whites they could play baseball. They also helped quell the irrational racial fears that so many whites were subject to—the product of generations of segregationist myth that painted black men as untamed, inferior beings. Hoskins's on-field performance as well as the fortitude he displayed convinced other Texas League owners it was time to employ blacks on their teams. Tulsa, Beaumont, and San Antonio integrated the next season. Hoskins also brought the national pastime home to African Americans in this part of the country. Blacks in Dallas, Houston, Tulsa, and other league cities gained spiritually and emotionally from watching a black man best whites in a once-segregated sport. They also benefited more tangibly, with the integration of Burnett Field's grandstand. In the end, Hoskins had just what Branch Rickey thought was essential for him to make Dick Burnett's Texas League gamble pay off. Coincidentally, Branch Rickey had played in Dallas as well, forty-seven years before Dave Hoskins. In 1905, Rickey, then a twenty-three-year-old graduate of Ohio Wesleyan University, was the Dallas catcher before moving up to the big leagues later that season.

Don Mossi, who also pitched with his friend in Cleveland, recalls the 1952 season in Dallas, when Dave Hoskins was the star of the Texas League.

Dave was a very nice guy. He was very personable, and he knew the situation. It was tough. I was surprised, and being very liberal myself, I couldn't understand the segregation at first. With the team, we'd get to the hotel and I'd look around and say, "Where's Dave?" I'd find out he was over at the black hotel. I never got used to the situation, and I didn't like it. You couldn't socialize with blacks. You couldn't drink in the same fountain. When a white man was walking down the street, you [African Americans] had to get into the gutter.

Dave kept his place. He knew people were looking at him, wondering what he'd do. He knew he couldn't say anything. He knew he had to just do his job. There were black families the team knew wanted to help out. They would pick him right up at the ballpark. He didn't even go on the bus, unless we were all going to the airport. But he kept to himself. He never really talked about what was going on. There were always fans who would voice their opinions. You'd go into towns, and people would say things, nasty things about Dave. He kind of held things in.

He was a breaking-ball pitcher. He threw a fastball, but his main thing was the breaking ball. He had good control. Dave was always working on something, on the side, in the bull pen, along the lines. When he pitched, it seemed that everybody wanted to watch him. That was just his year. I do recall the enthusiasm of a lot of blacks because of Dave. They were hollering for him wherever we went. Black fans had found somebody they could root for.

They had been so oppressed for so long. Now, they had somebody to be excited about. It made them feel pretty good. They wanted to take part in what Dave was doing. They had so little to take part in and enjoy then. Dave was something special. Until then, the whites had it all locked up.

Some of the southern boys on our team might have been buzzing back and forth about Dave early in the season. We had some real southern boys, too. But they didn't say anything. No one had a problem with Dave playing. It was bigger for the fans than the players. Everyone was just kind of watching to see what would happen next.

The sooner the people saw him, the sooner they'd get into their heads that blacks and whites could be together. If you could play ball, why not get the chance? Whites might as well have gotten used to this sooner than later.

What Mossi, his teammates, and others did not know in 1952 was that Hoskins's life was threatened prior to an Eagles game in Shreveport on 9 June. Hoskins ignored the threats and did what many other African American athletes of his era did: He played that day, taking out whatever anger and frustration he felt on his opponents, defeating the Sports 3 – 2 before a record crowd of 7,378. As reported in the *Shreveport Times,* the 4,403 African Americans at the ballpark "completely overflowed the right field stands, did the same to the left field bleachers and left at least a thousand standing along the right field fence. Although ground-rule doubles were in effect, only two balls were hit into the mob all evening." In a 4 March 1953 *Sporting News* article, Hoskins recalled that day:

I received three letters that morning, one at a time. First one said I'd be shot if I sat in the dugout. Second one said I'd be shot if I went on the field, and the third one said I'd be shot if I took the mound. I figured all three were from the same person. Probably someone just trying to scare me. I didn't tell Dutch Meyer, the manager of our club, because I was afraid he wouldn't let me start. Dutch doesn't know about it to this day. Even though I thought the person who sent the letters was only bluffing, I was a little scared when I went out to the mound. Later on, I didn't even think about it and it was just another ball game. We won it without any trouble . . . The people treated me very nice in Dallas and everywhere else, too. Once in a while a ball player or a fan would holler something at me, but you've got to expect that. All in all, I had no complaints.

Dave Hoskins won nine games and lost three as a spot starter and reliever for the Cleveland Indians in 1953. He played sparingly the next season and then bounced around the minors for several years, never returning to the big leagues. He died in 1970.

3 | Change, Tension, Resistance: 1953

If the Negroes are good players, they are extremely popular with the fans and boost attendance. Baseball has long been a melting pot for various nationalities and creeds. It is one of the world's most democratic institutions. We believe that the time is here when the player is accepted for what he can do on the field in helping his club win games. Naturally, if he is good, he is helpful at the box office.

—HOWARD GREEN, PRESIDENT, BIG STATE LEAGUE, 1953

Nineteen fifty-three was a year of anticipation, excitement, and caution for African Americans and southern whites. Southern baseball integration proceeded apace as more teams and leagues opened up their rosters to nonwhite athletes. While integrated baseball was helping to bring about the erosion of formerly impenetrable racial barriers, Dixie and the rest of the nation focused on a potentially more explosive development. As 1953 progressed and the baseball season began, much of America eagerly and anxiously awaited the United States Supreme Court's school desegregation decision in five consolidated cases arising from NAACP legal challenges to segregation in Clarendon County, South Carolina; Prince Edward, Virginia, Washington, D.C.; Wilmington, Delaware, and Topeka, Kansas.

Emotions ran high as blacks and whites contemplated the ultimate pronouncement on the constitutionality of segregated public schools.

Nearly everyone realized that a Supreme Court decision against school segregation would represent the beginning of the end to other aspects of de jure segregation.

However, in early April the high court dramatically delayed the release of its opinion until the 1954 court term. While disappointment echoed from many quarters after the announcement, many white political leaders and segregationists expressed relief. Many such politicians wistfully clung to the belief that the Supreme Court would never abolish public school segregation, and for the time being, their dire predictions of racial unrest and bloodshed resulting from a school desegregation ruling were held in abeyance.

A large number of southern whites, fearful of the looming court action, were also aware that baseball integration could well be the first in a wave of similar efforts. They had already witnessed subtle changes in Dixie, not only resulting from baseball democratization. They included court-mandated selectively equal access; integration of graduate university programs in states such as Arkansas; and increased hiring of African Americans in the urban workplace, as southern industrialization forced many employers to seek out blacks to fill expanding factory labor needs. With the Supreme Court now preparing to act, segregationists had reason to be especially passionate in their dedication to stopping any further damage to Jim Crow and southern white racial traditions. Although careful not to assert their outright refusal to obey a mandate from the nation's highest court, some southern governors openly discussed the consequences of declaring segregation unconstitutional. The response of Georgia governor Herman Talmadge, a committed segregationist, was typical. There would not be enough soldiers in the entire country, he said, to quell the bloodshed resulting from any court decision ending school segregation. Talmadge refused to believe the high court would act so irresponsibly, in his view, as to intrude into matters best left undisturbed, as they had been for many decades. "In addition to the precedent of law," he told the *Savannah Morning News,* "the court surely will consider other consequences of such a decision. I can't imagine that the justices would be so improvident to hand down such a decision."

Talmadge invoked the South's standard historical reaction to attempts to interfere with its "peculiar institutions," be they slavery in the 1850s or Jim Crow in the 1950s. By advising the high court not to trample upon long-held southern institutions and racial practices, Talmadge and his political allies were sending clear signals to their constituents, together with northern judges, politicians, and others: "Leave us and our traditions alone or suffer the consequences."

Just as their Confederate brethren did in 1861, southern governors and legislators made arrangements for their incipient conflict. This time, their battlefields would be courthouses, legislatures, and state houses across Dixie. Lawmakers in Georgia and South Carolina announced plans for legislation designed to preserve segregation regardless of the Supreme Court. Virginia governor John Battle and Mississippi governor Hugh White promised to call special legislative sessions in case the high court outlawed segregation. Governor White planned to introduce proposals to equalize white and black school programs, preserving the separate and effectively unequal facilities permitted by the Supreme Court's *Plessy v. Ferguson* decision of 1896. Portending the years of struggle ahead for America, Governor White stated, "If the decision is against segregation, I don't believe persuasion would have any effect. I've said before that an adverse reaction would create a serious problem in Mississippi for which I have no remedy. It will take a smarter man than I to find the solution."

The Eisenhower administration's plans to integrate schools on southern army bases by the beginning of the 1953–54 school year sparked a storm of protest in Dixie, providing a preview of the reaction to a more far-reaching United States Supreme Court pronouncement. Governor Talmadge warned the president he would be making a "great mistake" if his plans were implemented. The words of Congressman Arthur Winstead of Mississippi, a member of the House Armed Services Committee, resonated throughout the capitol and would be repeated by segregationists many times over in their years of futile resistance to integration: "We'll not take this lying down. We'll fight it."

Although the question of school desegregation would have to wait, southern baseball integration would not be delayed. Several teams and leagues, in the largest numbers to date, sought black ballplayers more actively than ever before. While some southern cities continued to resist proposals to integrate their minor-league teams, many in this region had become acutely aware of the financial benefits of having black players as drawing cards. For example, when the Brooklyn Dodgers and Milwaukee Braves staged a 1953 preseason game in Nashville (a city whose minor-league team was all-white), more than half of the 12,059 people in attendance were African Americans. Most of these fans were drawn to the game to see some of baseball's most prominent black ballplayers, including Jackie Robinson, Junior Gilliam, and Roy Campanella.

Elsewhere in Dixie, excitement ran high among African Americans about integration in the Class B Piedmont League, with eight teams in Pennsylvania, Maryland, and Virginia. An exhibition game between the newly integrated Portsmouth (Va.) Merrimacs and a team from the Oceana Naval Air Station attracted 1,250 African Americans, out of a total crowd of 1,915. When the league opened its regular season, seven African Americans took the field with their white teammates on four Piedmont League franchises. A total of 3,601 fans, including 1,091 blacks, watched the Merrimacs and their African American shortstop, Eugene White, "make their debut by walloping the lily-white Norfolk Tars, 10–3." In a quirk of historical irony, the Merrimacs, the league's first southern team to integrate its roster, were named for the Confederacy's first ironclad naval vessel from the Civil War. While some southern traditions occasionally yielded to change with varying degrees of resistance, others, including a reverential connection to the War between the States, did not.

Some teams continued staging various promotions featuring African American athletes, seeking to capitalize on the "Negro entertainment dollar" in any manner they could devise. On 8 August, the Peoria (Ill.) Chiefs arranged what was billed as "the first Negro wedding" in an organized-baseball park between Jim Fishback, Peoria's second baseman, and Alma Cornett. Fans gave the newlyweds $703.79, and the local Old Timers association donated a floral wreath and $54. Pampa, New Mexico, of the West Texas–New Mexico League, followed suit on 19 August, prior to a game against Amarillo, Texas. On that day, the largest crowd of the season, 2,599, paid its way into the ballpark to witness the wedding of Pampa Oilers second baseman Ben Felder. For a matrimonial send-off, the newlyweds were given gifts from fans and 10 percent of that night's ticket revenue. As an added incentive to prospective patrons to come to the ballpark, two African American pitchers, Pampa's Sam Williams and Amarillo's Eddie Locke, were scheduled to oppose each other in that night's game.

Arguably the most controversial color line yet to fall was the long-standing barrier in the South Atlantic League, nicknamed the Sally. In 1953, its fiftieth anniversary season, this circuit's Savannah and Jacksonville teams fielded a total of five black ballplayers. One of them was a skinny, nineteen-year-old second baseman named Henry Aaron. Integration of the Sally was a true milestone. This league consisted of old-line, traditional southern cities steeped in Jim Crow mores, such as Macon, Georgia; Columbia, South Carolina; and Montgomery, Alabama. Montgomery, the so-called Cradle of the Confederacy, was the first capital of the Confederate States of America and the place where Jefferson Davis took the oath of office as the CSA's president.

During the season, these five players often provided a boost to league attendance, which had sagged in recent years, drawing in the largest numbers of African American fans in the loop's history. South Atlantic League president Dick Butler noted in an interview with the *Pittsburgh Courier* that this was one of the prime reasons behind the circuit's decision to drop its color barrier.

> The weakest point of the league has been attendance. The entrance of the Negroes into competition with our other boys should reach the fans we haven't touched before. Until the novelty does wear off, it's possible the new lads will receive a little more abusive treatment from the stands than would be normal otherwise. In some cities, the trip down the first base line past the bleachers may get pretty long. But I believe that too will pass . . . That Negroes are now playing in the Sally League is natural. They're playing in the majors, all three AAA leagues, the Texas League and others all over the country. It's inevitable that they come here, and reasonable to assume that they'll one day be in virtually every league in organized baseball.

While Jacksonville was busy integrating its team and garnering increased revenues from the influx of African American and white fans eager to see Aaron, the league's new superstar, nearby Jacksonville Beach was undergoing a different experience. That city's Sea Birds, of the Class D Florida State League, backed away from integrating their team after a vocal remonstration by white citizens, including city government officials and the American Legion and chamber of commerce. Fred Schilling, the team's business manager, announced the Sea Birds' decision not to use African American players after a protest meeting was held in late March. Mayor I. D. Sams took the safe route for a southern white politician, saying he had to support the integration retreat "because of the pressure brought on me by citizens."

H. M. Shelley, secretary of the chamber of commerce, denied that racism was behind his organization's opposition. But his words rang hollow given the entirety of his remarks: "No race hatred is involved in it. It's just that patrons of the team felt they would rather have an all-white team." In a more revealing aside, Shelley indicated that since Jacksonville Beach catered to southern white tourists who might cavil at the presence of integrated baseball in their midst, the Sea Birds and the entire community would be better served by remaining among baseball's segregated locations. He also suggested that cities of the Florida International League (such as Miami, Fort Lauderdale, and West Palm Beach), which integrated in 1952, were better suited to the modernity of interracial baseball since they catered to arguably more tolerant northerners. Coincidentally, the Sea Birds' manager was Red Treadway, a former player who left his team in 1946 rather than play against the Montreal Royals and their new infielder, Jackie Robinson.

Although the Sea Birds backed away from integrating their squad, other Florida State League franchises went in the opposite direction. Leesburg's starting lineup featured two nonwhite players, shortstop Raul Fundora and center fielder Lincoln Boyd, formerly of the Negro American League's Indianapolis Clowns. The *St. Petersburg Times'* E. H. McLin, curious to see white fans' reaction to Boyd after the Jacksonville Beach controversy, attended an early season game in De Land featuring the visiting Leesburg Packers. He noted no overt racial disquiet over the presence of Fundora and Boyd, writing, "As far as we were able to observe, the reaction of white fans in the park toward the Negro players was very pleasant."

As exemplified by the situation in Jacksonville Beach, 1953 was also a year of tension and resistance. Despite the currents of baseball change, the Class AA Southern Association, which included Birmingham, Memphis, and New Orleans, remained steadfast in its rejection of African American ballplayers when the season began.

While several dramatic steps were taken to further the integration of southern minor-league baseball, opposition to such reform in some quarters sparked heated debate. In Birmingham, a city ordinance criminalizing interracial athletics was the focal point of controversy. Jim Tugerson, an African American ballplayer in the Cotton States League, filed a federal lawsuit in Arkansas seeking damages against the league because it refused to permit him to play for one of its teams.

With the South forced to wait until 1954 for the Supreme Court's segregation pronouncement, an atmosphere of uneasy peace pervaded the region. Dixie's practiced racial intolerance became even more poignantly obvious. A Miami, Florida, federal grand jury investigating the Ku Klux Klan issued a "catalog of terror that seems incredible," the *Baltimore Afro-American* reported. Grand jurors detailed violent acts dating from 1943 to 1953 for which they found the Klan culpable, such as the beating of an African American man by five Klansmen in 1949 for "sassing white women" and the bombing of a business in Orlando in 1951 after management did not heed a warning to provide separate windows for its black and white clientele. Most of the violence documented in the report was committed in the Orlando area of central Florida, where the grand jury noted that "such things have been going on for years." Other incidents occurred around greater Miami.

Bus drivers in Baton Rouge, Louisiana, went on a four-day strike to protest an ordinance mandating equitable seating for black and white passengers on city buses. Two drivers were fired for their refusal to obey the ordinance, prompting a sympathy strike by their erstwhile co-workers. More than twenty thousand white area residents joined in the protest, which ended when the law was invalidated by the state's attorney general. By contrast, African American leaders in Memphis warned of a citywide bus boycott to protest "threats and terrorizing of Negro passengers by two bus company employees." These drivers had unreservedly reminded black passengers of their secondary status under Jim Crow when they did not vacate their seats for white passengers who were unable to find their own places to sit.

With racial lines demarcated, the South awaited what would become one of the most important judicial proclamations in American history. Until then, whites and blacks could only imagine the contours of the impending change that would result in a decision by nine white male Supreme Court justices in Washington, D.C.

21 MARCH

PHOENIX, Ariz.—Perhaps the hardest-working rookie in a [New York] uniform is Bill White, rookie first baseman. Reason, White wants to go to a Class "C" league in the North rather than face discrimination if he goes into the Carolina League.—*Pittsburgh Courier*

At the end of spring training, Bill White did not get his wish. He spent a difficult 1953 season, his first in professional baseball, as the only African American player in Danville, Virginia. White had to be removed from several Carolina League games that summer because of heated shouting matches between him and hecklers. Furious with the fans' racist reactions to him and tired of abiding segregation, White asked Danville's manager to send him to a minor-league team in Minnesota. His request was rebuffed, in large part because White was the team's leading hitter. As described in the book *Crossing the Line*, White recalled that difficult summer. "Perhaps the Giants weren't sensitive to the problems I faced in the Carolina League. [But] the more fans gave it to me, the harder I hit the ball. They eventually decided to leave me alone, which was a victory over bigotry. Taking it out on the ball was, you might say, but one of the psychological effects of segregation on me. The other was—I rebelled. I yelled back at the name callers. I was only 18 and immature."

White hit .298 with 20 home runs and 84 runs batted in for the Danville Giants. The following year, he led the Class A Western League with 30 homers and 40 stolen bases. Three years later, he began a standout thirteen-year major-league playing career in which he compiled a lifetime .286 batting average. White was also a two-time National League All-Star

(1963–64) and a seven-time (1960–66) winner of the Gold Glove Award as the National League's top fielding first baseman. In 1989, twenty years after retiring as a player, Bill White was named president of the National League, the first African American to attain the presidency of a major sports league.

3 APRIL

A few days ago, I announced in this column that Edwin (Gum) Charles, local athlete, was in spring training with the Ft. Lauderdale Lions of the Florida International League and that if he made good, he'd be in town to play against the St. Petersburg Saints . . . We further stated that hundreds of Negro baseball fans would go to the park when the Ft. Lauderdale team came to town, primarily to wish Charles well . . . when we arrived at Al Lang Field Wednesday night and saw Carlos Santiago, shortstop, and German Pizarro, rightfield, both Negroes with the Saints, we were surprised and delighted. From now on, I am certain that every Negro fan in town will think of the St. Petersburg entry in the FIL [Florida International League] not as "the Saints" but as "our Saints." Already I have the same feeling for "our Saints" that the thousands of Negroes all over America have for those major league ball clubs with Negro players on their rosters.—*St. Petersburg Times*

Ed Charles, who carried his father's nickname, Gum, while playing in Florida, remembers his time in the Florida International League fondly. He returned to the league in 1953 after failing in his attempt to make the Saints the previous year. Playing then for the Fort Lauderdale Lions, he was one of four black ballplayers, together with Dave Barnhill, one of those who broke the FIL color line in 1952, George Handy, and John Davis. Of his many stops in eight years of playing minor-league baseball in the South, Charles's season in Florida stands out as his favorite.

There were a lot of fair-minded white people in the South who wanted to see things change, who wanted to do the right thing. They just wanted to treat you like a human being, and a lot of them did. I was very fortunate, growing up in St. Petersburg and being born in Daytona Beach. There was a greater tolerance between blacks and whites in Daytona Beach than in most of Florida. Growing up in St. Petersburg, I also found the climate there to be quite compatible.

Playing in my home state of Florida in '53, I felt quite comfortable. I didn't sense the intense racial divisions in Florida that would come in other areas. The cities that comprised the Florida International League were not the little towns, the remote villages where the division between the races was very intense, where you'd experience a harsher type of experience between the races. In cities, there was a little more tolerance. It didn't bother me to play in places like Tampa–St. Pete, West Palm Beach, Fort Lauderdale, Miami.

When I came into the Florida International League, I was comfortable. That's not to say that things had opened up enough that you felt part of the team. We couldn't live or eat with our white teammates. We had to go find places to stay in the black neighborhoods. I left the Fort Lauderdale team in June after I was drafted into the army. Looking back, I do not recall any incidents taking place of a racial nature [in the Florida International League]. Pepper Martin was my manager. Pepper was a great manager. He was very funny, and he was the right manager for me at that time in terms of his attitude and outlook about things. All Pepper wanted to know was if you could play. If you could, he had no problems putting you out there.

8 APRIL

DAYTONA BEACH, Fla.—General Manager Hank Greenberg of the Indians, after being informed that authorities at Winter Garden, Fla. had refused to permit two Negro players in the Cleveland farm system to perform there, has ordered that no games be played where colored players are barred.—*New York Times*

6 MAY

MIAMI BEACH, Fla.—Negro church delegates turned to Miami's Negro section for lodgings today after a move to turn over to them an ocean front hotel in an all-white area had been canceled because of telephone threats to the management. George Rone, [manager of the Betsy Ross Hotel, believed that] advance publicity had brought scores of threats . . . "If we hadn't received all this advance publicity, we might have been able to quietly perform a service needed here in the South," Mr. Rone said.—*New York Times*

9 MAY

TEXARKANA, Tex.—A near-riot was barely averted last week in the second game of a twinbill between Paris and Texarkana in the Big State League. The disturbance came about when Moe Santomauro of the Paris team resented a close pitch by Negro Cuban pitcher Pete Naranjo. Santomauro tossed his bat at the tan hurler and then charged to the mound. Immediately, players from both teams swarmed onto the field . . . closely followed by one thousand Negro fans out of the stands. "Oddly" enough, no blows were struck. Santomauro was [e]jected from the game while Naranjo was removed by manager John Davis.—*Pittsburgh Courier*

6 JUNE

TALLADEGA, Ala.—Congratulatory letters from all over the country have been received by Miss Marye Weaver, senior at Talladega College, who challenged the South's jim-crow law by refusing to take a back seat on an interstate bus traveling from Georgia to Alabama.—*Pittsburgh Courier*

8 AUGUST

GREENSBORO, N.C.—The time-worn practice of cross-burning was given a new twist in this college town last week when two shotgun blasts from an irate Negro resident dispersed a crowd of an estimated twenty-five white men after the local police had failed to do so.—*New York Times*

COLUMBIA, S.C.—A busload of Negro soldiers, driven to a police station after one of them sat by a white girl, were fined $1,573 on disorderly conduct charges . . . John I. Rice, city judge, said the white girl testified she asked the Negro soldier to move when he sat by her. He refused, she added, and other soldiers joined in the disturbance. State law requires segregation on buses. —*New York Times*

Texas League

Beaumont	Oklahoma City
Dallas	San Antonio
Fort Worth	Shreveport
Houston	Tulsa

When spring training began for Texas League teams, many were concerned with more than just readying themselves for the coming campaign. They were looking to catch their own versions of lightning in a bottle, also known as the next Dave Hoskins. In Alexandria, Louisiana, the Tulsa Oilers spring home, over two hundred hopefuls were in camp striving to land berths on the squad. One of the most closely watched players was Charles (Chuck) Harmon, the first African American ever to try out for the Oilers. In five previous minor-league seasons, Harmon had batted over .300 four times. In 1952 with Burlington, Iowa, of the Three I League, he led the circuit with forty-two stolen bases while batting .319. Harmon was among the top prospects of the Cincinnati Reds, the Oilers affiliate. He secured a place for himself with Tulsa by batting .361 in spring exhibition games.

When the regular season began, Harmon had an auspicious debut as Tulsa's first black player, driving in both runs in the home team's 2–0 opening day victory over Oklahoma City. African American players were not the novelty in 1953 that they were the year before. When the league opened its new campaign, several teams had blacks on their rosters: Bill Greason in Oklahoma City, Willard Brown and Jim Clarkson in Dallas. Harry Wilson and Charley White of the San Antonio Missions formed the first black pitcher-catcher combination in league annals.

After several weeks, Chuck Harmon's singular racial status on his team changed when the Oilers signed infielder Ben Lott. By mid-May, a third black player, outfielder Nino Escalera, joined the Oilers, giving Tulsa the distinction of carrying the most African Americans on its roster of any franchise in the Texas League. But for these men, their presence on the same ball club had a greater significance. Together, through mutual support, they were better equipped to tackle the rigors of a Jim Crow summer than if they had been alone on different teams.

Chuck Harmon was a product of small-town America, growing up in the southern Indiana community of Washington, a town where segregation was well established. At two of Washington's movie theaters, black patrons were required to sit in the balcony. A third such establishment, with only a ground floor, at first did not permit any African American customers. Gradually, the theater's owner showed a degree of tolerance, allowing blacks to occupy the last several rows of his movie house. Despite the segregation in Washington's business district, its schools were integrated, and Harmon lived in a racially mixed neighborhood, integrated primarily because there were so few blacks in Washington that they were scattered all over town.

As a teenager, he quickly developed into a basketball star, playing for two state high school championship teams. After a one-week stint in professional baseball with the Indianapolis Clowns, Harmon moved on to greater sports prominence as a basketball player with the University of Toledo, eventually earning a place in his alma mater's Athletic Hall of Fame. But baseball was his true passion. After a stint in the United States Navy, where he played service ball against Larry Doby, Harmon embarked on a professional baseball career. In 1947, he broke in with Gloversville-Johnstown, New York, of the Canadian-American League, becoming the first African American in that loop the same year Jackie Robinson broke major-league baseball's color line. Six years later, Harmon found himself a racial pioneer again, in the restrictive atmosphere of the Texas League, where he batted .314. Harmon helped lead Tulsa into the league championship series where the Oilers lost to Dallas.

For the Texas League in 1953, attendance declined by more than 116,000 from 1952. African American players were no longer guaranteed drawing cards solely because of their skin color, and the league lacked a marquee attraction like Dave Hoskins. But it was a sign of some progress that blacks were becoming an accepted, although not yet uniformly tolerated, part of the southern baseball firmament. In Tulsa, attendance increased dramatically over the season's last few weeks, not because of Chuck Harmon, Nino Escalera, or other African Americans, but for a simple, nonracial, baseball reality—the team's play improved and the Oilers found themselves in a pennant race.

> I [Harmon] had names called at me in high school in Indiana. One time, one of the rival players spat on me. I didn't do anything. I went down the floor and put in a few more baskets and held him from scoring. I knew what he was trying to do. When the game was almost over, he apologized when he was going down the floor. He said, "I'm sorry. I didn't want to do that, but my coach told me to spit on you to get you in a fight so you'd hit me and get thrown out of the game." He was a nice kid. If I had done anything, I would have gone over to the coach and knocked him in the head. You're trying to teach ethics to kids, and here's a coach trying to incite a riot, just to win a lousy ball game.
>
> Of course, nobody sees him spit on me. If I hit him, all they'd see is me haul off and hit him. I'd be the one. I'd get kicked out of the game, suspended from high school. If you had a college career, everything would be gone. This would affect all the black players in sports. That's why they tried to get Jackie, call him all kinds of names. If he would have thrown a fist at somebody like that, there wouldn't have been any black players in the major leagues for I don't know how long.
>
> I followed Jackie when I was in high school. I used to read about Jackie Robinson and his brother before him, [and football players] Lester Strode, Kenny Washington, in the black newspapers, the *Pittsburgh Courier, Chicago Defender.* The other [white] papers, every once in a while, would say something about black players. But usually you didn't see anything. The black papers had a lot about sports and who was doing well. When I was with Toledo, we went to the NIT [National Invitational Tournament] finals one year. That's when the NIT was *the* tournament. The

NCAA [National Collegiate Athletic Association] was hardly heard of. We played in Pittsburgh. We had three blacks on our team, and St. John's of Brooklyn beat us in the final game. Naturally, we were in the paper all the time.

Offhand, I didn't think anything about spending the year in Tulsa because that's where the Reds farm club was. To make the major leagues, you had to go where the farm clubs were. They did not have a AAA club, so AA at Tulsa was the highest [level] they had except the major leagues. I had no idea about anything in the Texas League except that it was in the South. I was sure the Reds weren't going to send me someplace that wasn't safe.

Tulsa was very segregated. The ballpark was segregated. You thought about it, but there really wasn't anything you could do about it. When I first went to Tulsa, we stayed with a black family, a man and his wife. When Escalera got sent down there, we found a house that was empty, so we stayed there, Escalera and his wife and me and mine.

The team in Tulsa was upset when they found out my wife and my daughter were sitting up there in the stands. They didn't realize my daughter is black and my wife is white. They got real upset. They were afraid something would happen, some of the fans might get rowdy. I was on the verge of getting sent out because if my wife couldn't sit there, maybe it would be best for me to leave.

My wife said she didn't have to go to the ballpark. They were afraid that if she sat in the black section, the blacks would be upset because this white lady was sitting down there. I told the general manager that there's no such thing. "They've seen light-skinned black people before." He said, "She looks white." I said, "She is white! She's got French, Indian, Black, and German ancestors." I have to give the Cincinnati Reds credit for what they did. They told the Tulsa owner that I was going to stay there. So I stayed. They [Tulsa] called Cincinnati, and they told Tulsa that I stayed there.

I won the first game for them in extra innings. I was hitting very well for the first month. My wife didn't come out until about the first or second week of the season. A lot of the players had played with me at Burlington, Iowa, in the Three I League. The wives would all get together. When we went on a road trip, they'd stay at each other's houses. They didn't think anything of it. Ballplayers' wives are ballplayers' wives. It turned out I led the team in just about everything.

We traveled by train and didn't have any trouble. We rented the whole car. We usually got off the train and went right to the bus. There was no need to linger in the stations. They were segregated.

A lot of incidents happened in Shreveport. It just happened that every time we went in there, Escalera and I would tear 'em up. We would get no less than two, three hits a game. He would lead off, and I'd hit a single or double, and he'd score. It was fantastic what we would do. In one four-game series, we swept the first two, and we each had three or four hits apiece. On the fourth day, we were warming up at the ballpark, taking infield and batting practice. Some of the fans hollered at Shreveport manager [Mickey Livingston], "Hey, when are you going to get yourself some of them niggers so we can win some ball games?" I almost fell over. You didn't want to let them see you laughing, but it was funny. It was a left-handed compliment.

I never tried to figure out why Shreveport was this way. In reflecting back upon it now, the low-class whites in the South were really lower class than the blacks in their own eyes. A lot of the whites called them "poor white trash" to their faces. If they say that to their own relatives, what are they going to say about you? You consider the source. Of course, you can fight, but you'd be fighting a losing battle. You can't just look at what fighting is going to do to you. It's those behind you, those that are coming up. If you want to make it better for them, you've got to walk the straight and narrow. You've got to endure the harassment to make it possible for somebody else. If you don't do it, there may not be anybody else.

We were playing in Beaumont. Don Mossi, who [later] pitched for Cleveland, was lent to us because we needed some pitching. You know how dark Mossi is. With that Texas sun, even the whitest ballplayer looked dark. That sun was beating down on him. He happened to be pitching that day. He hadn't been in there with us before. Escalera was taking batting practice, and I followed him. We got down to Mossi, and he went up there to take his cuts. One of the women in the stands said, "Hey, Herbie, look there. They went and got themselves another nigger. You know we're not gonna beat 'em now." I thought I would die. I told Mossi, and he fell off laughing.

Right after we finished a series in Dallas, they were holding the train for us. It was getaway day, so they told us to remember to bring all our stuff to the ballpark. "We're leaving right after the game. You've got to hurry up and get dressed. There's no loitering in the clubhouse, having an extra beer or anything like that. They're going to call the game at a certain time, so be sure to get ahead."

I told our clubhouse guy, "John, you've got on the clubhouse board that there are going to be ten, fifteen cabs waiting for us after the game to take us to the train station. We can't ride in the white cabs." He said, "You'll be able to ride in them because we hired them. They belong to us." I said, "Okay, John, but be sure you check on that."

That night, after the game, Escalera and I and this other black kid on the team [Ben Lott] happened to be near the end. They had about three or four cabs left waiting. John said, "Get in the cab. It's okay." So we did. There were one or two cabs left, for the trainer, the manager, and others traveling with us. Here are all these fifteen cabs going down a wide street in Dallas, going to the train station. We were near a left-hand curb because we had to make a turn in another block or two. A police car came along. They were just looking at all the cabs. I know they're saying to themselves, "Well, I wonder what's going on with this bunch of cabs." We were slowing up to make the turn, and they looked over into our cab, and as we went by, the driver of the police car hit his buddy and said, "Look there!" He looked over, and they threw on their lights. I knew what they were saying.

We pulled around the corner, and they pulled around the corner with their lights and siren on. They pulled us over. Two or three cabs in front of us stopped to see what was going on. The police came up, opened the door, and said, "You niggers get out of this cab!" The driver said, "What's wrong, officer?" He said, "You can't be riding these niggers in these cabs." The driver said, "I'm sorry, sir, but these are the Tulsa Oilers. This is just one of the cabs that was hired by them specially to carry them to the train station. They're holding the train up for them." The police said, "We don't give a damn who they are. They've got to get out of this cab. You get your supervisor on the phone." He got him on the radio, and then the police said, "Well, I'm going to give him this ticket, and he's got to show up downtown tomorrow." We got back in the cab and went on.

When we get to the train station, we were only a couple of blocks from the station when we stopped; everybody else was standing outside the cabs wondering what was going on. One of my teammates came up and asked, "What's going on, Chuck? Nino?" I told him they wanted to arrest us because they didn't want us in the cab.

We had to rush in and get to the train. We were walking along, and he said, "Boy, Chuck, I don't see how you guys do it." I said, "What do you mean?" He said, "All us white guys got to do is worry about that fastball, that curveball. You guys got to worry about where you sleep, where you're going to eat, and how you're going to get to and from the ballpark. You've got to travel over to the other side of town. With all the extra time this takes, you guys still go out there hitting over .300 every day, and we're hitting nothing. I don't see how you guys do it. You guys have got to take all this crap." That was a compliment. That was the territory. Instead of getting mad, you get mad at that ball, hit that ball harder. Every time we went to these towns, guys always said,

"Where were you and Nino last night? We never see you two guys around the hotel. You got some women in this town? Come on, take us with you some night." We were too ashamed to tell them we were not allowed to stay in the hotels. They didn't see us in the restaurants for the same reason.

Of course, they called you all sorts of names, but they just went in one ear and out the other. They didn't come right up to your face and say anything. Instead, they'd say things like "Look at all those niggers out there. Get that nigger out." That doesn't bother me. But if I were walking down the street and they'd come out and say, "You nigger, you" and like that, you may feel different. If you have an accident, bump into somebody, confront somebody, or walk into a restaurant and they tell you to get out of there, stuff may happen. It would be a different feeling than out on the ball field because there, they're trying to get you to lose the game. I still wouldn't try to do anything, because it was just a waste of time. The only thing you could do is lose and get in trouble. You were alert about the South, about the things you could and couldn't do.

I put up with it because it was the thing to do. If you know the obstacles out there and you've got to defeat them, you put up with it. It's just like a knuckleball. If a guy's got a good knuckleball and you know he's going to throw you knuckleballs, you learn how to hit it. You know it's hard, but you still have to do it because he's not going to throw you anything else.

It's not a crusade, where you say, "I'm going to Tulsa as the first black player, and I'm going to make it possible for other blacks to come along. I'm going to do this and I'm going to do that." That doesn't even cross your mind. First, before I can do any of those things, I've got to make the team, just like a white ballplayer. Your mind is on making the team, not being a crusader. You can't be doing those two things at the same time. You can do it by being the best player out there and playing ball. The other will come along naturally. I looked at making a good-enough impression so that the fans like you. If they do, you're going to make it.

I know I left a little bit of Jackie behind me. When I signed in '47, it was just a year after Jackie signed in '46. I'm playing in Gloversville, New York, in the Canadian-American League. I was the only black on our team. You might say I was the pioneer in that league, but I never thought about it. I was just worried about making the team.

In 1954, Chuck Harmon became the first African American player in the history of the Cincinnati Reds, the major league's oldest franchise, dating back to 1869. Harmon played 289 games in his four-year big-league career, from 1954 to 1957.

4 | Two Different Places: 1953

The South Atlantic and

Piedmont Leagues

South Atlantic League

Augusta	Jacksonville
Charleston	Macon
Columbia	Savannah
Columbus	

Negroes in baseball was sure to come South. It has been a gradual movement, but one that was inevitable. And I personally say: What's the difference if the boy is a good ball player. Anyway, There's nobody that can stop it."
—FAN AT OPENING DAY IN SAVANNAH, 14 APRIL 1953, QUOTED IN THE *Atlanta Journal*

When the decision was made to integrate the Sally, there was no agonizing search for suitable players. The Philadelphia Athletics sent Savannah two top prospects, and the Milwaukee Braves sent three to Jacksonville. Fleming "Junior" Reedy, a Savannah native, batted .290 for Lincoln, Nebraska, in the Western League in 1952, his first year in organized baseball. Savannah's other African American player, Elbert "Al" Israel, won the Class B Interstate League's batting title with a .328 average. For Jacksonville, Henry Aaron (batting .336 for Eau Claire, Wisconsin, of the

Northern League), Horace Garner (batting .318, with 23 home runs and 107 RBIs, for Evansville, Indiana, of the Three I League), and Felix Mantilla (batting .323, with 11 home runs, for Evansville) had all won outstanding-rookie awards in their leagues the previous season.

As the season opener loomed, every franchise in the Sally was aware of what was about to happen in their tradition-bound circuit. These teams, with the exception of Montgomery, had their own tentative plans to hire black ballplayers but were waiting to see how these line breakers fared before making their own bold statements. The hesitation of the Montgomery Grays to integrate their team dovetailed with the refusal of the Detroit Tigers, the Grays' major-league affiliate, to employ blacks at the big-league level.

Coincidentally, Jacksonville and Savannah opposed each other in the season opener. Before 5,508 fans at Savannah's Grayson Stadium, the Jacksonville Braves defeated the Indians, 6–4. The *Savannah Morning News* reported that more than 2,500 African Americans, "who completely filled one section of the grandstand, the bleachers down the left field line and one section of the left field bleachers," attended the game, which drew the highest number of fans of any of the league's 1953 openers. This was a dramatic change from the opening game in Savannah fifty years before, the *Morning News* recalled, when 100 blacks "were in attendance but their seating proved precarious. About the seventh inning stretch, a makeshift stand built on the side of a tenement collapsed and that ended over-the-fence looks."

Throughout the season, African Americans visited South Atlantic League ballparks in unprecedented numbers. In Jacksonville, the average number of black fans per game increased twofold from the 1952 figure. Jacksonville's visits to Columbia, Charleston, Montgomery, and Columbus produced some of those cities' largest crowds of the year, largely because of increased attendance by African Americans. Fan response was so enthusiastic that officials for other teams contemplated adding their own black players in 1953, although none did until the following season.

As the season progressed, teams throughout the Sally installed extra seats to accommodate the increased numbers of fans, black and white, who were flocking to ballparks. "The management yesterday was requested to reserve a section in the colored stands for some two hundred Negro fans who are coming over from Savannah to attend today's game," the *Florida Times-Union* reported on 12 July. A Jacksonville civic organization, the Downtown Lions Club Knothole Gang, sponsored a program that gave free Braves tickets to children. Although few white youngsters availed themselves of the opportunity to see a 28 April game between Jacksonville and Columbia, African American children nearly filled the segregated seating area located in the left field bleachers, a situation that repeated itself throughout the 1953 season. By May, the Macon Peaches had set aside an additional 265 seats in the grandstand for black fans, noting that attendance by African Americans had been almost the same as that of whites.

On 18 May, a crowd of 3,426 patrons, the year's largest, turned out in Augusta to see the Jacksonville Braves and their league-leading hitter, Henry Aaron. In one early season game between Jacksonville and Columbia in South Carolina, the drawing power of Aaron and his team-mates was obvious. Fifteen hundred African American fans came out to watch the Saturday night contest, a tremendous crowd compared to those in 1952, when only 54 black fans on average bought tickets to individual Sally games in Columbia. Overall attendance in South Carolina's capital was also much better than average, where patronage for a typical April game customarily totaled under 1,000. On 24 April, 2,500 patrons (995 African Americans) showed up on a chilly night to catch a glimpse of visiting Jacksonville. "And the fans," the *Florida Times-Union* related, "white and negro alike, cheered lustily as Aaron homered, singled and doubled; with Mantilla pulling off a slick double play at a crucial moment; and Garner homered four hundred feet to give Jacksonville its seventh straight victory." Three months later, on 21 July, Columbia's largest crowd of the season, 5,048, watched first-place Jacksonville best the Columbia Reds, 2−1.

Although townspeople came out in record numbers in most Sally locales, this did not obscure the fact that the league's five new drawing cards were black men playing in one of the most segregated parts of the South. Even white, mainstream newspapers, which generally tended to minimize or ignore stories about racist outcries from fans, could not disregard certain comments from the grandstands. According to the *Savannah Morning News,* reporting on a Jacksonville game in Columbia, "There was a lot of 'go back to the cotton fields' remarks and booing from the stands," which the paper (also typically) downplayed, noting "but little of it seemed to have any overtones of viciousness."

Before the season opener, Aaron, Garner, Israel, Mantilla, and Reedy received highly unusual admonitions from Sally umpires. They were instructed not to rock the boat by arguing any calls or retaliating against their opponents if they were spiked or beaned by a pitched ball. Nonetheless, during one week in July, Felix Mantilla's forbearance in the face of racism from players and fans reached its limit. Jacksonville and Macon engaged in a bench-clearing brawl after Mantilla, who had been hit in the head with several pitches already that season, was beaned again. This time, instead of backing down as ordered, he challenged John Waselchuk, the hurler whose pitch had struck Mantilla. On his way to the pitcher's mound, Mantilla was restrained by teammate Horace Garner, ostensibly to prevent a riot, since many black and white fans were poised to come onto the field to challenge one another. Policemen quickly rushed onto the diamond, where they formed a ring around the stands. This intervention deterred the fans and averted a violent confrontation. Days later, in Augusta, Mantilla was ejected for arguing an umpire's call too strenuously. He was subsequently fined ten dollars.

America's black press responded enthusiastically to the success of the Sally's line breakers. Having black men playing interracial baseball in South Carolina, Georgia, and Alabama represented a significant sea change in southern racial realities.

> If someone had predicted ten years ago that Negroes would be playing with the ball clubs at Savannah, Georgia, and Jacksonville, Florida, neither of which is noted for its liberalism, that person would have been subject to the quizzical stare and the appraisal, "Man, you're crazy." Even Ripley, then living, would have backed off such a prediction as a "Believe it or Not." Nevertheless, it's true—and what's more, integration has not resulted in Doom's Day, as professional race-baiters like [Georgia governor] Talmadge, [Senator] Eastland, and [South Carolina governor] Byrnes would have you believe will result from the merest mixing of Negroes and Caucasians.—*Pittsburgh Courier*

The 1953 Sally season also demonstrated that adding black athletes to team rosters was not necessarily the solution to lagging attendance. While Jacksonville with its African American players attracted large numbers of fans to the ballparks, Savannah was less successful. The explanation for the disparity can be found by examining the teams themselves.

Jacksonville, which won the 1953 pennant, played consistently well throughout the year and was led by the South Atlantic League's Most Valuable Player, Henry Aaron, one of the best major-league prospects in the minors in 1953. He captured the batting title (.362 average) that season while leading the league in runs scored (150), hits (206), and runs batted in (125). On the other hand, Savannah struggled early in the season before coming on strong in the second half, finishing in fourth place, with a 68–73 record, and locking up a play-off berth in the season's final days. Jacksonville's home attendance of 142,721 was more than double the team's figure for 1952. Although Savannah also drew larger numbers of fans in 1953 (84,142), the increase (6,000) was far less dramatic.

The Sally's 1953 attendance boom justified, in an economic sense, the league's decision to integrate. But integration was not a panacea for minor-league teams. Despite the Sally's record crowds in 1953, seven of the eight league clubs reported that their fortunes were hurt by baseball's new bête noire, television. Sally teams and other clubs throughout the country added television, together with poor weather, to their list of reasons why many fans were staying home rather than coming out to ball games.

Henry Aaron, a native of Mobile, Alabama, began his professional career in 1952 as the shortstop for the Negro American League's Indianapolis Clowns, earning a monthly salary of $200. Aaron was discovered by the Clowns after he starred in an exhibition game between Indianapolis and the semiprofessional Mobile Black Bears the season before. By June 1952, Aaron was being scouted by several major-league organizations, particularly the New York Giants and Boston Braves. He eventually signed with Boston and was assigned to the Eau Claire Bears. The Clowns were paid $10,000 for their shortstop—$2,500 immediately with the promise of another $7,500 if the unproven young infielder could remain with the Braves organization for at least one month.

When Aaron was assigned to Jacksonville in 1953, he was aware of the historic role he was about to play. But Aaron was nevertheless unprepared for the realities of being one of the first African Americans to play baseball in the South Atlantic League. By the end of the season, the highly visible nineteen-year-old's determination to succeed had helped show white southerners that black ballplayers could perform as well as, if not better than, whites. By ignoring the taunts and insults of fans, Aaron demonstrated he had the self-discipline to overcome any kind of adversity.

A lot of people were watching integration in the Sally League. Baseball had to be seen everywhere. Teams all over the major leagues were integrating. They were planning to have black ballplayers, so they had to put them somewhere. Why not put them in the South? They could just as easily play here as anywhere else. You have to also remember that a lot of teams wanted to come south because of the weather. They wanted to go someplace where they could have their teams, their rookies, their young players, get off to a good start and not worry about whether they're going to be playing in cold weather.

I wasn't prepared at all for what would happen that year. When I played in Jacksonville, there were things that happened to me that happened to Jackie Robinson before and after he got to the big leagues. Baseball was having problems in Georgia, in the South, and all over.

When we came here, Horace Garner, Felix Mantilla, and myself, we were three of the top prospects in the Braves organization at that time. I'm sure that the Braves knew we were going to have some problems. But they also knew that if we could just set aside all of the things that were happening and play baseball, we were going to prove to everybody—our teammates, the people that were in the stands, the people that were all over the league—that given the opportunity, we were going to play baseball.

We were not there to start anything. We were there just to play baseball. I don't think anybody had to remind us of what we were there for. There were a lot of things, when Horace Garner, Felix, and myself played in the South Atlantic League, that happened just because we won a ball game. You had people that were hanging around. Crowds that were hanging around. That just meant one thing. They were hanging around to stir up something. People said things to us, calling us names from the stands, but we ignored it, as long as they don't touch you or put their hands on you, then you have no recourse. Just let them say what they want to say.

I couldn't put my finger on which city in the league was the worst for me to play in. I would say all of them. In fact, at the beginning, even Jacksonville could be included. Columbus was as bad as Jacksonville. Jacksonville was as bad as Montgomery. They all had their problems. They just weren't used to black and white players playing together.

Looking back on that season, I start laughing. I say, "I can't believe that it happened." But it did. There were probably a lot of things that happened that I was not aware of. Letters were sent to the manager. Letters were sent to the general manager. I never did happen to open a lot of letters then. I'm sure there were some death threats.

I do remember some things that happened just before the All-Star Game. The governor of Georgia [Herman Talmadge] didn't want me to participate in the All-Star Game [which was played in Savannah]. That didn't surprise me, nor did it bother me. I was prepared, if I could play, to come to the game and play. I didn't care if the governor wanted me there or not. I was there playing as a South Atlantic League All-Star, and I was going to the game. It just so happened that I got in a rundown with a catcher, and he stepped on my big toe and clipped the nail off. I wasn't able to go to the game, so that solved that problem.

The next year, [Jacksonville] had Juan Pizarro, the left-handed pitcher, and they kept building on what we had done. If we had failed, if we had come to the South and started arguing, fighting, and not having a good year, there would have been something for the press to talk about. There would have been something for the league to talk about. It would certainly have been something for everyone to say, "I told you so." By the Braves' sending us here to play baseball—and I had probably one of the best years I ever had in baseball, and Horace and Felix both had good years, and Felix and I got to the major leagues off this team—we proved that by just being given the opportunity, we could play baseball.

We were able to look back at some of the things that happened in that year and laugh at some of the ignorance. Believe it or not, at night, you laugh about it. That's one thing that made you go out the next day and say, "I can't believe that people are this ignorant," and go out and do better. It was a motivator.

Aaron reached the major leagues with Milwaukee in 1954, beginning an illustrious twenty-three-year career in which he established himself as one of the greatest players in baseball history. He set several major-league records but is most renowned for one: hitting more home runs (755) than any other big leaguer. In 1982, six years after his playing career ended, Henry Aaron was elected to the Baseball Hall of Fame.

One of Aaron's teammates in 1953 was Jim Frey, future major-league player, manager, and team executive. In 1952, Frey played at Evansville, where he befriended Horace Garner, who died in 1996. There, in the Midwest's Three I League, the two young men developed a strong bond, generally unfettered by racial restrictions. But this changed in 1953, when their friendship was tested by the realities of Jim Crow.

Horace Garner was one of the players I became friendly with and stayed friendly with over the years. When I was the general manager with [the] Chicago [Cubs], he'd come up [from Cedar Rapids, Iowa] and visit me.

I always thought Horace Garner was one of the good guys I met. I idolized him when we met in Evansville. He was older. I was around twenty; he, late twenties. I always looked up to him. In the Evansville ballpark, it was 477 feet to center field. Horace used to hit balls out over that wall. I couldn't do it even in batting practice.

He and I played cards and spent time together. I was inquisitive about the black leagues [Garner had played for the Indianapolis Clowns in 1949]. He told me about the great players he had seen. We developed a friendship. We spoke a lot before the games, as any young men would speak to each other. But with Jacksonville, Horace and I were separated by the conditions. He didn't like to talk about all the things that were happening.

In '53, we went to spring training and trained in Waycross, Georgia. We were pretty much together there. I didn't notice much of anything. The first situation I got was in Savannah. When we came out of the clubhouse, we had to walk through the stands, right past the fans. They were awful. They were lined up on both sides of us. Their remarks to the black players were absolutely horrible. I thought to myself how horrible that was to the black players, to have to hear this.

I grew up in Cincinnati, in an area called Bridgetown, at the edge of the residential area. When I was about ten, my dad hired a black man to do some stonework around our house. I hung around and was interested in what he was doing. One day, I heard my dad say, "That's enough for today. We'll finish up later. I'll drive you home." I rode with them. On the way back, my dad said we had to get him home before sundown. "Why?" I said. He said, "The Negroes have to be out of town by sundown. That's just the way it is." That kind of struck me. It made an impression.

By the time I got to Jacksonville, the seed had been planted, I guess. I was sympathetic to the black players I came in contact with. When I saw segregation firsthand and heard the daily verbal abuse, it was something I didn't like. It was hard on everybody. Multiply this many times for blacks and what they had to deal with.

In Jacksonville, they had a separated grandstand. They'd charge fifty cents for blacks. I played left field, where the black stands were. On the final night of the season, the black fans presented me with three different boxes, with shirts, clothing, and other things. I treated them with respect. I guess everyone didn't do that.

All of the parks had areas where black fans could sit separated from the white stands. It was redneck country. Many of the young white men were raised with a hatred, or they had a fear that the black man would succeed. The verbal abuse they took was awful. It went on all the time. It wasn't just in Savannah. It was everywhere. My most vivid experience was standing at the end of the dugout and hearing this awful, terrible, fanatical abuse by these young white guys. It was amazing there weren't more problems. When I watched the Jackie Robinson tribute the other night, I thought they did a good job, but I don't think people today understand what it was like then.

I became aware of how difficult it was to be a black player or black person, period. Growing up, we were middle-class people. My dad was the kind of guy who talked about opportunities. You have an opportunity, work hard, and you get ahead and make something of yourself. My experience with blacks in the South was they never grew up with this feeling. They never had the same opportunities I did. They were limited. The worst part had to be growing up with built-in restrictions. They weren't allowed to have dreams of uplifting themselves.

I never saw any black player who did anything other than put their heads down, play well, and weather the storm. They had to. If they didn't, they could get sent home. None of us wanted to go home. Hank Aaron was very quiet. He would just come, play, and go. I always took this as some built-in anger. Black players kept the anger inside. A lot of players I met were like this, like Bob Gibson. They were quiet. They played the game. But years later, once they were established, they spoke out and talked about what happened.

The acceptance of blacks into pro baseball, and subsequently into other pro sports, meant it was to the teams' benefit. They'd have better teams. It was a financial thing since they could make more money. As it became clear whites were accepting blacks, it gave other people the confidence to go out and try to do more— people like Martin Luther King. They could believe change was possible. Athletes could do this. We were on a stage. People looked up to us and followed what we did.

When he arrived in Savannah, twenty-two-year-old Al Israel was considered a good hitting infielder who could also play the outfield. He came from a true baseball family. His older brother, Clarence, was a professional in the Negro leagues, and his younger brother, Dewey, was a standout amateur and semiprofessional player on the sandlots around Rockville, Maryland, a suburb of Washington, D.C.

Al Israel received his first taste of competitive baseball while playing for an American Legion team in Rockville. From there, he moved on to a professional career that began in 1947, when he and Clarence played for the Negro National League's Homestead Grays. The elder Israel had established himself the season before, when he helped the Newark Eagles win the 1946 Negro League World Series with a clutch pinch-hit single off Kansas City Monarchs pitcher Satchel Paige.

Al Israel's career was sidetracked until 1950, when he played in the Negro leagues again, this time for the Philadelphia Stars and their manager, future Baseball Hall of Famer Oscar Charleston. Israel left baseball in 1950 and eventually took a job as a guard at a naval hospital in Washington, D.C. His playing days seemed over until the spring of 1952, when manager Buck Etchison persuaded Israel to suit up and play for his Harrisburg team in the Class B Interstate League. Receiving a six-month leave from his employer, Israel packed and left for Harrisburg. As things turned out, Israel was away from his hospital job for five years.

It was with Harrisburg that Israel had his first brush with baseball racism. Coming home on the team bus following a game, one of his teammates started bad-mouthing blacks, eventually coming around to using the word *niggers*. When Etchison heard the epithet, he wasted no time, warning his player that he would be off the team if this slur was used again. That was the first and last racial incident on the Harrisburg squad that year.

When Al Israel was asked to play for Savannah in 1953, he was unaware of the significant role he and his four fellow African American ballplayers were assuming in the South Atlantic League. Although he had already experienced racism in baseball and in his hometown of Rockville, where, for example, the public rest rooms were segregated, this did not prepare Israel for what awaited him in the Deep South towns of the Sally League.

Junior Reedy was my roommate in Savannah. There weren't but two of us, two blacks and sixteen whites. I had heard about Jackie Robinson coming through Savannah and Georgia, playing exhibition games. But I had not realized that no black had ever played in the Sally League before me. The president of the Sally League [and] the manager and general manager of Savannah asked us if we were willing to go to Savannah because we might be called names and different things might happen. I told them yes.

[Philadelphia Athletics minor-league director] Hank Peters was the nicest guy. We were in spring training in Florida. We didn't have any facilities, like drinking fountains. So we drank out of buckets, and we also used the same towels. Everybody used the same thing. There wasn't discrimination.

After spring training, the night we opened up the regular season, I was inside, and Reedy was out practicing. When I came outside, Junior Reedy told me, "Al, they got a white bucket and a black bucket." I said, "They have *what?* That's not for me." That was too far. I wasn't used to it. I thought it was going to be like spring training. I went over to drink out of the white bucket, and one of the guys came over and said, "That's not your bucket." I said, "We didn't do this in spring training; why should they start it here?" The manager was Les Bell. He came over and talked to me. He said the difference between Savannah and spring training was that now we were in a different place. I said, "I'm about ready to go home. You go talk to Mr. Peters because I'm not going to play."

Hank came around and told the guys, "Look, I just heard about these buckets. I didn't know anything about them. Al Israel is one of the best ballplayers down here, and I'm not going to let him go. If any of you other guys want to go home, go ahead. But he's not going." So he moved the buckets, and we did what we did in spring training, no more segregated buckets.

You got called names. In Savannah, they had to put people out of the stadium for yelling, "Nigger, you can't play ball," "Watermelon," and "Dice shooter." I stopped [segregated ballpark] seating in Savannah, Georgia. My wife came to see me in June. She didn't come to see me until June, because we had one kid in school. She asked me where she was going to sit. I said, "With the ballplayers' wives." I said, "You know they have white on one side, black on the other. You sit with the white people." She said, "I might not come." But she came, and she sat with the wives. That night, all the black people moved over there [to where my wife was sitting]. Nothing was said. Then, from the whole time I was down there, blacks and whites sat together.

The team stayed in a hotel about twelve miles out of Savannah. A lot of nights, we'd come in from a long trip and everybody would go to the hotel. I stayed with people in the city. When we got to the hotel, Les Bell would have to go inside, call to the city to get a black-owned city cab to come nine or ten miles to pick me up. Me and Reedy had to sit on the bus until they came and picked us up. Meantime, there were ten or fifteen white cabs sitting out there, and we couldn't ride in them. Junior was from Savannah. He stayed with his wife. I stayed with Mr. King, who was a black guy. I got used to it.

I had my car, so I would go to Reedy's house to eat, or he would come by my house. We met another guy who owned a cab company. He used to loan us his car and wouldn't charge us. On the road, we didn't stay in hotels. We would stay with private families. But in Columbia, we had a hotel, a black hotel—also in Charleston; Montgomery, Alabama; and Charlotte. In Augusta and Macon, we stayed in private homes.

When Jacksonville came to town, Hank Aaron, Felix Mantilla, and Horace Garner came over to our house, and my wife, Frances, used to cook breakfast. We'd have sausage and hotcakes and coffee, grits, stuff like that. Mantilla was from Puerto Rico, Garner was from down [south], and Hank Aaron was from Alabama. They were used to that food. A home-cooked meal was much better than those restaurants where we'd been eating. They would always come in for two or three days. They'd come the first day and be at their hotel. That night, we'd play, and I'd invite them over the next day for breakfast. That night, they might come by. We'd go to a movie or something, or they might eat something. The next night, they'd be heading back to Jacksonville.

They were regular guys. Hank Aaron was a good guy. Both of us wanted to make it. But I knew within myself that Hank would because he used to knock me down when I was playing third base with line drives. I said, "That's one ballplayer." He could hit that ball.

I spoke my mind. Maybe that was one reason I never made it to the big leagues. I said what I wanted. I didn't want to drink out of that bucket, so I didn't drink. I was ready to go home if they didn't accept what I wanted. They looked at me like, you know, maybe I was a troublemaker. But I wasn't. There were just some things I didn't take.

I had good teammates. I had no trouble in Savannah. The other players in the league were okay. We got along pretty good. I figured that Jackie's playing in Brooklyn would make it easier for the rest of us. But I didn't know it was like it was down there, like the cabs, like sitting in the back of buses—when a white guy got on, you had to sit in the back of them—and drinking out of the fountains—you couldn't drink out of them. I didn't know this.

Sometimes, Junior and I used to talk about what we were doing. But Junior was kind of used to it. He was born there. He understood it a little more than I did. He helped me get used to living down there. He showed me around, told me what you were supposed to do and what you're not supposed to do, like not going certain places.

Jackie Robinson, Willie Mays, Doby, and all of them only barnstormed through [the South]. We stayed down there six months. We were the ones who caught everything. I don't hear too much about what we did that year. It was a little strange, but we put up with it. I always thought that what we did that year was a big help to integration. [But] we just don't get recognized. I'm proud of what I did. I hope I could be remembered for it.

After 1953, Israel spent one more year with Savannah. While playing winter ball in Venezuela in early 1955, he injured his arm, an injury so severe that it caused him to miss the entire 1955 season. Israel came back in 1956, beginning the year with Abilene, Texas, of the Big State League where he set career highs in batting (.326), home runs (12), and runs batted in (72). He also found a different racial atmosphere here.

> It was just like black and white people had been together all the time. It was integrated. There were blacks there before we got there. They were kind of used to it. Nobody paid race no mind. They had three or four years of black players before I got there, unlike some places I played in '52 in the Interstate League. We had places like Hagerstown, Salisbury, and Wilmington, Delaware, which were the same way it was in Alabama and Georgia. The reaction from fans was the same. And in '52, all those places were segregated. You got called the same names and this and that. But I didn't pay any attention to it. I was there to play ball.

Israel left Abilene when he was promoted back to the Sally at the end of the 1956 season. But by now his arm was giving him problems again. He finished 1956 with Columbia, returning there in 1957, his final season. After his baseball career ended, Israel went back to his old job at the naval hospital, where he worked several more years. He spent the remainder of his life in Rockville, spending time with his grandchildren and driving a school bus. He died in 1996. The Israel brothers' athletic achievements are honored by a park in Rockville that bears the family name.

Piedmont League

Hagerstown	Portsmouth
Lynchburg	Richmond
Newport News	Roanoke
Norfolk	York

In the minors, the success of the colored player in the South will furnish an additional conversation piece. All down the line he has continued to prove that

on the field of competition he can give the fans their money's worth and here in Virginia, his arrival in the Piedmont League has been a howling success . . . The colored ballplayer has enjoyed his best year in organized baseball in '53 and from where we sit the opportunity to add to his laurels will increase many fold in the years to come.
—*Norfolk Journal and Guide,* 19 SEPTEMBER 1953

The Middle Atlantic region's Piedmont League established precedent early, before the start of spring training. The York (Pa.) White Roses, who were new to the league in 1953, were also the first to break the color barrier, with Willie Tasby, Joe Vann Durham, Pedro Arroyo, Al Gibson, and Campy Mieres already on the roster when the team joined the loop. To keep up with their northern trendsetting competitors, Portsmouth (Jim Mason, Brooks Lawrence, and Charlie Peete), Richmond (Whitt Graves and Garnett Blair), and Newport News (Charlie Neal and John Glenn) quickly followed suit, giving this circuit the largest contingent of African American players to start a color line – breaking season of any southern minor league to date. The only teams without black players, Lynchburg, Roanoke, and Norfolk, were owned by major league teams (the St. Louis Cardinals, the Boston Red Sox, and the New York Yankees, respectively) that had no African Americans on their own rosters and, for New York and Boston, few in the minor leagues. Hagerstown, an independent franchise, initially did not express any interest in acquiring black players.

Emblematic of this league's generally welcoming attitude toward integration was Portsmouth owner Frank Lawrence's invitation to the three African Americans who were excluded from Jacksonville Beach to try out for the Merrimacs. Although shortstop Eugene White made the team coming out of spring training, he did not last beyond the season opener. Clyde Golden, a pitcher, wound up on the disabled list, and Rutledge Pearson was not offered a contract.

The presence of black players did result in increased attendance by African Americans, although generally not in numbers large and consistent enough to prevent several Piedmont League teams from teetering on the edge of insolvency. In fact, the Roanoke franchise disbanded before the end of July. Developments were quite different in Newport News, where attendance was up over 300 percent compared to 1952. While the season-long competitive play of Newport News, a Brooklyn Dodgers farm team, was an attraction itself, management had also fostered good relationships with African American fans for years. In 1948, for example, the grandstand at War Memorial Stadium was among the earliest in the southern minor leagues to desegregate. At the Piedmont League's 1953 All-Star Game in Newport News, the *Norfolk Journal and Guide* reported that "the overflow crowd completely eliminated the segregation pattern and despite the fact that the fans were seated, shoulder-to-shoulder, [Newport News president Jack Lewis] has yet to receive a complaint from any fan." Nearby Portsmouth was also recognized as providing its black patrons with first-rate accommodations, nearly comparable to those of Newport News.

Contrasting with the relatively tolerant atmosphere in these tidewater communities was that of Norfolk, the Piedmont League's largest city. Norfolk's Myers Field was one of the circuit's most segregated ballparks, with a separate gate and poor seating for African American fans, whose bleacher section was deep in the left field corner; the "partly covered colored grandstand" was between third base and left field. The Jim Crow entrance forced blacks to wait at their designated gate, sometimes as late as a game's fourth inning, to gain admittance to the ballpark, while the whites-only entrances stood empty. The appearance of African American players in Norfolk emboldened local residents to demand reforms of the ballpark's Jim Crow facilities. The area's black newspaper, the *Norfolk Journal and Guide,* noted this imminent sea change: "Norfolk's colored baseball fans have been among the league's most faithful home boosters and they deserve better treatment . . . They've endured inferior accommodations for many years in silence and it appears that they have finally decided to quit supporting Norfolk where it hurts the most—at the box office."

By midseason, Norfolk's blacks started boycotting the local team, often taking their business to nearby Portsmouth. Despite winning the pennant and league championship in 1953, the Norfolk Tars' attendance had dropped by more than ten thousand from the 1952 figure, largely because of the steep decline in black patronage.

Following the season, team management changed, and Norfolk's new owners took note of 1953's sagging attendance. In 1954, they mounted a concerted effort to woo African Americans back to the ballpark. The campaign included discount tickets (sixty-nine games for ten dollars) and the first meeting ever held between team officials and black community representatives, who promised to continue their boycott unless the Tars' ballpark facilities were improved. Shortly after this conclave, the team announced that the main grandstand would be integrated and the separate entrance gate policy, abolished. When the 1954 season opened, Norfolk also featured two black players and an African American trainer. By the end of the year, the Tars had won the pennant and also topped the Piedmont League with a total attendance of 129,918.

As teammates with York, Joe Durham and Willie Tasby played in the Piedmont League's only integrated city, in a circuit whose remaining seven cities were segregated. But Joe Durham knew about Jim Crow. He was a native southerner who grew up in Newport News. The city had no Little League baseball for black children, so Durham and his friends had to fend for themselves, developing their skills in a more unstructured setting than whites. Durham's father died two weeks before he was born, and Joe was raised by his grandparents. Durham's grandmother was small in stature, only about five feet tall, but she had a powerful presence and speaking voice, and she taught her grandson that it was unacceptable to simply dislike people. Instead, she cultivated in him the value of getting to know them as individuals, regardless of color. It was this skill that Durham put to good use while playing in the South.

A local high school athletic standout, Durham turned professional in 1952, signing and playing with the Chicago American Giants, of the Negro American League.

> There just wasn't a whole lot said. You went out and played your game. People didn't bother you. They were just amazed with some of the things you could do. Norfolk had this great team over there, but we played them pretty tough. People seemed to appreciate us coming in and giving them a heck of a game. Hagerstown was the worst team in the whole damn league. They were really bad. I used to hate to go there.
>
> We opened the season in Hagerstown. I'm telling you, I never

heard so much stuff in my life. But that's all drowned out when you come up with three doubles. Then, you forget about it. Newport News was really the only place that drew well. They gave me a night down there. I got several gifts, and they had ropes in the outfield, with people standing behind the ropes.

The trips weren't that long. Being in York, we had the longest trips, but the longest one was from York to Roanoke. It's only about 215 miles down to the Newport News area. We played Newport News and Portsmouth on the same trip, Norfolk and Richmond on the same trip, and Lynchburg and Roanoke together. Hagerstown was not that far from York.

When we went to Newport News, Tas and I stayed at my house. We had a buddy of mine in Portsmouth who would meet the team bus on the James River bridge every day. He would listen to the games on the radio, and when the game was over, he'd drive over to the bridge and pick us up. There was no tunnel in those days from Newport News to Portsmouth. Taking the James River bridge was the quickest way to Portsmouth. We stayed with him in Portsmouth when the rest of the team stayed in the hotel.

When we left York, everything was still segregated down there. Growing up in Newport News, I was used to that sort of thing. Being segregated didn't bother me. The only thing that bothered me was not being able to see my teammates all day, conversing, mingling with them, playing cards.

Joe Durham eventually played in the big leagues with the Baltimore Orioles and St. Louis Cardinals in 1954, 1957, and 1959. On 12 September 1954, Durham became the first African American ballplayer to hit a home run for the Orioles.

Willie Tasby had three minor-league seasons under his belt when he arrived in York with a reputation for outspokenness and power hitting. He batted .283 for Class C Pocatello, Idaho, of the Pioneer League in 1952 while belting 22 home runs and driving in 115 runs.

In Idaho, his unique status as one of the few blacks in the area did not prevent Tasby from having one of the best times he ever had as a professional athlete. Accepted by fans and not faced with segregation, except in Salt Lake City, Tasby enjoyed an excellent season. But he also received an education in baseball politics. Before one game, he overheard manager Ed Fernandes talking to that night's starting pitcher, Virgil Giovanni. Tasby recalls what happened next:

> Ed Fernandes came in and said, "Virgil, I think if we keep their two nigs off the bases, we won't have trouble with this team." Virgil wouldn't shut up. He wanted him to talk. He wanted me to hear. Man, I couldn't hardly get myself together. There was another black player on our team, Steve Hill. I went out there and said, "Ed, I heard you. I was in the toilet when you came into the clubhouse, and I heard what you said." He said, "That was no reference to you and Steve." I said, "Are you crazy? God damn it, if I had been on that team, it would have been me. When you call them that, you call me that. I'm not going to play tonight. I quit. I'm Willie Tasby, but when I'm behind your back, I'm a nigger."
>
> Virgil came up to me and talked me into playing. Man, I had a hell of a night, three or four hits, a couple of home runs. I was mad.

This may well have been where Tasby picked up his reputation for being outspoken and a troublemaker, labels he feels kept him out of the big leagues until 1958, despite the fact that he had played well at virtually every stop he made in nine minor-league seasons before his promotion. Tasby was angered and hurt by the racism and segregation he encountered in baseball, and he experienced these emotions often in the 1953 Piedmont League.

> When we got to York, it was okay there. Joe and I roomed with a black lady in York in an integrated neighborhood. We had no problem in York. But right down the road from York was Hagerstown. That was as bad as Mississippi. That was one of the worst places I played in my life. It wasn't even in what you'd call the South. It's in Maryland. But you see, Baltimore and Washington

used to be bad too. I really can't think of real bad trips or bad scenes except in Hagerstown, in that Piedmont League. We got called everything except our names there, all of the derogatory names. Of course, we beat the hell out of them every time we played there. But we still had to hear them.

In Newport News, we really didn't hear anything. The fans were not brutal. That city had a Dodger affiliation. They had a lot of black guys on the team. In fact, they had guys who were ready to go to the majors, but there was no room for them with Brooklyn. So the Dodgers paid them good money to play minor-league ball. These guys were driving cars as nice as Duke Snider's. That was a pretty nice town. Of course, I stayed with Joe's family there. I didn't stay in a hotel. Incidentally, Willie Mays was down there that year. When we were in town, he'd let us have his car to ride around.

In all those Virginia towns, the only hassles were not so much the fans but finding some place to eat. If they had black restaurants in those towns, they would close early. The game was over, and we couldn't eat. They didn't have any 7-Elevens then. I don't even remember us finding a service station for us to buy peanuts or anything. What you had to do, if you thought about it, was get yourself some kind of knickknack during the day. We had to wait [to eat a real meal] until the next morning. Sometimes, Joe and I would go someplace where he knew people from traveling in the Negro leagues.

I was bitter. I stayed mad all the time. Joe was mad too, but he realized the best thing for us to do was have a hell of a year and get the hell out of there. I'm acting like I was going to be there forever. I'd just go off. He'd keep me cool. Eventually, I got used to it.

If you hit a home run directly in front of me, I'd look to go down. They'd knock you down. That was baseball back then. You expected it. In the minor leagues, it was real bad. If you hit a home run leading off, and I'm hitting fifth and there's three white guys hitting in front of me, nobody came close to them. When I came up, the ball was up in my face. We expected it. All that did was motivate us.

The name-calling and the places we had to stay were the worst things that happened to me. In Hagerstown, we stayed in some kind of a rooming house. We had to eat at the black American Legion. There were no problems with their players, but I think their players really wished the fans would leave us alone. We played outstanding ball against them. They motivated us. We kicked their asses. I remember one night in Hagerstown. We had Pedro Arroyo playing shortstop. If somebody hollered something in the first inning, maybe they should have let sleeping dogs lie. The minute they started, we would get together. Pedro would say, "I'm going to get on and steal them all." We had guys who would hit as high as four or five home runs, some guys twice in a game. I had a lot of good days in Hagerstown.

The other players wished the fans would leave us alone. It seemed like we wouldn't start doing these things until the fans got on us real bad. When this was going on, we'd look at the faces of our white teammates to see how they were taking it. Some of those guys didn't like it. First off, before we really knew how our teammates were, we would watch their reactions. We never really got any negative reactions [to us] from the players on that team. The white guys on our team were really nice guys. We were just like a family. We had some great guys who came forward and to our defense. One was our first baseman, Marv Jones. We called him Footsie. Ray Lindquist was another. He was real fiery. He would holler back, "Shut your goddamn mouth." He would yell some type of southern name at the fans. He would grab his crotch. He would say, "Come on and bite me." They would make us feel good.

We had a great manager, Mark Christman. But they sent him someplace else and sent us George Hausmann. I didn't like him. I told him that. I was a prospect at the time. Every chance he got, he wouldn't play me. But he had to play me because I was a prospect. He didn't care about the segregation. He knew we didn't like it when we got to places like Hagerstown. I actually think I caught him laughing at some of the things they would say, because I watched him all the time because I didn't like him. I watched for his actions and reactions.

When we got together with other black players, we didn't talk about what was going on. We already knew what it was like because we were living it. We just enjoyed each other. We tried to make each other feel comfortable because that's all we had. They had that "no fraternizing" rule but we fraternized—not on the field. We didn't give a damn if they liked it or not. After the game, we all went out together.

We never really talked to any black people in the towns we played in, because they had to stay there. All they said to us was, "Glad you beat 'em. Hope you beat 'em every time you come." And then they'd look around to see if anybody was listening.

During the winter of '53, I went to Puerto Rico. That's where I broke my right leg. I was very outspoken with Baltimore after the franchise moved from St. Louis in '54. I wasn't pleased with the way they handled me. They called guys up to the big leagues ahead of me who, so to speak, couldn't carry my bat, my glove, or anything else. They had me on some kind of blacklist because I had spoken my mind to them because I knew that they were doing me wrong. We were like cattle. They would send you a contract and would tell you to sign it or else. If you don't, you sit or they might cut you. I knew that I had to do things two or three times better than white guys. Nobody had to tell me this. I knew. I let them know this. I told Baltimore, "You know you're not giving the best players in your organization a break."

If I played center field and you [a white man] played center field, I've got to run, hit, and throw. If you would just hit or just field, you'd get the job. If I didn't go two-for-four almost every day, you'd play. If you had a bad series, you knew you weren't going to play. The white guy would play. He really had to play himself out of the lineup. There was nothing you could do except talk to each other and do your job.

There were a lot of black guys who should have been playing baseball. Look at Satchel Paige. Dizzy Dean said, "If Satchel Paige was a white man and the Cardinals had him, between me and my brother, we could go fishing in July because we would have won the pennant." If there had never been segregation, they would have had more than sixteen teams years ago, and there would have been a lot of good players.

I feel as though Baltimore kept me back in the prime of my career. I wasn't given an opportunity. When they did call me up, it was because another team wanted me. You were told to keep your mouth shut. Otherwise, you would get the brand of being a troublemaker, bad for the team. I wouldn't do a lot of talking to reporters, because I was angry.

I didn't feel good about what I did, because I did mine [breaking the color line] reluctantly. I didn't think I should have had to do it. My philosophy was that baseball wasn't nearly as good to me as I was to baseball. I was born in America. I should have been able to play anytime, go anyplace I was able to.

5 | Resistance!

1953

The Cotton States League and Birmingham

Cotton States League

El Dorado	Meridian
Greenville	Monroe
Hot Springs	Natchez
Jackson	Pine Bluff

We don't interpret playing colored players on our club as being detrimental to any club. We hadn't anticipated this sort of reaction. We thought there might possibly be a little resentment and we offered to compromise to use Negro players only where they are welcome.

—A. G. CRAWFORD, PRESIDENT, HOT SPRINGS BATHERS, 1953

Amid the currents of change that were wafting through the South stood the Cotton States League, a solidly regressive baseball amalgam of eight teams in Arkansas, Louisiana, and Mississippi. This league couched its resistance to integrated baseball in nonracial terms, but it nevertheless made clear that African Americans were unwelcome on the professional baseball diamonds of this part of Dixie, especially in Mississippi, home to four league franchises—Jackson, Meridian, Natchez, and Greenville. The Cotton States League's resistance to integration in the spring of 1953 was one of the most vociferous of any taking place in the southern minor leagues and roiled this corner of the South.

Jim and Leander Tugerson were a pair of right-handed-pitching brothers out of Florence Villa, Florida. Jim was a big, tall man who could throw hard; Leander was more of a finesse pitcher, specializing in off-speed and breaking pitches. Leander made his professional debut with the Negro American League's Indianapolis Clowns in 1950, and his younger brother followed in his footsteps the next season. In 1952, Jim posted a record of 14 and 2 with the Clowns while batting .325. Leander won 7 of his 10 decisions with an ERA of 2.12.

On 1 April 1953, with spring training about to begin, the Hot Springs Bathers, seeking to bolster a team that finished last in 1952 and to attract larger numbers of fans to the ballpark (the team's attendance of 37,796 was the league's worst that year), announced the Tugersons' addition to the roster, breaking the Cotton States League's color barrier. The brothers came as a package deal, with Jim as the more desirable quantity. To secure Jim, Hot Springs tendered his older brother a contract as well. Although the Bathers' board of directors unanimously approved their signing, the team was aware of how such a bold step would play in a league where the other franchises had previously agreed, ostensibly, not to make any unilateral decisions to sign African American players. With spring training nearing its conclusion and opening day on the horizon, the stage was set for a battle royal over the pitchers' fates.

As early as January 1953, the Bathers declared their intention to sign black ballplayers for the upcoming season. Cotton States League president Al Haraway did his utmost to discourage such a radical move, commenting to the *Hot Springs Sentinel-Record,* "The people in our league were not yet ready to accept a breakdown in racial barriers. I realize it is difficult for Hot Springs with its cosmopolitan population from everywhere to grasp the thinking of Deep South people . . . I advised against signing [the Tugersons] and requested they do not attempt it at this time knowing the hornet's nest it would stir up."

That the Hot Springs Bathers, in a city about seventy miles southwest of Little Rock, were the first to break the league's color barrier is not surprising. With thermal springs, turn-of-the-century bathhouses, and a national park located inside the city limits, Hot Springs was Arkansas's pre-eminent tourist destination, and it enjoyed a decidedly different, more open atmosphere than other league cities. These attractions, as well as the city's racetracks and gambling parlors, helped bring large numbers of people here from disparate parts of the South. This gave Hot Springs what Haraway referred to as a "cosmopolitan population" compared to those of other Cotton States League communities.

In announcing their decision, the Bathers also declared that their new players would only play at home so as not to incur the wrath of disapproving whites and teams around the league. The Cotton States' other Arkansas-based clubs, El Dorado and Pine Bluff, together with Monroe, Louisiana, supported the integration of their circuit in principle. Hot Springs quickly discovered where the primary opposition to the Tugersons would come from.

In quick order, Mississippi clubs threatened to quit the league if the Tugersons remained under contract. Previously, at the request of a Pascagoula resident concerned about mixed boxing matches in that state, Mississippi attorney general J. P. Coleman ruled that interracial boxing was illegal in his jurisdiction, claiming it was against state "public policy," although he noted that no statute or other written law existed on this point. State public policy could be inferred from such documents as the Mississippi Constitution of 1890, which mandated segregation and outlawed interracial marriage. Coleman subsequently extended his decision to encompass baseball and other team sports.

In a three-hour league meeting in Greenville on 6 April, Hot Springs offered a compromise: They would play the Tugersons in Arkansas and Louisiana only, avoiding Mississippi completely. League directors rejected the Bathers' attempts at conciliation, voting 6–0, with Pine Bluff abstaining, to take control of the recalcitrant team—in essence ousting Hot Springs from the league. The vote was affirmed by Al Haraway, who claimed it was consistent with Cotton States League bylaws. Haraway also pronounced Hot Springs' actions treason against the league since league directors had previously agreed not to decide unilaterally to sign black players. In effect, he was attempting to define the debate's terms as political and procedural by claiming the league was merely following its rules rather than barring two players because of their race. Haraway's efforts were for naught since no objective observer could conclude that this tempest concerned anything other than race and maintaining Jim Crow in this corner of the South. Hot Springs immediately appealed the league's decision to George Trautman, who was, effectively, the commissioner of minor-league baseball.

The league's position on the controversy also interfered with the Bathers' spring training since no other Cotton States teams would play exhibition games against the renegades from Hot Springs. With no professional competition available, the Bathers played several matches against local semiprofessional teams and a squad from the Naval Air Station in Memphis.

Reaction to the league vote, both pro and con, was swift. On 7 April, Leslie O'Connor, a former assistant to major-league baseball commissioner Kenesaw Mountain Landis and an adviser to the Bathers, summarized the sentiments of many when it came to the league's "standing in the schoolhouse door," blocking an attempt to achieve a measure of racial justice:

> I consider this the most grievous error ever committed by baseball. This is especially true in view of the conditions which confront our country and baseball at this time. The league's action is contrary to the liberal sentiments of the American people, and especially of baseball officials, players and fans and is wholly inconsistent with the ideals of our national game.—*Hot Springs Sentinel-Record*

The Tugersons, at the center of the dispute, were similarly outspoken about the decision that put their careers on hold. In a remarkably frank letter printed by the *Hot Springs Sentinel-Record,* they plaintively addressed their comments to local residents, asking when they too would be accorded the same basic privileges as white southerners:

> Why do we get all the breaks down and never up? Are we fit to work in your homes, your fields only? We can talk for you and help elect you when it's time for voting. When you were young, was it fair for a Negro maid to raise you? Now we are the forgotten ones.

There are times when we can look over our past and can't smile because you haven't been fair to us in the South. We don't want to, as Negroes, stay with you or eat with you. All we want to do is play baseball for a living. This, too, is a job. We are still working for you. We only take orders from the field manager to do the job he asks us to do. If we don't try to do the job, we will lose it, just as we would lose it if we were working in your homes as a maid, cook, butler or chauffeur.

We were in need of a job and the Hot Springs Bathers gave us jobs as ball players as a means of support. We hope this is not embarrassing to the city of Hot Springs which has been so nice to us. We don't wish to keep the city from having a baseball team, or its loyal fans from seeing America's greatest pastime sport. We sincerely thank the management of the club for giving us an opportunity few other cities in the South would do. If we have to leave, we pray that all of the people of the South have as understanding a heart as you here. But as long as the club wants us to, we will stay here and fight.

In this part of Dixie, the Tugerson soap opera was front-page news in early April of that year. As the (Little Rock) *Arkansas Gazette* editorialized on 8 April: "We have an idea that the Cotton States League is standing against a tide it cannot long resist. Negroes have earned a secure place in organized baseball on merit. They play without restriction everywhere now except in the Deep South . . . We can't see any social problem is involved here. The fans are the final arbiters, and the turnstiles will record their verdict."

One letter to the editor of the (Little Rock) *Arkansas Gazette* in response reflects how this dispute touched the nerves of many white southerners:

Personally, I do not see any harm in a Negro playing in the game as far as any particular game goes; but if there is no social barrier in the game, there should be none in the social gatherings as a result of those games . . . Now, if you can whole heartedly endorse a mixture of races in your family and do not mind the consequences, then let us say you are . . . broad-minded . . . On the other hand, if you have any consideration for the personal preference of those who wish to keep their pride of heritage, then you will grant those people the right to that preference . . . I have personally discontinued my interest in baseball . . . I lost all interest when the managers lost their morals.

This letter, which was signed "Observer," provoked the following response from another reader:

I am sure that "Observer" must also have "lost" his interest in eating because I am certain that the processing plants employees are in many cases colored. Does the man live in a home that was built entirely by whites? Does he sleep on sheets washed only by the "untainted race"? . . . My advice to "Observer" is to get himself a copy of the Constitution of the United States, with all its amendments, some good books on economics, morals and etiquette and crawl into a hole until he learns what makes this country of ours great."

Several area newspapers editorialized about 1953's hottest controversy in southern minor-league baseball.

[The Bathers] have agreed to play the Negroes at home only or at any other league town which asks for them . . . The clubs so opposed to the Negroes are uncompromising in that they would not be willing to allow the Bathers to keep them confined here. They argue that this would just be a start of breaking down the "color line."—*Hot Springs Sentinel-Record*

As far as we can determine, no Hot Spring players object to having Negroes on the team. We haven't heard any great opposition from Hot Springs fans or from any other Arkansas city. The biggest objector is Natchez. There has been some outspoken opposition in Greenville . . . We are not convinced that a third rate baseball league is any place to make a fight for equal rights because entertainment and not need is involved . . . We believe that the excellent performances of American Negroes in national and international interracial competition provide an answer to the propaganda of our Communist adversaries who say that the Negro has no chance in America . . . We will understand the inclination of Greenville Negro citizens to stay away from the games if the decision is made against the use of Negro players. In the long run, fair play is going to prevail . . . Why can't we realize we're living in a world which is a lot more concerned about saving mankind's undeserving skin than in the skin color of baseball players.—*Greenville Delta Democrat Times*

Willis Hudlin, owner of the league's Jackson Senators, told the *Jackson Clarion-Ledger* that he did not believe the circuit was ready for black players. Mississippi's capital had a reputation for providing an unfriendly atmosphere for visiting African American athletes. In 1951, basketball's Harlem Globetrotters canceled a scheduled game after it became obvious that their African Americans players would not be welcomed on the court by Jackson's white fans.

Natchez was similarly resistant to integrated baseball and the Tugersons, as reflected by this editorial from the *Natchez Democrat*.

The signing of the two negro players was an affront and insult to the rest of the league teams. Hot Springs owners knew the action would cause a furor, yet they never consulted other league members in advance or even notified them of intentions to get the negroes. No one, who is interested in fairness, would take such a far-reaching step that could endanger the whole future of the league. In short, the Hot Springs owners were guilty of a brazenness that would not be tolerated in any gentlemanly company and they deserve what they got.

Natchez, a small city on the Mississippi River in the state's southwestern corner, was a center of opposition to the Tugersons' presence in the Cotton States League. On 13 April, Natchez's baseball directors voted to "keep the faith with the citizenry here and to uphold their personal convictions," declaring that they would hold the line against Hot Springs even if it meant withdrawing from the league. With Greenville and Natchez opposed to seeing the color line fall and Jackson and Meridian reportedly wavering, unsure if the issue was worth forfeiting their franchises over, the Cotton States League anxiously awaited George Trautman's decision. They did not have long to wait. On 15 April, Trautman reversed the league, ruling that Hot Springs be reinstated and the Tugersons be permitted to play, finding that "the employment of Negro players has never been, nor is now, prohibited by any provision in the major-minor league agreement." However, despite the seeming finality of Trautman's decision, Haraway and the league continued their resistance. Rather than submit to integration, they threatened to dissolve the circuit should the Tugersons remain with Hot Springs. The Bathers' board of directors met to decide its next step. Jim and Leander Tugerson, not wishing to be the cause of further controversy, asked to be sent elsewhere, and a Canadian semiprofessional baseball team offered them unsolicited contracts.

Six days after Trautman theoretically forced open the Cotton States League's door to the Tugersons, the Bathers decided to fight no longer. With opening day and the prospect of league dissolution looming, the team sent the brothers to Knoxville, of the Class D Mountain States League. Although the league's crisis appeared to be over, the entire affair left a sour taste in the mouths of many area residents, particularly African Americans.

In Greenville, black residents and civic organizations joined together in an unprecedented effort to protest the conduct of the Cotton States League and their hometown team, the Buckshots. For the first time in city history, these individuals and groups united to call fellow black citizens to action in the cause of racial justice. A hotly worded resolution called for a boycott by African Americans of all local Cotton States League games in 1953. These people decided to say enough—enough of Jim Crow, enough of inequality, enough of being treated as second-class citizens. They pledged to put an end to their years of support for an all-white team that repaid them by refusing to permit blacks to play in Greenville's ballpark. The document called the Buckshots' actions concerning the Tugersons "a slap in the face in view of the fact that we the Negroes in this part gave unstintingly of our time, money, presence and moral support. We feel that the Greenville Buckshots policy making [group] was very generous with their slaps in the face and kicks in the teeth of some of their most loyal supporters. Signed: Inter-Denominational Ministerial Alliance; Washington County Negro Democratic Club; Washington County Negro Business League and Negro Voters League of Washington County."

It was baseball and the lost promise of integration that prompted these African Americans to take a stand against racial injustice, at a time when such outspokenness by southern blacks was discouraged, suppressed, or unknown, two years before Rosa Parks became a national figure for battling Jim Crow. The tangible success of this boycott is difficult to assess since Greenville's 1953 attendance increased by fourteen thousand over the previous year's total. But its effect on attendance was not the crucial issue. Rather, the important point was that Greenville-area blacks had taken a stand in an era when this just was not done, and their collective rebellion set the stage for future activism.

With the controversy seemingly behind them, Cotton States League teams opened their 1953 season with the color line still intact. Hot Springs, without missing a step from 1952, quickly settled into seventh place in the standings and attendance. Team revenues declined because of sagging numbers at ballpark turnstiles and several rain-outs, problems that afflicted the entire league. As the team's pitching staff struggled, at one point using as many as fifteen hurlers, management looked elsewhere for help. By mid-May, the Bathers, down to only four pitchers and struggling financially, were desperate. Seeking a solution to their myriad problems, the Bathers summoned a hard-throwing right-hander who had won six of his eight decisions in 1953—Jim Tugerson. One of the men who had brought the league to the brink of extinction one month earlier now headed back to Arkansas, where he was scheduled to pitch on 20 May against the Jackson Senators.

As expected, the atmosphere in Hot Springs on the night of Tugerson's return was highly charged. Fifteen hundred fans packed the grandstand to see the prodigal pitcher finally appear in a ball game, while several hundred more prospective patrons lined up to buy tickets outside the ballpark. African Americans living in the area made plans for a large contingent of black fans to turn out. E. S. Stevenson canceled a meeting of the Hot Springs Negro Civic League so its members could take part in the local extravaganza.

But there would be no prolonged debate concerning Tugerson as there had been in April. With Hot Springs' largest crowd of the season on hand and before a pitch could be thrown, Al Haraway ordered the game forfeited to Jackson, thus bringing a swift conclusion to chapter two of the league's color line saga.

Jack Bales was the Bathers' catcher that season. This role gave him as much contact with Jim Tugerson as any other player. A native of Hot Springs, he was also intimately familiar with his neighbors' sentiments regarding the furor over his teammate:

I told people here they [blacks] can play ball. If they can make it, fine. Just give them a chance. The town was segregated, but there were always a lot of blacks working in the baths with whites. On Bath House Row [downtown], blacks had their own hotels, but they also worked with whites in white bathhouses. They worked in illegal gambling. Some blacks made a lot more money than whites did. Whites were used to being around blacks here. I never saw the Ku Klux Klan here or anything like that. There were no problems with them pitching here.

Jim had a lot of talent. He could really throw. We didn't have any problems [with his being on the team]. Jim never did say much. He was quiet and pretty levelheaded. He knew what was going on. He accepted it because he wanted to pitch. Both he and Leander, they just wanted to pitch. That night against Jackson, Jim started out to the mound. I was warmin' him up. After a while, we stopped, and I said, "Don't make much sense to keep throwin'. We won't play tonight." He looked at me. He smiled and said, "You're right." When they exchanged lineup cards, the umpires said the game was forfeited. We knew we weren't going to play that night. They got a telegram before the game saying if Jim pitched, we'd forfeit. Jim and I walked off the field together.

After the forfeit, Haraway announced that Hot Springs' recall of Tugerson violated a secret commitment the team had made on the eve of Trautman's April reinstatement decision. According to Haraway, the Bathers had promised not to recall the Tugersons without the consent of four unnamed league teams, presumably those in Mississippi. This time, despite lusty booing from fans on the night of the forfeit, the Bathers did not buck Haraway's edict, shipping Tugerson back to Knoxville, where he pitched the rest of the season. But Hot Springs did appeal to Commissioner Trautman, who once again sided with the Bathers, overturning the forfeit. As each side hurled legalistic volleys at each other, the league's color line remained intact. Hot Springs resumed its lackluster season, drawing 730 fans to the first game since the forfeit, a 15 – 1 drubbing of Jackson. For the remainder of the 1953 campaign, no team made any further attempt to break the Cotton States League color barrier. While Hot Springs struggled, Jim Tugerson and his new team prospered. Upon his return to the Knoxville Smokies, team revenue and attendance soared. Tugerson was a primary reason why this team, so strapped for cash earlier in the season that it had to forfeit one game because it ran out of baseballs, found itself in good financial health by mid-July. The Smokies, in a backhanded appreciation of Tugerson's prowess, soon acquired two new nicknames: the Darkies and the Dark Stars.

On Jim Tugerson Night in June, twelve hundred fans, including five hundred African Americans who were admitted free, paid tribute to their star pitcher, who responded by pitching a one-hitter over Maryville-Alcoa, Tennessee. Jim Tugerson went on to enjoy his finest year in professional baseball with the Smokies, winning 29 regular season games, tying him for the minors' best in 1953. He also compiled a 3.71 ERA and led the Mountain States League with 286 strikeouts while batting .308 and hitting 5 home runs. In the play-offs, Tugerson was instrumental in Knoxville's capturing the league championship by winning 4 games (for a season total of 33) and hitting a clutch home run to ice Knoxville's comeback 14 – 11 victory over the Maryville-Alcoa Twins in the postseason finale. After the game, Tugerson was carried off the field triumphantly on his teammates' shoulders. But Jim's baseball success had a bittersweet quality to it. Amid his success, Leander suffered an arm injury that ended both his season and his career. Jim Tugerson returned to Hot Springs once more before the season ended, during the league's All-Star Game in July. While the league president and team directors were awaiting the start of an All-Star banquet, they were handed court papers naming them as defendants in a federal lawsuit filed by James C. Tugerson seeking fifty thousand dollars in damages against Al Haraway, the Cotton States League, and its constituent teams. This caused such an uproar that the Mississippi teams threatened to pull out of the All-Star festivities and take their players back to the Magnolia State.

In his suit, Tugerson alleged a conspiracy among the defendants to deprive him of the right to fulfill his contract with the Bathers because of his skin color, claiming their actions were unlawful under the United States Constitution, various federal statutes, and Arkansas state law. Tugerson claimed he had been deprived by the defendants "of opportunities of advancement in his career as a professional baseball player . . . and . . . of the right to follow his lawful occupation in the place of his choice and to carry out his contractual obligations."

Essentially, Tugerson sought a judgment declaring this conspiracy and segregation unconstitutional and a ruling that the Cotton States League had no legal right to exile him to another circuit against his will. This latter claim was similar to one made almost twenty years later by another baseball player, Curt Flood, who brought a suit challenging baseball's reserve clause, the system that allowed teams to trade or otherwise dispose of players as the franchises saw fit. Flood's suit, although ultimately unsuccessful, led to the creation of free agency for major-league baseball players.

But Tugerson was attempting something on a grander scale. He was challenging the constitutionality of southern segregation in a federal law-suit in 1953, at a time when few people could imagine the courtroom victories and grassroots activism that would propel the nation toward racial justice. Many also saw the lawsuit as a first strike against baseball's monopolistic tendencies, including its court-sanctioned immunity from federal antitrust laws. Jim Tugerson and his quest quickly became a cause célèbre in the black press, which extolled the courage of this baseball player. The *Norfolk Journal and Guide* reported that "if Tugerson is successful in proving his contentions it will pave the way for other suits that will contest the validity of the reserve clause and other practices that have labeled the game a monopoly. Tugerson is prepared to fight all the way." But when rumors arose that Tugerson might drop his lawsuit, the paper was quick to criticize his anticipated retreat: "Only last week, Tugerson was full of fight . . . but now, the Box has learned, the idea to sell Tugerson to the majors—an admitted effort to get the hurler to drop his Civil Rights suit—has paid off ... The righthander has failed his supporters in the clutch, if the current reports are true, and in doing so he gave the game's exponents of racial segregation a firm foundation for future action against the advent of colored players in their lily-white loops.'"

Contrary to this supposition, attempts to persuade Tugerson to drop his suit ultimately failed, and he decided to pursue the case until a decision was rendered.

In the end, Tugerson proved to be ahead of his time, as a baseball player in the Cotton States League and as a crusader for civil rights. On 11 September, ironically the same day Knoxville won the Mountain States League title, United States District Judge John Miller granted the defendants' motions to dismiss the lawsuit, striking out most of its damage claims. Judge Miller correctly ruled that Tugerson's constitutional rights were not violated since the Constitution only protects individuals from government conduct and does not apply to the actions of private persons or corporations, such as the Cotton States League's directors and teams.

In the rest of his opinion, the judge did not stray from established doctrine: He rejected Tugerson's allegations of racial discrimination. At this point, Congress was still more than ten years away from passing federal civil rights laws that would have given Tugerson a basis for his lawsuit. Similarly, the Supreme Court had yet to extend the reach of post–Civil War era laws to encompass allegations of racial discrimination such as Tugerson's. Although Judge Miller dismissed all of Tugerson's claims under federal law, he sustained the one claim under Arkansas law, that the pitcher's contractual rights with Hot Springs had been interfered with. However, it was unlikely, given other portions of the opinion, that Tugerson could have prevailed on this claim before a southern jurist such as Judge Miller. He was unable to buck the strictures of his times to find a legal basis for Tugerson to hang his cap on.

Jim Tugerson did not appeal this decision, agreeing to the dismissal of his case in December. Although he had been scouted by the Pittsburgh Pirates and the New York Giants in Knoxville, Tugerson never reached the major leagues. He spent the rest of the 1950s pitching in the Southwest for

Dallas and Amarillo, never coming close to the success he achieved with the Smokies.

Jim Tugerson died in 1983 in his home state of Florida, at the age of seventy-three. Leander passed away several years later. Although the brothers were ultimately unsuccessful in breaching one of the South's stiffest baseball color lines, they achieved much, nonetheless. Spurring African Americans to collective action, inspiring black baseball fans in a region where they previously had nothing to cheer about, and undertaking a prescient fight for racial justice in the courts are all part of their legacy. Jim and Leander Tugerson transcended their roles as baseball players, leaving indelible impressions on a small corner of the Deep South.

Birmingham

I remember at the end of the '56 season, Birmingham had a chance to be in the Dixie Series, and my teammate with Houston, Bill Greason, said to me, "I'm from Birmingham. If they win, we may have to go in there and fight the Ku Klux Klan."
—RUBEN AMARO, 1996

Just as the Cotton States League stands out as one of the South's most obstructionist minor-league circuits, Birmingham earned a similar reputation for being stubbornly resistant to change in society's racial order. Alabama's largest city was often at the center of controversy as professional baseball in the South took its first steps toward opening the door to African Americans.

As early as 1950, Birmingham made clear that interracial athletics were not welcome inside city limits. In September of that year, the National Football League's Detroit Lions were scheduled to play the Washington Redskins in Birmingham's third annual Pro Bowl exhibition game. However, the presence of Wally Triplett on Detroit's roster made this more than just a football scrimmage. Triplett, a former All-American halfback, was African American. As far as Birmingham's power structure and most whites were concerned, it was unacceptable for Triplett to play, dress, eat, or associate with his white compatriots on the gridiron. To permit the game to proceed, a "gentlemen's agreement" was reached allowing Triplett to warm up with the Lions but not play in the game.

To prevent the repetition of such an awkward situation, the Birmingham City Council passed the following ordinance on 19 September 1950:

> Sec. 597. NEGROES AND WHITES NOT TO PLAY TOGETHER
> It shall be unlawful for a negro and a white person to play together or in company with each other in any game of cards, dice, dominoes, checkers, baseball, softball, football, basketball or similar game.

The ordinance criminalized interracial sports, providing for a fine of one hundred dollars and/or imprisonment for up to six months for violators upon their conviction.

When the New York Giants and the Washington Redskins arrived in town in 1951 for the fourth Pro Bowl, the Giants' Emlen Tunnell and William Jackson were not even accorded the opportunity to practice with their teammates, as Triplett had been the year before. Instead, these African Americans were forced to sit in the grandstand while their teams battled each other on the field. This match proved to be the last in the series, which was suspended following the game's conclusion. The specter of interracial professional sporting events in Birmingham did not arise again until 1953, when the success of the city's minor-league baseball team threatened to reopen the issue. The Barons opposed Nashville for the Southern Association championship, with the winner to face the Texas League victor in the annual Dixie Series. Tulsa and Dallas, contenders for the Texas League title, both featured African American players who would presumably accompany their teams to Birmingham for the series.

Faced with an imminent crisis and also seeking to attract major-league baseball and football teams to Birmingham for exhibition contests, Mayor James Morgan and City Commissioner R. E. Lindbergh relied on an opinion by the city attorney, who said the ordinance was unconstitutional. They boldly announced their votes to repeal applicable portions of the law. Dallas or Tulsa could then bring their black players to the Barons' Rickwood Field. Their two votes provided the needed majority on the three-member city commission. It was no coincidence that Morgan and Lindbergh chose to act at this time, when the third commissioner, Eugene "Bull" Connor, was vacationing in Canada. Connor, a staunch advocate of white supremacy and a leader of the city's segregationists, enthusiastically enforced the ordinance in his role as police commissioner.

Their stance provoked an immediate response. Local newspapers editorialized in favor of the repeal while many Birmingham citizens wrote Morgan to express their concerns.

> I should like to thank you and Robert from the bottom of my heart for your stand and statement concerning your intention of repealing that disgraceful law concerning segregation that is on our statute books. The law is a disgrace to our town.

> Why is the law being changed in favor of a few baseball games? Is baseball any more important than any other reason for having the law? Is the City of Birmingham finally bowing to the anti-segregation sponsors?

> It seems to me it is a shame that our city ordinance cannot be altered in a case of race mixing while playing in any game of sports. Colored and white work together in most all our corporations little or big in our city and harmony is attained. Surely we can do the same in baseball.

At the city commission meeting where the official repeal vote was to be taken, on 22 September, an overflow crowd of more than 150 white men turned out to voice its vociferous objections to any alteration of the ordinance. Before the meeting, opponents of the repeal had bought time on several Birmingham radio stations to air commercials urging segregationists to go to the meeting and express themselves. Such vocal opposition, and Birmingham's elimination from Dixie Series contention, removed the imperative for immediate action, and Morgan backed away from his repeal efforts, thus leaving the interracial sports ban in effect.

But this contentious issue did not disappear. Faced with the prospect of the Southern Association's Atlanta Crackers bringing a black player to town during the 1954 baseball season, and still courting several major-league teams for exhibition appearances, Mayor Morgan and the city commission, led again by Morgan, voted on 26 January 1954 to repeal those portions of the ordinance dealing with baseball and football games. Then the city announced that the Milwaukee Braves and Brooklyn Dodgers would come to Birmingham for a two-game series on 2 and 3 April. Subsequently, the St. Louis Cardinals and Chicago White Sox were booked, creating a four-day baseball extravaganza that promised to feature as many as fifteen African American players.

However, opponents of integration mobilized in more force than they had the previous September. Three weeks after the repeal, the Birmingham City Commission was greeted at City Hall by a crowd of four hundred vocal segregationists, clamoring for the ordinance's reinstatement. Former judge Hugh Locke, claiming that the local white citizenry had been overlooked by the commission, vowed to gather the required five thousand petition signatures to force a popular referendum. With the United States Supreme Court poised to render its long-awaited school desegregation decision, many Birmingham whites were worried about what the future held for segregation in Dixie. Faced with the looming prospect of judicially mandated change from Washington, D.C., local segregation supporters were not prepared to accept the weakening of Jim Crow restrictions in their own backyard. The repeal of the sports ordinance became a symbol of racial tolerance, a glimpse into a possible future that was unacceptable to large numbers of Birmingham's white residents.

After just a few weeks of effort, Locke kept his promise, obtaining ten thousand petition signatures, double the amount needed to place the interracial sports ordinance on the June ballot. During the petition drive, xenophobic repeal opponents exploited the fears of many whites regarding desegregated schools and racial mixing in social contexts. In seeking out signatories, Locke's adherents encouraged voters to sign the petition by asking the following charged question: "Do you want your children to go to school with negroes? If not, sign here."

With dispositive action on the ordinance looming in the spring, Birmingham citizens from all walks of life voiced their opinions on the vote they would cast in four months. In letters to Mayor Morgan, the city commissioners, the chamber of commerce, and the local paper, area residents voiced their opinions about the integrated athletics referendum.

Commissioner:

May I express my belated but violent disapproval of your action in abolishing the color line in baseball, football and track in the City of Birmingham, Alabama . . . Since the act has already been committed our only recourse is for action at the polls and when you run for office again. You may rest assured this will still be fresh in my memory at that time.

Mayor James Morgan:

My dead husband worked for you when you first ran for Commissioner, you and Mr. Conners [*sic*] on that one thing, that you would keep our city segregated, remember? Think it over Mr. Mayor. I do not want to take a thing away from our Negroes. Give them their own sports fields and pools and schools.

Dear Mr. Nolan [president, Birmingham Chamber of Commerce]:

We feel very deeply on the segregation problem and if Negro players were allowed to play in this game we would be unable to offer our support. We have done lots for the Negroes of Birmingham, and expect to continue to do so, but we must draw the line when it looks to us like this game might be the opening wedge to break down segregation. We realize that the Supreme Court may eliminate it legally at some time in the near future, but we still feel morally responsible for doing everything we can to maintain it.

In a letter to the editor of the *Birmingham Post-Herald,* a reader commented,

There will always be a barrier between the different races and different religions as long as the world stands. One race will say they are better than my people, the other will say they are as good as I am and then the war will start, maybe with just a few but it would be big enough to start hard feelings. Why not just keep it divided like it always has been? It seems to me everyone has been getting along all right.

While many voters opposed Morgan, others supported his drive to bring integrated athletics to Birmingham.

Gentlemen:

I am a native white of Alabama and have always believed we could make the South a more prosperous section if we could help the Negro rise above the economic level so many seem satisfied to see them in. Certainly I am aware of the laziness, the irresponsibility and other bad characterisation [*sic*] of so many of the Colored race—but who is to blame for that? We Southerners, of course. Improper and inadequate educational facilities—making every effort to repress the race at every turn . . . It won't work any longer and we might as well face the true situation.

Dear Mr. Morgan:

I have followed you in all of your under takings [*sic*] . . . My admiration for you . . . has risen considerably since there will be no compromise of the order to abolish the old outdated ordinances that hurt us all through the past years . . . Please, please dont [*sic*] permit them to force you to accede to their stagnated demands.

Since the repeal vote was scheduled for June, it could not stop the early April exhibition series involving the four major-league teams. One week before the series commenced, a group calling itself the Preserve Segregation Committee sent telegrams to White Sox manager Paul Richards and St. Louis skipper Eddie Stanky asking them to bench black players on their teams to "preserve our segregation traditions and customs in the South." Paul Richards wasted no time in replying, sending his response by telegram: "I am very sorry, but that question of racial segregation was settled more than 2,000 years ago on Mount Calvary . . . Christ Jesus died for us all."

Birmingham's racial barriers fell without catastrophe in April 1954. More than twenty-one thousand fans witnessed integrated baseball in this city. But black fans, who overflowed their designated seating area and outnumbered whites during the set's first two games, were dissatisfied with the poor quality of Rickwood Field's accommodations. African Americans were not allowed to sit in the whites-only grandstand, which was two-thirds empty. Instead, they sat on two-by-eight-inch wooden planks without a roof over their heads. The *Birmingham World* reported that "the so called 'Negro grandstand section' is so poorly located that no Negro patrons are able to keep up with the progress of the game since they cannot see the scoreboard . . . I heard a large portion of Negro fans complain that 'we feel as if we had stopped at a country store for a sandwich and we had to go around the back of the place and be served from a hole cut in the back wall.'"

In May, the Supreme Court confirmed the worst fears of segregationists, handing down its landmark *Brown v. Board of Education* decision. This ruling, representing a major crack in Jim Crow's armor, moved many integration opponents to become more strident, vowing to resist not only this decision but also any other similar effort to change the "southern way of life," including repeal of the Birmingham interracial sports ordinance. The *Brown* decision spurred many in Birmingham to go to the polls on 1 June and stand against the integrationists.

On election day, Birmingham's white voters overwhelmingly rejected the ordinance's repeal. By a margin of nearly 3 to 1—19,640 to 6,685— voters reversed the commission's action and endorsed an even more restrictive law. The new voter-approved ordinance prohibited the same interracial sports and games as before as well as golf, track, and "any mingling at the races, swimming pools, beaches, lakes and ponds." Petition campaign leader Hugh Locke was quoted by the *Birmingham Post-Herald* as claiming that the segregation vote "indicates that the people of Birmingham are not going to take breaking down of segregation lying down. And it tells it to the people of the United States. It was necessary to preserve our southern traditions."

While the vote made Birmingham's immediate stance on racial matters quite clear, it also firmly established a notorious reputation that stained the city's soul for years to come. Birmingham's distinction as the South's most polarized and most reactionary community when it came to integration proved to be well deserved, as events of the 1950s and 1960s soon illustrated.

For the remainder of the 1950s, interracial athletics was an alien concept in this city. The 1 June vote was an unmistakable signal that the vocal white majority in Birmingham would also resist the integration of the Barons baseball team and the region's most significant minor-league holdout, the Southern Association. If this circuit was going to integrate successfully, proponents of change would need to overcome powerful opposition in a bastion of segregationist sentiment—Birmingham, Alabama, where resistance to integration became the hallmark of a community incongruously nicknamed the Magic City.

6 | A Year of Decision: 1954

If the Northern people want to mix up with the colored, let them do so and I would suggest sending all the colored folks up there to be with them and see how it works. For us Southerners, nothing doing! We all of the South are the best friend that the colored folks ever had and will always be so long as they stay in their places—and there is rarely a good Southern colored man who wants any change.

—LETTER TO THE EDITOR OF THE *Birmingham Post-Herald*, 6 JUNE 1954

Hailed as Decision Day by America's black press, 17 May 1954 indelibly marked this date as a landmark in United States history. On Decision Day, the United States Supreme Court unanimously declared public school segregation to be unconstitutional in the much-anticipated *Brown v. Board of Education* decision. The ruling, both dreaded and eagerly awaited, had an immediate impact throughout the country. As reactions across the ideological spectrum were recorded and responses to the Court's action planned, Supreme Court justice Robert Jackson's previous statement about *Brown*'s legacy loomed prophetically over the swirl of public opinion: "I foresee a generation of litigation."

Southern politicians' reaction to the ruling, reported by the *Pittsburgh Courier,* was swift and mostly vitriolic. Georgia governor Herman Talmadge declared, "Georgians will not tolerate the mixing of the races in the public schools or any of its public, tax supported institutions." In the weeks before the high court acted, Talmadge, who believed segregation was the most important issue facing the South since the Civil War, proclaimed that his state would not permit school integration, vowing to call out the National Guard to prevent the mixing of black and white students. Senator Richard Russell of Georgia denounced the Court's ruling as a "flagrant abuse of judicial power," and Senator Harry Byrd of Virginia referred to the decision as "the most serious blow that has yet been struck against the rights of the states."

Other political leaders who supported segregation were more temperate in their remarks. Senator Russell Long of Louisiana said, "Although I completely disagree with the decision, my oath of office requires me to accept it as law. Every citizen is likewise bound by his oath of allegiance to his country." South Carolina governor James Byrnes preached caution, warning citizens to "exercise restraint and order." Although Byrnes was less than incendiary in his post-*Brown* remarks, he had previously made his stridently segregationist views well known, announcing his commitment to oppose any desegregation ruling forcefully. In Georgia, South Carolina, and Mississippi, where state legislatures had previously voted to privatize their school systems and thus remove them from the effect of a high court opinion governing public schools, preparations were under way to implement these obstructionist measures. By contrast, Oklahoma governor Johnston Murray and Maryland governor Theodore McKeldin announced that their states would obey the ruling.

African Americans reacted jubilantly to the decision, realizing that *Brown* was a major step forward in the battle against segregation. The eventual demise of Jim Crow and de jure segregation was no longer a distant notion. This goal was now more clearly attainable than ever before.

In New York, Dr. Ralph Bunche, winner of the Nobel Peace Prize, was so distracted by the news that he forgot to pick up his money after cashing a check at a bank. Thurgood Marshall, who argued the case for the NAACP before the Supreme Court, triumphantly declared to the *Pittsburgh Courier:* "This should be the happiest day of many, many years for Negro Americans. [The] stigma of second-class citizenship is on the way out."

At its June conference in Atlanta, the NAACP pledged vigor in following up on *Brown*. The organization laid plans to appeal directly to local southern school boards to abide by the decision and end segregation voluntarily; those that refused would be taken to court. Members discussed litigation strategies to combat state efforts to resist the decision and impede integration efforts.

Just days before the high court acted, Thurgood Marshall spoke to five thousand people at an emotionally charged freedom rally in Mississippi. His words, predicting both southern defiance of the Supreme Court and the NAACP's determined reaction, could well have been on the minds of the Atlanta delegates as they considered the decision and its aftermath: "Tell the Governor and the Legislature that I don't care how many laws they pass or what tricks they use to keep the Negro down, those laws still have to be measured by the U.S. Supreme Court . . . Come hell or high water, we'll be free by 1963."

Within a month of Decision Day, a different type of conclave was held in Richmond, Virginia, one where the parameters for the white South's campaign of massive resistance to *Brown* would be drawn. Governors from Georgia, South Carolina, North Carolina, Mississippi, Louisiana, Alabama, Florida, West Virginia, and Virginia attended the meeting; lower-level representatives from six other southern and border states were also present. It was in Richmond, former capital of the Confederacy, that Dixie's governors prepared to do battle again in the cause of protecting white southern traditions, agreeing to obstruct the despised court ruling.

By contrast, Catholic schools in Nashville were integrated by order of the city's bishop, and West Virginia, the District of Columbia, and Kentucky took steps to open up their public school systems to both races. But while West Virginia's Board of Education integrated all of the state's public colleges within a month of the *Brown* announcement, two colleges in Louisiana refused to admit African American students seeking to enroll for the fall term. By July, the Louisiana Senate passed three bills designed to impede integration by mandating segregation in public elementary and secondary schools throughout the state. In Sheridan, Arkansas, Russell Henderson resigned from the local school board in protest after the board reversed its decision to integrate the Sheridan school system when confronted with angry white parents denouncing the new policy and demanding retribution from members who voted for integration.

As 1954 progressed and reactions to the Supreme Court's ruling played out, the atmosphere down south was anything but settled. Initial exuberance and contempt over *Brown* yielded to uneasy anticipation of disquiet and conflict as both sides in the integration battle realized that the decision was merely the first blow, albeit an enormously significant one, in what loomed as a protracted campaign over Jim Crow's future.

Southern minor-league baseball was not insulated from the wave of emotions and change that was cascading through Dixie. While many segregation supporters may have more or less accepted integrated baseball in their midst before *Brown,* this would no longer be true. In light of the decision, they belatedly saw integrated baseball for what it always was: a significant erosion of Jim Crow restrictions. Such a calamitous occurrence, in the eyes of segregationists, could no longer be countenanced.

From now on, a "no exceptions" policy would be their rule. Many African Americans playing baseball in the post-*Brown* South, had to endure even greater racial hostility than their predecessors, both in and out of the ballpark. Birmingham's vote against interracial athletics and the formation in Mississippi of the nation's first White Citizens Council, an organization destined to proliferate and become notorious throughout Dixie for fanatical resistance to integration, were but two indicators of the South's new racial parameters and how difficult it would be to fulfill the promise of *Brown.*

In 1954, Al Israel was playing his second season in Savannah. During an early season trip to play the league's newest entry, the Charlotte Hornets, Israel learned how inhospitable North Carolina could be to African American athletes. "I had trouble in Charlotte. I said something to one fan who was yelling at me. 'You know, you're paying to see me play, and I love to play ball. You're telling me I can't play, but still you come and pay to see me.' That night, when I come out of the ballpark, I had to be escorted out by the police because a whole bunch of white guys was waiting for me with sticks and bottles. I didn't pay attention to that. I didn't pay it no mind. We were there to play ball."

Joe Durham played for the Texas League's San Antonio Missions in

1954, following his color line–shattering year in the Piedmont League. Although African Americans had played in the Texas League since 1952, racism remained virulent in much of the loop and, by extension, across the South.

In '54, San Antonio was the most liberal in the league. Shreveport was the worst. I played left field, next to the fifty-five-cent bleacher seats for whites. They would talk all evening. They would talk about my mother, call me names. They'd call me the *n* word a thousand times. They'd talk about my hair, and say, "You berry-head." I remember I fouled a ball off my shin. A little old lady— she must have been 75 years old—jumps up and says, "I could kill you, you little black bastard!" I would have laughed if my leg wasn't hurting so bad. I thought it was comical, myself. If you let those things get to you, you're never going to be able to play. As long as they don't come out there and put their hands on you. They were just talkin', yellin', and screamin'. Sticks and stones will break my bones, but names will never hurt me.

I didn't even look that way. I never paid any attention to it. I had some good days there, though. In fact, I led the league in triples that year. I hit 17, 7 of them in Shreveport, 4 with the bases loaded. I must have hit well over .400 there. It didn't bother me.

Black ballplayers of that era had to have a little something extra to go along with their playing talent because of things you had to endure. You had to tell yourself not to let anything get in your way or distract you. There was nothing you could do. [You would] just get up in the morning wherever you were, have your breakfast, go to a movie. They used to have a lot of afternoon movies, starting around twelve, one o'clock. You didn't have to be at the ballpark until around five, five-thirty, because most of the games in those days didn't start until eight o'clock.

In Beaumont, I had this person who owned a [black restaurant], good barbecue and whatnot. They had excellent food, all fresh veggies every day. He would take me out to the ballpark and, after the game, pick me up and bring me back to town. I'd have something to eat and go home. That was the worst city for housing. I lived in one of these boardinghouses, tourist homes.

They only had one bathtub in the building, and it was a two-story building. I think each room had a little washbowl. I'd take my shower at night at the ballpark after the game. In the morning, I would sponge myself. I wasn't getting into that bathtub. That was a way of life. To deal with it, you do the best you can. The best place was Houston. We stayed at the White Crystal Hotel on Lyons. They had a restaurant that seated about 250 people, and you didn't have to worry about the food. The rooms were nice, with radios, and a few had telephones. Dallas and Oklahoma City were nothing to write home about.

[Segregation] was one of those things that happened. I'm sorry that there wasn't a day when you could have a lot of fun and not worry about anything. The only thing that bothered me was not being around my teammates in the day. The thing about all this was, the only time you saw your teammates was at the ballpark, which made it a little difficult. I had to wait until I got to the ballpark and before batting practice to say hi to Ryne Duren or Jim Pisoni or one of the other guys. If not [for segregation], I probably would have been a better hitter than I was. I would have added some points [to my batting average]. I think it could have bothered a lot of other guys who played in those situations.

During the 1954 baseball season, African American athletes found themselves in a widening circle of southern locales. Players continued to be assigned to greater numbers of southern teams and leagues as more color lines fell across the region. However, acceptance of baseball integration, and the reception these line-breaking ballplayers received, varied from city to city and league to league.

The Atlanta Crackers took perhaps the boldest step forward in integrating southern baseball in 1954, when they added Nat Peeples to their roster, thus desegregating their Class AA circuit, the august Southern Association, one of Dixie's long-standing racial holdouts, with a color line going back to its founding in 1902. African Americans in Atlanta and other league cities were excited about the prospect of integrated baseball in the Southern Association. The thought of having Peeples compete against whites inspired many blacks across the region to dare to dream that his entry into the league would be the catalyst for the reformation process in association cities. But the Crackers' decision would face fierce opposition.

Meanwhile, rumors that the Class C Evangeline League's color line would fall rippled through New Iberia, Louisiana, before a scheduled match against Texas City, Texas, one night in May. Believing that nonwhite minor-league players would hit the field for the first time in this Louisiana community's history, 1,719 fans jammed into the Pelicans' ballpark. Out of this unusually large crowd, 632 African Americans filled the segregated grandstand, which normally seated at most 350.

When the game began, the rumors proved true as Tony Bonilla and a player identified as Naranjo made history for the Texas City Pilots, a 1954 newcomer to the eight-team league, which had two franchises in Texas and six in Louisiana. That the Pilots integrated their new loop was not surprising, since they had played in the now-defunct Gulf Coast League the season before, when that circuit had used nonwhite players for the first time. Even the unseasonable forty-degree chill did not deter fans from turning out to witness their own slice of history, though the *Pittsburgh Courier* did report that "some razzing by white fans when Bonilla appeared at the plate" occurred. Although a preseason "gentlemen's agreement" had kept the Evangeline League segregated until now, no formal segregation policy existed, as in the Cotton States League in 1953, to discourage individual teams from choosing to hire black players.

Weeks into the new season, dissension raged in the Class D Georgia State League. This circuit featured six teams located in small Peach State towns. Trouble began when H. N. McMichael, owner of the Sandersville Wacos, threatened to pull his team out of the league if three clubs that had two African American players apiece, Dublin, Vidalia, and Douglas, were permitted to continue using them in ball games. The league previously had featured nonwhite players from Cuba, Puerto Rico, and other Latin American countries, but 1954 was the first year that teams carried African Americans on their rosters. The prospect of watching American-born southern blacks play with and compete against whites, some of whom were also from Dixie, was too much for some locals, including McMichael, to bear. This affront brought integration too close to home for those opposed to the ballplayers and the racial mixing they represented.

But league president Bill Estroff defied the protests and announced the league's commitment to integration, telling the *Sporting News* that it was "a case of survival" to allow the teams to field these players. Economic interests again made the difference for another southern league seeking to integrate its teams. Dublin reported a dramatic attendance surge attributable to its minority ballplayers. Compared to 1953, when often fewer than one hundred fans filled the local ballpark, Dublin was averaging twelve hundred patrons per game by early May 1954, when league-wide attendance had tripled over the previous year's. At a league meeting on 2 May, Estroff pronounced the controversy resolved, stating that Sandersville and the African Americans would all remain in the league. "Of course," said Estroff, "there has been some feeling about the use of Negroes in the league but that has been true all over the South where Negroes played for the first time . . . This year we are . . . giving our own Southern Negroes an opportunity to advance in their chosen profession. These boys understand our traditions and customs and speak our language and will be governed accordingly. Frankly, I don't see anything to get excited about." Little more than a month later, McMichael, undoubtedly facing his own financial tribulations, acceded to Estroff's view when he added two African Americans, Bill McNeely and Walter Davis, to his Sandersville team. But the increased attendance that resulted from integration was only a temporary answer. Like so many minor leagues, the Georgia State League, burdened by low revenues, inadequate fan support in its small towns, lack of financial assistance from the major leagues, and other problems, folded after the 1956 campaign.

The promise of increased revenues also influenced the inveterately recalcitrant Cotton States League. Mired in debt and plagued by rain-outs, unseasonably cold weather, and low attendance, the league dropped its previously fierce opposition to integration. In July, Hot Springs' new owner, Charlie Williamson, asked team officials in Monroe, Louisiana; Meridian, Mississippi; and El Dorado and Pine Bluff, Arkansas, about their reaction to his plan to add African Americans to the Bathers. These teams, all of which were enduring small crowds and financial difficulty, welcomed Williamson's plan as a potential boost to their collective fortunes.

Armed with this support, Williamson so informed first-year league president Emmet Harty, who called an emergency league meeting to discuss the Hot Springs proposal. Confronted with no serious opposition from the league or its teams, Williamson signed eighteen-year-old Uvoyd Reynolds, a star player for Hot Springs' Langston High School. On 20 July, Reynolds started for Hot Springs and went hitless before an unusually large home crowd featuring 750 African Americans. Before Reynolds's debut, blacks usually numbered no more than 125 at Bathers home games. Two nights later, Joe B. Scott, a twenty-seven-year-old outfielder and alumnus of the Negro American League's Memphis Red Sox, joined Reynolds in Hot Springs and recorded one hit in four at-bats as the Bathers lost to the Meridian Millers, 19 – 12.

Their presence was a remarkable one-year reversal for the Cotton States League. The circuit's acceptance of integration was undoubtedly aided by the presence of a new, more flexible league president and by the absence of Jackson and Natchez, clubs whose racially recalcitrant stances in 1953 played a pivotal role in their eventual demise. When Meridian signed Carl Heron on 26 July, the franchise became the first in Mississippi to include a black player on a team with whites. In Greenville, Mississippi, attendance doubled when Meridian or Hot Springs came to town, with black fans routinely outnumbering white patrons. The "public policy" justification that had been used to keep integrated baseball out of the Magnolia State in 1953 was not raised anew in 1954, when the league's color line was eliminated in an effort to stave off bankruptcy. However, this proved to be an ephemeral solution. The Cotton States League, previously tormented by floods, hurricanes, and locusts and now buffeted by declining revenues, went out of business in 1955.

Montgomery, Alabama, was another former naysayer that integrated its team in 1954. The Montgomery Rebels became the first previously all-white team in Alabama to hire black ballplayers, when John Davis and George Handy were added to the roster. While integrated baseball had much symbolic importance throughout the South, perhaps nowhere was it as historically ironic and significant as in Montgomery. After all, this was the Cradle of the Confederacy, the city where the Confederate States of America was born, the city whose team's very name evoked memories of the South's "lost cause."

The Rebels hoped to capitalize on the increased interest African Americans showed in South Atlantic League baseball during 1953, when the end of the circuit's color barrier brought more black fans to the ballpark than ever before. Thirteen thousand African Americans paid their way into Rebels home games that season to watch the Sally's first black players, four times more than did so in 1951.

Montgomery's black community responded enthusiastically to the presence of their own African American players in 1954. Tuskegee Institute, the prestigious black educational and research institution, sponsored a ticket drive. For the first time, black businesses formed a booster club to help promote Rebels baseball. Thanks to this excitement, 6,214 fans attended the season's first game, the highest figure for any Sally opening-day contest that year.

The most intense reaction to baseball integration most often occurred in the smaller towns and communities hosting southern minor-league baseball. In these locales, blacks and whites rarely interacted in any meaningful way, unlike in many large cities, such as Dallas and Atlanta, whose more cosmopolitan populations and attitudes often resulted in relatively greater racial tolerance. Therefore, the racial climate was often more highly charged in smaller communities, such as those of the Class C Mountain States League, which had teams in such small cities as Kingsport and Maryville-Alcoa, Tennessee, and the hardscrabble coal town of Harlan, Kentucky.

Leo "Muscle" Shoals was the player-manager for the 1954 Kingsport Cherokees. Having begun his career in 1936, Shoals had experienced much of what the minors had to offer, including integration, since the Mountain States League featured black players in 1954. Shoals was also a star in this region, having established a reputation for himself as the foremost home run hitter of his era in minor leagues located at the intersection of Virginia, Kentucky, Tennessee, and North Carolina. Shoals recalls the vitriolic reception his team, which included black players, was given by fans when they played a weekend series in Harlan. Residents of this community, like many others across Dixie, took their racially motivated anger out on Shoals for the unpardonable affront of leading a team with nonwhite athletes into their town.

We went to Harlan, Kentucky, and that was mean country. They were having a big thing at the ballpark that Saturday night. They had a big promotion because they were losing money. There were a lot of people there. I took my black ballplayers and my white ballplayers in there. They were leading, up until the eighth inning. Then, I hit one out, and that put us a run ahead. My God, that calmed everything down. In the meantime, some fans in the bleachers had hit our pitcher [who was] warming up in the head with a cinder. The pitcher was black. I ran out there, and his head was cut. There was some blood. No police. Couldn't find any.

The last play of the game, there was a pop-up. The ball game's over. We win. I told the batboys to grab the bats. I'd take the ball bags. I grabbed the roster sheets and started out through the crowd. Boy, as soon as we got through the gate, the people were waiting for me. Oh, God, they got right up into my face and said, "You nigger-lovin' son of a bitch!" They were standing four or five deep and yelling everything. There was an old woman—she and her husband ran the hotel. He had a white linen suit on. She had on a white outfit and a big white hat and pocketbook. She stood on top of a step and said, "I ought to beat your damn brains out." Boy, was she agitated.

I was afraid somebody was going to jump on my back. If I ever got on the ground, you can't tell what might happen. In the meantime, I saw a guy I knew. Every time we got to the ballpark in Harlan, he'd run up and say, "Hope you get beat," and run. We laughed at him. So here I see him in the crowd. He's right in front of me. It comes to my mind that, by God, I'll work that booger. I'll talk to him. I eased up and up to him. He was going along with that old woman with the pocketbook. So I said, "Ease up a little bit. Let me through." I edged closer to him and the clubhouse. First thing I know, they lost me. When I got through the crowd, I ducked and made it into the clubhouse. We locked the door.

The next day, I went to the club president and said, "I'm taking my boys home." He said, "What about the game Sunday?" I said, "There was no police, no nothing. I've got to have protection." He promised to have police, deputies, plainclothes, and I wouldn't have to worry. He gave me his word. So we went to the ballpark. But our black pitcher was afraid to warm up. Fans were lined up along the fence down the foul line. Some of them had rocks. But they had some of those plainclothes guys. They yanked them out of there. I'll bet they took out a dozen. That's one thing I'll always remember. I have to give that pitcher a lot of credit. But he wanted to play ball.

Shoals's experience in Harlan was not his only brush with baseball racism in 1954. When the Mountain States League folded on 20 July, Shoals and many of his teammates moved about 120 miles south to Knoxville, where they joined the Class B Tri-State League's Smokies. Aldo Salvent was one of the players Shoals took with him. The Cuban-born third baseman broke his new league's color line in impressive fashion, collecting three hits and batting in three runs in his first two games to help Knoxville top the Greenville (S.C.) Spinners. Salvent was well received at home and when the Smokies played later in Asheville. However, he remained on the bench, unable to play in Anderson, South Carolina, because of that city's ban against interracial sports. But on 1 August, Salvent's presence prompted the Spartanburg Peaches to withdraw from the league after their 5 – 1 defeat by the Smokies. Before the first pitch, Knoxville promised not to use Salvent against Spartanburg, but the third baseman was nonetheless inserted into the lineup midway through the game, chalking up his team's first hit of the night. After the game, Peaches president R. E. Littlejohn Jr. ordered his team to leave Knoxville and return home without completing their scheduled four-game series.

Just as efforts to integrate the Tri-State League had threatened to tear the league asunder two years before, Spartanburg's actions forced the circuit to deal with this issue anew. Leo Shoals remembers the racial realities confronting his team's attempt to play Salvent against the league's South Carolina franchise. "The guy who owned the ball club told me Spartanburg had a law, can't play no blacks. Anderson did too. Some towns had it, some towns didn't. But the owner told me, "My God, he'll play." He was a rough old guy. Salvent was a pretty good ballplayer. He was going to play because our third baseman was jakin' it a little. He wasn't hustling. Salvent was ready."

Littlejohn's rationale for his abrupt decision to abandon the Tri-State was by no means novel. Indeed, similar racial rationalizations were heard in the Cotton States League in 1953. According to Spartanburg's owner, Knoxville had broken an agreement not to use black players during the 1954 season. Littlejohn declared, "It was not a racial issue. I had made a pledge to the park board before the season opened [about not using black players], and I had to keep my word."

Three days after the controversy erupted, the Tri-State League announced a solution. To preserve league harmony, Aldo Salvent would be removed from the Smokies' roster and sent to a team outside the circuit, as Charlotte had done with David Mobley in 1952, when his presence had engendered objections and threats of league dissolution. Salvent never returned to play baseball in Tennessee, finishing the 1954 season in Hagerstown. As Leo Shoals recalls, "Salvent was homesick. But I wanted him in Hagerstown. He said, 'They'll just take out more taxes from my paycheck in Hagerstown.' He was getting a pretty good raise to go there, but he was worried about those taxes. So they agreed to pay his taxes and he went to Hagerstown." Salvent returned to Hagerstown for the 1955 season. He spent the remainder of his playing days in the Mexican League, where in 1959 he batted .317 while posting career highs in home runs (29) and runs batted in (108).

There was a larger consequence to Salvent's exile from the Tri-State. Just as the Tugersons' battle in the Cotton States League prompted collective action among African Americans in Greenville, Mississippi, Aldo Salvent's removal from the circuit became the catalyst for similar action in Rock Hill, South Carolina. On 9 August, days after Salvent left for Maryland, African Americans picketed outside Rock Hill's ballpark

before a game against Spartanburg voicing their objections to his treatment by the league and Littlejohn. Rock Hill officials reported no incidents arising from the protest except for an 80 percent decline in African
American attendance at that night's game. Only eleven blacks were
counted in the segregated grandstand, where perhaps seventy-five usually sat. Outside, picketers dramatized their desire for democracy in baseball, carrying signs that poignantly declared, "If we can't play, we won't
pay. We fought at Hiroshima, but we can't play in the Tri-State." This was
the first time that these Rock Hill citizens, spurred on by Littlejohn's
racial obtuseness, had banded together to protest segregation at their
local ballpark.

Events in the southern minor leagues mirrored what was occurring
elsewhere in America. Change and struggle were constant companions.

19 MARCH

WASHINGTON, D.C.—[The FBI was investigating a spring training
incident in Florida involving eight of the Washington Senators'
nonwhite minor-league players who were training with the Chattanooga Lookouts.] According to reports published here, officials
of Winter Garden, Florida suggested to officials of the Washington farm system that they get [their] Negroes out of town by
sundown . . . The Negroes were moved to Orlando . . . [Lookouts
general manager Zinn Beck] said an unidentified man wearing a
police uniform drove up to the ballpark and ordered team officials
to have those Negroes out by sundown and don't bring them back.
—*Pittsburgh Courier*

10 APRIL

INDIANAPOLIS, Ind.—When the basketball team of Indianapolis'
all-Negro Crispus Attucks High School played in the Indiana state
semi-final tournament recently, it had the support of all other
public and parochial schools in the city. This was a precedent-
shattering action on the part of the Indianapolis schools . . .
Cheerleaders from eight sister schools in the Hoosier capital city
joined the Crispus Attucks yell leaders at the two games in which
the team played.—*Pittsburgh Courier*

17 APRIL

NEW ORLEANS, La.—An estimated 5,000 colored fans were among the spring's record crowd of 8,009 which watched the Cleveland Indians outslug, 10–5, the New York Giants . . . Three sections provided for colored fans in segregated Pelican Stadium were overrun a half-hour before game time. A fourth section was made available after it had been cleared of a few scattered whites.—*Pittsburgh Courier*

12 MAY

A group of Negroes representing the Inter-Denominational Ministers' Alliance, Washington County Negro Democratic Club, Negro Voters League of Washington County, Washington County Negro Business League and Negro fraternal organizations announced they would stay away from all Cotton States League games in Greenville [Miss.] in protest against the Bucks' ban on colored players.—*Sporting News*

4 SEPTEMBER

NORFOLK, Va.—A dull roar, like the muffled explosion of a far-away artillery shell, was a signal Sunday night that white people in the Coronado section of Norfolk will stop at nothing to get Negro families out of the area. The bombing of 4400 Albert Avenue, which followed by about a week a previous attempt to dynamite the house, was the most serious attempt to date to terrorize colored people who have recently bought homes in the section.—*Pittsburgh Courier*

11 SEPTEMBER

CAMDEN, Ala.—Tom Abernathy, Talladega newspaper publisher and first Republican to wage an aggressive campaign for governor here in recent years, said last week that the May 17 U.S. Supreme Court ruling [in *Brown v. Board of Education*] "pointed directly at the bedroom door and it will get there by and by unless we stand with calm resolution in the way."—*Pittsburgh Courier*

A 3 June letter to the editor of the *Birmingham Post-Herald* from a white Birmingham resident underscores the obstacles that still lay ahead on the road to integration in the South.

> The company my children keep, the churches they go to, yes, even the school they attend . . . the kind of people they associate with; yes, even the color, should be my privilege to choose as a free American . . . I do not feel myself any better than any God fearing, respectful Negro; but I do claim the right not to live with him, go to school and church or swimming with him . . . I for one will never agree to nonsegregation and will teach my children the same.

Southern Association

Atlanta	Memphis
Birmingham	Mobile
Chattanooga	Nashville
Little Rock	New Orleans

Nat Peeples was a twenty-seven-year-old outfielder when he slipped into his Atlanta Crackers uniform during spring training. Another alumnus of the Negro leagues, this Memphis native began his professional career with the Kansas City Monarchs and the Indianapolis Clowns in 1950 and spent the next three years in the minor leagues as a member of the Brooklyn Dodgers and Milwaukee Braves organizations.

His appearance with the Crackers sent ripples of excitement through the black communities of Atlanta and other Southern Association cities. Team owner Earl Mann, who had withstood Ku Klux Klan threats and other racial opposition when he championed the appearance of Jackie Robinson and the Dodgers in Atlanta five years earlier, was again seeking to set precedent here. Given Mann's history of racial pioneering, league observers had long expected that his team would be the first to end the Southern Association's Jim Crow tradition. Indeed, Mann had sought to bring African American players into the league before 1954, but his efforts had been consistently thwarted by segregationists in Georgia and other Southern Association locales, Birmingham in particular. So Nat Peeples was understandably incredulous when he received the letter at his Memphis home informing the outfielder he had been assigned to a Southern Association team.

> The Atlanta Crackers sent me a contract. At first, I thought it was a mistake. No Negroes had ever played in the Southern Association. I sent it back without signing. About a week later, they sent the same thing right back. The postman was a white guy. When the letter came back, he said, "Didn't I bring this a week ago?" He looked at the envelope and said, "The Atlanta Crackers?" He couldn't believe it either. That's when I called Milwaukee and spoke with the general manager.
>
> That's when they said, "That's right. You're going to spring training with Atlanta." I spoke with Mr. Earl Mann. He said, "We were waiting for you. What's wrong? What took so long?" I said, "I thought it was a joke." He said, "No. We're going to try." We had about eight Negroes in the Braves organization. They had Wes Covington, Juan Pizarro, Felix Mantilla. I said, "Why'd y'all pick me?" He said, "We sat around a table and talked about it. We decided that you were the best guy." I said, "No. What y'all did was put names in a hat and draw them. That would have been a little better." He said, "No. You're the best one."
>
> I was sick about it because back in 1954, I didn't know how it all was going to work out. I played through the South when I was with the Kansas City Monarchs. I knew what those towns were like. Earl Mann said, "Well, come to spring training, and we'll see what happens." And that's what I did.
>
> When I left Memphis to go to spring training, the general manager came to Memphis, and we rode down on the train together. We had a Pullman coach together. We did a lot of talking. He told me what to expect, the names and things. He said, "When you're called these names, you must be like Jackie and take it. You're down south." I understood how things would be. But I thought things

might be all right because we rode down on the train together. In spring training, the manager, Whitlow Wyatt, told me about the problems Jackie Robinson had. He was preparing me."

The Milwaukee Braves wanted to end the league's color ban. Their inability to send any black players to the team's Class AA affiliate was a constant source of frustration. For these athletes to move up the professional baseball ladder, they were forced to skip a level and jump from Class A to Class AAA or even the major leagues. While some players, such as Henry Aaron, were talented enough to weather such a dramatic promotion, most were not and were forced to languish in Class A longer than they deserved or move up to AAA before they were ready.

While Milwaukee and other major-league organizations could have championed integration more forcefully than they did, the teams instead chose the path of least resistance in the South. They opted not to rock the boat and acceded to their skewed perceptions of local white mores and traditions rather than insisting on the abolition of all color lines. In the final analysis, major-league baseball's lack of strong action was not surprising, since many big-league clubs were themselves slow to sign black players, while others—namely the New York Yankees and the Boston Red Sox— had yet to integrate their own teams in 1954, seven years after Jackie Robinson donned a Dodgers uniform.

Even the Dodgers had no interest in breaking down barriers with the Mobile Bears, Brooklyn's Southern Association farm team. When queried on this point in April 1953 by an *Atlanta Journal* reporter, a Dodgers executive responded in effect that his team's barrier-shattering days were over. "Brooklyn," he said, "is doing no more pioneering . . . We'll send Negro players to the Southern only after some other club, or clubs, have made such a move."

Earl Mann, however, was ready to take it upon himself to change the Southern Association, partly because he hoped to benefit. Peeples's entry into the league was also being scrutinized by some of Mann's league rivals, the Chattanooga Lookouts, the Nashville Vols, and the New Orleans Pelicans, who were thought ready to add their own black players should the Crackers' venture succeed.

In his first Atlanta appearance in a preseason exhibition against Milwaukee, Peeples recorded the Crackers' only hit before 1,950 African American fans out of a total crowd of 6,920. Despite the presence on the ball field of more-prominent black big leaguers, such as Milwaukee's Aaron, Billy Bruton, and Jim Pendleton, it was Peeples who generated the most attention, receiving frequent ovations from the grandstand, especially from black patrons, who cheered even his most routine outfield putouts. In his first at-bat, Peeples received greater acclamation than anyone on either team except Milwaukee Brave and former Cracker Eddie Matthews. .

During the two-game series, Peeples talked about the coming season and its historic ramifications with the Braves' Henry Aaron, an expert in breaking southern baseball color lines after having spent 1953 in the South Atlantic League. Peeples recalls, "Hank, Billy Bruton, and I stayed at the same hotel. Hank told me, 'It's going to be bad, Nat. I don't know if they'll let you play. I heard they're going to send you to Jacksonville to take my place because they're trying to win another pennant there. The Braves want you to go to Jacksonville.' I wasn't surprised. Hank and the rest wished me luck. Then they left and I stayed."

When spring training concluded, Peeples had made the team on the strength of a stellar exhibition season in which he batted .348 and hit 6 of Atlanta's 14 home runs. Crackers manager Whitlow Wyatt proclaimed, "He's the best left fielder we have." The stage was set for history to be made in Mobile, Alabama, where the Crackers opened the regular season against the Bears.

Peeples and his teammates were well aware of that first game's unique significance. Chuck Tanner, Peeples's closest friend on the Atlanta team, recalls the atmosphere at Mobile's Hartwell Field on 9 April as he and the Crackers' twenty-seven-year-old rookie opened the 1954 Southern Association campaign: "We loosened up together before the game. In Mobile, I sat with Nat in the dugout. I knew he was the first black player. After the game, I talked to him. He knew that I was his genuine friend. I think the fans enjoyed seeing him play. I thought they treated him like a baseball player. A lot more black people came to that game because they knew he would play."

More than 6,700 fans, 1,500 of whom were African Americans, were on hand at Hartwell Field to see Nat Peeples's inaugural game. He was greeted by a "mixed chorus of boos and cheers" when he pinch-hit in the fifth inning and tapped the ball back to the pitcher in his only appearance of the night. Peeples's debut with the Crackers was hailed as a significant breakthrough in the Deep South. Many thought his presence might even provide an impetus for change in such recalcitrant, racially polarized locales as Birmingham and Memphis. After all, Atlanta, the region's largest metropolis, was also considered the South's crown jewel. Should baseball integration succeed there, the ripple effect could well carry it to other cities and different parts of society, perhaps encouraging the integration of other aspects of southern life. Optimism among black southerners ran high as Peeples and the Crackers embarked on their new season.

> Put it down that Peeples will be remembered as a trailblazing "symbol" in the Southern Association in the fashion that Jackie Robinson is with the Brooklyn Dodgers. There had to be a "first." Fate decreed that Peeples play this role. It is the fervent wish of everyone that he measures up to the test which has been squarely placed on his shoulders. However, if he fails then no one must lose heart. The "symbol" must not be used either to exploit racial ambitions or failings. It would be a disservice to the player and to the race to have him carry on his shoulders the full strivings of those who see in him an end to all the discrimination that hampers competition in the area. Yet he is a wedge in the doorway. That no one would deny.—*Atlanta Daily World*

Such hopes were dashed two weeks into the season, when the Crackers announced Peeples's demotion to Class A Jacksonville, ostensibly so he could see action on an everyday basis. He had played sparingly for Atlanta, losing his starting job to a teammate and going hitless in four official at-bats while receiving one walk. Peeples did not have the opportunity to play a single regular season inning in Atlanta before leaving town involuntarily. While his demotion may indeed have come about because the Braves changed their mind and now believed he was not ready to make the jump from Class B Evansville (where he had played in 1953) to AA Atlanta, it is also true that the league had been putting pressure on Earl Mann to end his foray into Southern Association racial matters. Although Mann denied it at the time, he was nevertheless advised to dispatch Peeples and avoid a confrontation over his presence in the league. Whatever the reason for his demotion, Peeples left Atlanta without being given a full and fair opportunity to demonstrate his ability. Four official at-bats in less than two weeks are simply not enough on which to base a determination of a baseball player's ability.

Nat Peeples had a good season with Jacksonville—a .288 batting average, 7 home runs, and 47 runs batted in, but he was not the same player after his experience in the Southern Association. He was deeply disappointed not to be given the chance to show that his stellar spring training with the Crackers was no fluke. "It just took all the fire out of Nat," recalls Ed Charles, a fellow Braves minor leaguer who talked with Peeples about his time in the Southern Association. "I noticed his whole attitude changed. He was quite hurt by it. It hurt him to the point that he didn't have that drive, that intensity. It bothered him a lot."

For the rest of his career, Peeples was never again given the opportunity to play in Atlanta. No further serious efforts were made to integrate the Southern Association. This league went down in history as the nation's most racially intolerant baseball organization. Peeples spent five more years bouncing around the minor leagues. After playing his final season in Mexico in 1960, he returned home to Memphis.

I had problems in the little towns, coming back from spring training. Douglas, Georgia, Dalton, Georgia—the folks there didn't like us. They hollered a lot of things—"black Cracker," "liver lips," and things like that. It was something. That's when I got scared. We played exhibition games there. We played against other organizations' teams. But they were all-white. I was the only black player. This was where all the name-calling was. But it wasn't all the fans. It was just a few. A lot of them clapped. But I could hear those other fans because they were right down near the dugout. A couple of guys would say, "As long as I lived, I never thought I'd see a black Cracker." Chuck Tanner said, "Did you hear that?" I said, "Yeah, I did. I'm sitting right here looking at them." I understood what it was going to be like.

We stopped one time in Douglas. They told us they'd fix me a place in the kitchen. So I ate in the kitchen. I looked up, and Tanner, Dick Donovan, and three or four more guys came back there and ate with me. That made me feel real good. [Usually,] the guys had to bring food to me on the bus. I couldn't go into the restaurants. Chuck Tanner was one of the nicest guys on the team. He sat with me on the bus. He sat with me on the airplane. Tanner said, "Man, I don't understand how you do it. We stay in an air-conditioned hotel. You stay in a house with no fan." I said, "Well, no choice. You just got to go along with the flow."

We opened the season in Mobile. We rode together as a team on the train, but I knew what was going to happen once we got to town. When we got off the train, there was a colored cab waiting for me. The cab took me to a colored lady's house where I stayed. The house I stayed [at] in Mobile had one fan. The lady there said, "Mr. Peeples, I'm going to let you have the fan." Well, after eleven o'clock, when I was asleep, she sneaked in my room and took it. She wasn't going to lay there and sweat all night. She must have thought, "He's had enough cool air already." I told Chuck Tanner about it. Man, did he laugh.

The fans were real nice. I got a good ovation. I didn't have any trouble out of the fans, because of [St. Louis Cardinals manager] Eddie Stanky. That was his hometown. He just came out to the ballpark to see me play. They let him come down to the dugout. He came over and sat in the dugout and told me about being with Brooklyn when Jackie Robinson broke in. There were no problems with the Mobile players, because they were from the Dodgers. I played for two years over in the Dodger organization. I knew most of them.

When I came up to bat, the catcher was someone I knew from '52, when we were in Elmira. He said, "How are you doin', Nat?" I said, "All right." He said, "That's great. I hope you make it, but it's going to be a pretty tough job." I understood. That's what Stanky told me when I got back to the dugout. We played two games in Mobile. Then we took a plane back to Atlanta.

When I got to Atlanta, I talked to Jackie twice. He heard about me being down in Atlanta. He called me from Brooklyn. He told me, "Let's keep it cool. Your job is going to be worse than mine because you're down south." He told me that everything was going to work out all right. That made me feel good. I knew Jackie from when I was with the Dodgers in spring training in '52. I talked to Jackie and Pee Wee Reese in Vero Beach. Jim Gilliam was there too. There were a lot of colored guys with the Dodgers. We went to town together.

Back in Atlanta, I went to talk to Mr. Mann. He called me in his office. The team was getting ready to go on a road trip. The Braves told him I was going to Jacksonville. When Aaron left Jacksonville, they told Earl Mann [the team needed] somebody there to take his place. He told me, "Well, I tried it, but it ain't going to work right now. It ain't the right time. They're just not ready yet. I couldn't get nobody to go with me. We'll have to wait awhile." He said [to Peeples], "But what about Jackie?" He was up in New York. I'm down south. Earl Mann said the president of the league told him it wasn't going to work. "Ain't nobody tried it but you. It ain't gonna work like that. There have to be two, three, or four teams to try this. No one else wants to try."

Mr. Mann had told me he had called all of the towns in the Southern Association. Mobile said they'd play whoever we brought there. He said Birmingham and Memphis were the only towns that said I couldn't play. That really was bad, especially because I was born in Memphis. I couldn't understand it at first. But at that time, I said, "Well, this has never been tried before. No black has ever tried to play in the Southern Association."

That's when they sent me to Jacksonville. I wasn't surprised. I knew they weren't ready. I played three years in Jacksonville. It didn't make any difference that Hank played there in '53. When I was there, it was like it was all just starting. Hank told me about the names they called him. "Man, you should have heard the names," he told me. In '54, we won the pennant, but still we had trouble in those towns like Savannah, Macon, Augusta. But it was still better in Jacksonville than Atlanta because I wasn't the only one there. It would have been easier if another team had a black player. I wouldn't have been the only one they could pick on. But no other team tried. I was left as the only one.

They didn't try to bring in any other black players after me. Those teams told Earl Mann not to bother. They just weren't ready yet. But in Atlanta, there were no problems. Everything worked out pretty nice. I feel pretty good about what I did because no other black players tried to play in the Southern Association. I don't regret what I did, but I can't say I'd do it again. I'd have to think about it. I'd like to be remembered for what I did. I tell people, but they still don't believe me.

When Chuck Tanner and Nat Peeples were with the Crackers, Tanner was the veteran, in his ninth minor-league season. Before spring training began that year, Earl Mann coaxed Tanner, who was contemplating retirement, into one more campaign with Atlanta, where he had been since 1951. With a thousand-dollar bonus and a salary equal to the major-league minimum, Tanner returned to the Crackers and had his best season to date, batting .323 with career highs of 20 home runs and 101 RBIs. The next year, he began a major-league career that spanned four decades. After his playing days ended, Chuck Tanner managed three big-league teams and won the World Series with the Pittsburgh Pirates in 1979. He will always believe that his friend's experience in the Southern Association is what kept Nat Peeples from his own career in the big leagues:

> He was one of the best players I was associated with. He should have played in the big leagues. He was big and strong, could hit the ball, and he had desire. He played hard. He was good enough to play in Atlanta. Nat never said much, but I liked him, and we were friends. I played catch with him and always talked with him. I went with him as much as I could. We would warm up together. He was a quality person. He was my friend. I ate in the kitchen with him because I felt bad and I didn't think that was right. I didn't think that was fair, that they'd do that to a fine human being or to anybody. Heck, where I grew up, we were all nationalities. In New

Castle [Pennsylvania], I played ball with black guys. We'd eat together. They were my friends.

Where I stayed in Atlanta, at the Hotel Ponce de Leon, there was a black porter. He used to say, "Mr. Chuck, Mr. Chuck." I'd say, "No, no, no. My name is Chuck. You call me Chuck." He just looked at me. He was a nice young kid. One day, I was in my room and said, "You call me Chuck. I'm no better than you. I'll call you mister." He said, "Oh, no. Don't do that, or I'll get fired." "When you come in this room," I said, "you call me Chuck." He was surprised, and I think he was scared. He did call me Chuck, but only in the room, where there was just the two of us.

I didn't even see [Nat] when he left. I didn't know he was leaving. Nobody really came around to give us an explanation about why they sent him out. I heard that there would be boycotts in the Southern if he played. I personally feel that this hurt him [when it came to] making the big leagues. It demoralized him. Imagine if they say, "You can't play here because of the color of your skin." Don't forget that he was a young kid and didn't understand it. He did not make the big leagues, because his heart was broken somewhere along the line. It knocked that little bit of fire out of him. It took a little piece out of him.

He's a pioneer. Just like Jackie Robinson and Larry Doby were pioneers in the big leagues, there's one black ballplayer that was going to be the pioneer [in Atlanta]. Looking back, Earl Mann, he really liked Nat Peeples, and the Braves selected him because of the person he was plus his superior ability. He was quiet, and he was a tough kid. He would be the image of Jackie Robinson in the Southern. They figured Nat would have to go through the same things Jackie Robinson went through. They thought Nat would be best suited to go through all of the things in the South. They felt he could handle it better than anybody. Nat was really a pioneer in the Southern because he was the only black to ever play there. I know if I had to go through all of that, my heart would have been broken, too.

7 | The Battle Is Joined: 1955

It is my request that athletic teams of . . . the University System of Georgia not be permitted to engage in contests with other teams where the races are mixed . . . or where segregation is not required among spectators at such events. The South stands at Armageddon. The battle is joined. We cannot make the slightest concession to the enemy in this dark and lamentable struggle. There is no more difference in compromising integrity of race on the playing field than in doing so in the classrooms. One break in the dike and the relentless seas will rush in.

—GEORGIA GOVERNOR MARVIN GRIFFIN, 1955

After *Brown,* southern segregationists united to prevent the end of their racially divided society. Much like Dixie did on the eve of the Civil War, many southern whites mobilized to fight Washington's interference with their way of life as more court decisions declaring segregation to be unconstitutional were handed down. As the battle to preserve segregation was joined in 1955, violent resistance to integration began to manifest itself with alarming frequency throughout Dixie. Indeed, over the next four years, more than seventy people fell victim to racial violence in the South. Before the end of another sweltering Dixie summer, the murder of an African American teenager in Mississippi would horrify millions, revealing the malevolent emotions that *Brown* had laid bare.

This year also marked the true beginning of the civil rights movement. On 1 December 1955, Rosa Parks was arrested in Montgomery, Alabama, for refusing to vacate her bus seat for a white passenger, as required by state and city law. Her defiance sparked African Americans to collective action and launched the Montgomery bus boycott, providing the impetus for an epoch-changing decade of grassroots activism.

As 1955 began, the conflict over segregation moved to the baseball diamond. For the first time since Louisiana's attempt to ban integrated athletics in 1952, another state legislature sought to reverse baseball's democratizing influence. On 12 February, Georgia state representative Willie Lee Kilgore introduced a bill outlawing interracial athletic competition in the Peach State. Kilgore's proposal carried criminal penalties to enforce its stricture, with a fine of two thousand dollars or imprisonment for up to eighteen months for those convicted of violating the ban. This bill was quickly embraced by several of the state legislature's segregationists, including Representative C. C. Perkins, who introduced his own version of Kilgore's legislation.

Outside the legislature, opponents of these bills quickly mobilized. Georgia State League president Bill Estroff denounced both proposals. Invoking the economic benefits of integrated baseball, Estroff spoke out forcefully against the athletic ban in the 23 February edition of the *Sporting News*:

> I strongly feel that this legislation would set us back 20 years. Last year, our league operated as a Class D organization in Vidalia, Dublin, Hazelhurst, Douglas, Sandersville and Statesboro. Those are good old-fashioned south Georgia cities. Colored ballplayers were used in our league last season without a single incident. Our leading hitter was Bossard, a Negro, with Douglas. In past years, we had been operating at a loss in most towns. Last season, attendance picked up and we were able to show a profit. We feel that if this law is passed . . . it will put our baseball operation out of business. All of us regard it as vicious legislation and we vigorously oppose it.

Baseball integration had made racial converts out of Estroff and other southern minor-league executives. Motivated more by economics than by moral outrage over Jim Crow conditions, these men nevertheless championed the presence of African Americans in their cities and towns. As respected business and community leaders, they used their positions to influence legislative and policy decisions in ways the South was unaccustomed to. Indeed, five years earlier, the Georgia State League's president could likely not have envisioned defending integrated organized baseball in Georgia. But times had changed. The end of southern baseball's color line had created new allies in the cause of fighting for racial equality.

The lobbying by Estroff and others paid dividends. On 18 February, the legislature adjourned without acting on the proposed athletic ban. However, defiant even in defeat, Representative Perkins signaled his commitment to revisiting the issue. Alluding to Estroff's claim that Perkins's bill had pronounced regressive effects, the Carroll County representative thundered, "Well, if this would set us back 20 years, I say 'let it set us back!'" Before the year ended, Perkins's words rang true as segregationists once again made interracial sports the focal point of conflict in Georgia.

Six weeks after Georgia's foray into the post-*Brown* politics of interracial athletics, the retrograde Southern Association again moved onto front pages throughout the region. On 1 April, the New Orleans Pelicans, AA affiliate of the Pittsburgh Pirates, dropped the five nonwhite ballplayers who were listed on the team's spring roster. Three of the athletes, R. C. Stevens, Herb Bush, and Ben Daniels, who had spent spring training with the Pelicans in Huntsville, Texas, were sent to teams outside the association before the season began on 7 April. Another player, Cuban Roberto Sanchez, never reported to the team's Huntsville camp. The fifth athlete, Roman Mejias, spent spring training with Pittsburgh, impressing Pirates president Branch Rickey, who was attempting to cajole the Pelicans into retaining him on their regular season roster. Mejias had caught the Pirates' attention the year before. While playing for Waco, Texas, in the Class B Big State League, the outfielder enjoyed a remarkable fifty-five-game hitting streak en route to compiling a .354 season batting average, with 15 home runs and 141 RBIs.

However, unlike Nat Peeples the year before, these prospective line breakers were not even given a chance to play regular season ball in the Southern Association. Jake Nowak, Pelicans general manager, declined to keep Mejias, claiming that the other black prospects were not talented enough to remain in New Orleans. "If we can't find two Negroes of Southern League ability," Nowak said, "we will not have one on the team. One Negro player would be at a tremendous disadvantage. We want two or more or none." Nowak's decision to resist the Pirates' attempt to place Mejias on the New Orleans roster was ironically juxtaposed with the beginning of three major-league exhibition games in the Crescent City, featuring more than twenty black ballplayers altogether.

Nowak's contention that there were no black players available to team with Mejias was justifiably rejected by most African American observers. If the Pelicans were truly committed to integration, they would have secured the necessary players, as many other Dixie teams had previously done. The speciousness of Nowak's argument was also revealed by these prospective line breakers themselves, who demonstrated their baseball abilities and readiness for the Southern Association while playing for teams far from Louisiana.

For example, R. C. Stevens, deemed incapable of playing AA baseball, was traded to the Hollywood Stars, a team in the major-league-quality Pacific Coast League. He remained there all season, batting .241. Three years later, the man considered not good enough to play for bush-league New Orleans was playing in the majors for Pittsburgh. Following his exile from New Orleans, Ben Daniels won fourteen games in combined service for Billings, Montana, of the Class C Pioneer League, and Lincoln, Nebraska, of the Class A Western League. After winning fourteen games for AAA Columbus, Ohio, in 1958, Daniels was promoted to the big leagues, where he pitched nine seasons for Pittsburgh and Washington. Roman Mejias enjoyed a major-league career as well, playing seventy-one games for the Pirates in 1955, the first of his nine years in the majors.

As these performances reveal, Nowak and the Pelicans clearly had at least two players of AA caliber available to team with Mejias. It was team management's racial bias and pressure from segregationists in Louisiana and elsewhere in the Southern Association, not deficient baseball skills, that prevented integration of their team.

The shabby treatment of these four men and the transparently unsupportable justifications for sending them away from New Orleans infuriated African Americans in the Crescent City and across the state. Throughout

1955, hundreds of letters were sent to the *Louisiana Weekly*, imploring blacks not to attend Pelicans games and decrying the Jim Crow attitude of team ownership. Indeed, the club's perceived snub of black fans sparked a boycott of the Pelicans by African Americans. This embargo, championed by Jim Hall, the *Weekly*'s sports editor, began shortly after the 1955 season opened.

One *Weekly* reader sent a particularly impassioned letter to Hall, imploring him to do all he could to inform New Orleans's African Americans about the Pelicans' affront and call on these citizens not to patronize the AA team. Saying it was a "matter of principle" not to watch the Pelicans in 1955, this reader also questioned the commitment to the cause of racial equality of anyone, white or black, who paid their way into AA games in New Orleans that summer. A united front and boycott were necessary not only to send a message to Nowak and the Pelicans' owners but also to demonstrate solidarity in the overall fight against racial segregation. "Negroes shouldn't have to pay to have 'Jim Crow' kick them in their face," the letter concluded.

While emotions in New Orleans were running high over the boycott by African Americans, there was seemingly less controversy some three hundred miles to the northwest, in Shreveport, where black Texas Leaguers had visited since 1952. However, familiarity here did not breed acceptance. This city, near where Arkansas, Louisiana, and Texas meet (in an area known as the ArkLaTex), had a notorious reputation for being particularly hostile to minority ballplayers. In 1955, Willie Tasby played for San Antonio in the Texas League, his first year in AA after two seasons with Class B York, of the Piedmont League.

> I played against a guy, Mel McGaha. He was the manager for Shreveport. Boy, he was a real rebel. McGaha was in the dugout, pointing at his head so the pitchers would try to hit me. I met him later on in the big leagues and told him I remembered. He tried to whitewash it, but I wouldn't let him. That's something you don't forget. In San Antonio, we had Ryne Duren, who played there a year or two before I got there. At that particular time in his career, Ryne Duren, really didn't know where his pitches were going. He

had thick glasses. He'd purposely take his glasses off, and if anybody on Shreveport came close to me with the ball, he'd throw at guys in the on-deck circle. We had Duren, Howie Fox, a big right-hander. Those guys threw hard. We didn't have too much trouble around McGaha when they were there. They protected us. We also happened to have a manager who didn't go along with that bullshit.

Shreveport was the worst. The black people sat down the right field line in the bleachers. It was so bad that if the black guys popped up, the black fans would jump up and applaud us, trying to make us feel good. If we got a hit, oh, man, they would just go crazy. If we hit a home run, they got drastic. They would wait for us outside the ballpark. The whites would try and drown them out, but they couldn't, even though there were more whites. Those people really tried to make us feel good.

I regretted going to that ballpark. Those people could think of more derogatory names than I had heard in my life. They wouldn't let up. You had a feeling those people would come out there and shoot you. That's the way they acted. They gave you the impression that if you beat their team, someone would be waiting outside to do harm to you. That's how bad it was. The police were standing right there, but you got the impression that they'd be the leaders if something happened. The amazing thing about all of this is that I stayed angry. It motivated everybody, even guys that had a milder temper than me. Everybody excelled. Man, you'd go to towns like Shreveport in a semislump and motivate yourself. That's the only thing you had going for yourself. We turned the stuff they were throwing out around. Seemingly, it worked.

Louisiana was one of the worst places for African American ballplayers in the '50s, according to the black men who played in various southern locales and to Jack Bales, who teamed with the Tugersons in Hot Springs in 1953, two years earlier. Bales was playing in his eighth minor-league season in 1955 as player-manager for the Class C Evangeline League's Lake Charles (La.) Giants. His previous experience with African

American teammates and opponents sensitized this Hot Springs native to associating with blacks on a relatively equal basis, preparing him well for his tenure with Lake Charles, a team with its own minority players. Although not transformed into a civil rights crusader by his baseball encounters, Jack Bales nevertheless became more open-minded when it came to race than he would have been if he had never stepped onto an integrated baseball field.

For some reason, it was bad in Louisiana. Black players had to be different than white players in the South. They couldn't curse, argue a call, or cause a fight. They had to ignore all the hollerin'. They had to stay under control. If they didn't, there'd be trouble.

When I was managing in Lake Charles, I was called all kinds of things, like "nigger lover." There was one guy in Baton Rouge who sat up in the bleachers all by himself on a raised seat. He'd raise himself up and call me "nigger lover." I didn't argue with him. I'd ignore him. After the first time, he never called me that again. He and I got along real good. I was just doing my job. I guess he figured that out. I guess he figured out that we were all just doing our jobs.

One of the ballparks, I think New Iberia, had barbed wire on top of the dugouts. When we got there, they told me to get out of there if the folks came out of the stands after us. They said, "Get out 'cause they'll cut you." I went and told my players. I told my black players to watch out. If anything happened and people came after them, they should follow me 'cause we're out of there. We traveled in cars. I would have the three or four black players travel with me in my car. It was fine with me. They knew how I felt, so it worked out well.

I had played with blacks before, in New York in the Canadian-American League in 1950. The players were accepted up there, especially in Canada, better than in the South. In the Three I League [in 1951], we had a Mexican pitcher. He was small and thin. They'd always ride him. They'd call him "Taco," "Pablo." One game, he'd had enough. He took the ball and threw it into their dugout. Then he threw down his hat and glove. He yelled, "You wanna piece of me!?" They quieted down after that. They didn't yell anymore that night.

I got used to black players. But I've always been the type who believes in giving everyone a fair shot. If you can play, then play, and that's it. The black players knew me. They knew I didn't mess around. I'm not a big one for socializing, but I never have been. I kept to myself. I had a wife and kids. We didn't socialize. Whites stayed with whites, and blacks stayed with blacks. I don't believe whites and blacks should marry, but I think everyone should have a chance.

As the baseball season wound down, tragedy struck when the body of a fourteen-year-old African American named Emmett Till, bruised, bloodied, and weighted down by a 150-pound cotton gin fan, was pulled from the Tallahatchie River in Mississippi. Visiting from Chicago, Till had been staying with his uncle, Mose Wright, when he was kidnapped early in the morning on Sunday, 28 August, and later lynched and murdered. Till's offense, flirting with a white woman, was an unpardonable sin to segregationists. While buying bubble gum at a local store, Till, unaware of such southern racial taboos, had "wolf whistled" at the white store owner's wife.

Such an affront to segregationists' sensibilities could not go unpunished by those who believed in strict racial separation. To the unreconstructed segregationist, African Americans had to stay in their traditional position of subservience or suffer the consequences at the hands of their "betters." No Supreme Court decision would ever change this reality for unrepentant racists. On the morning of Till's abduction, Wright pleaded with his nephew's tormentors for his life. As the terrified teenager was shoved into a waiting car, Wright, according to the *Jackson Clarion-Ledger,* begged the kidnappers not to take Till away, beseeching them unavailingly, "Just take him out in the yard and whip him and I'll be satisfied." This was the last time Wright saw his nephew alive.

The brutality of Till's murder mortified people across America. Reaction to his death was swift. Roy Wilkins, NAACP executive secretary, issued a statement declaring, "It would appear that the State of Mississippi has decided to maintain white supremacy by murdering children. The killers of the boy are free to lynch him because there is in the entire state no remaining influence of decency."

Among African Americans, particularly those in the South, this crime tragically demonstrated that despite the progress that had been made, the race hatred spawned and fostered by Jim Crow remained a powerful force to be reckoned with. Their sense of grief, loss, and anger was not mollified by the swift arrest of three men who were charged with the murder and kidnapping of a fourteen-year-old boy.

Two men were brought to trial quickly. On 24 September, an all-white, all-male jury deliberated for one hour and seven minutes and acquitted half brothers Roy Bryant and John Milan of murder, despite seemingly overwhelming evidence against them. Tragically, Till's lynching was not unique. It was but one of several to occur in the Deep South of 1955.

Events of the next three months put this tragedy into perspective. As the South's rabid segregationists did all they could to keep Jim Crow alive, events beyond their control demonstrated the ultimate futility of massive resistance. Integration continued its inexorable progress. In two November rulings, the Supreme Court declared segregated public recreational facilities, such as parks, swimming pools, golf courses, and playgrounds, to be unconstitutional and opened beaches and bathhouses in Maryland and Georgia to people of all races. While many cities across the South, such as Houston, Dallas, and Wilmington, North Carolina, had previously opened their public facilities to both whites and blacks, these latest court rulings provided the force that was necessary in more recalcitrant communities to begin prying open Jim Crow's doors.

As significant as these Supreme Court rulings were, the white South was perhaps more surprised by a ruling of the ICC. On 25 November, the ICC took unusually bold action, ordering the end of racial segregation on interstate trains and buses as well as in public waiting rooms. Until this time, railroads operating in the South typically dealt with Jim Crow by adding to their trains segregated railroad cars exclusively for African Americans.

Since its founding in 1887, the commission had largely accepted segregated travel accommodations, deciding that they did not violate the Interstate Commerce Act as long as the separate waiting rooms, railroad cars, and other facilities were equal for both races. But on 25 November, the ICC, influenced by *Brown* and other recent court decisions declaring the concept of "separate but equal" to be unconstitutional, changed course, ruling: "The disadvantage to a traveler who is assigned accommodations or facilities so designated as to imply his inherent inferiority solely because of his race must be regarded under present conditions as unreasonable . . . It is hardly open to question that much progress in improved race relations has been made since [1887] and more can be expected."

These decisions were controversial not only throughout the South but within the ICC itself. Commissioner J. Monroe Johnson of South Carolina provided the sole dissenting vote on the eleven-member commission. This son of the South criticized his colleagues for overreaching, and said the commission "should not undertake to anticipate the [Supreme] court and itself become a pioneer in the sociological field." Another southern commissioner, Texas's Everett Hutchinson, did not participate in deciding these cases, announcing that he was "necessarily absent" from their consideration.

The 25 November decisions prompted indignant defiance by segregationists in several southern states. State regulators in Alabama, South Carolina, Louisiana, Mississippi, North Carolina, and Georgia declared their intentions to defy the ICC and retain segregated travel throughout their jurisdictions. These states, as well as Florida, Kentucky, Oklahoma, Arkansas, Tennessee, and Virginia, all had state laws requiring segregated travel. The reaction of South Carolina attorney general T. C. Callison, reported by the *Atlanta Journal,* typified that of his colleagues across much of Dixie. The ICC's rulings meant nothing without court action to support them, he said, adding that he had every intention of maintaining the status quo: "I don't think it will affect handling of traffic in this state."

The opposition engendered by the ICC's actions further motivated segregationists, providing them with additional incitement to resist federally mandated integration. On 1 December, Georgia governor Marvin Griffin announced his intention to ban state colleges from playing against schools with African American athletes, requesting that the state's board of regents take the necessary steps to comply with his wishes. Griffin acted one month before Georgia Tech was scheduled to play in the Sugar Bowl football classic on 2 January 1956 against the University of Pittsburgh and the Panthers' African American running back, Bobby Grier.

Griffin's announcement surprised many throughout the state, in large part because the Georgia Tech – University of Pittsburgh clash had been arranged weeks earlier, without eliciting any criticism from the governor. Before Griffin's unexpected statement, interracial collegiate sports were a relatively uncontroversial issue in Georgia. Colleges and universities had played interracial athletic games since 1950 without the contretemps Griffin's plan would now engender. Both the University of Georgia and Georgia Tech had previously competed against integrated teams, with no attempts to halt their matches. However, the situation was different in 1955. In the post-*Brown* era, the climate in Georgia was too highly charged to allow a transgression against the color line to go unchallenged.

One day after Griffin's announcement, in the early hours of 2 December, two thousand people, mostly students, took to Atlanta's streets to protest against the governor's proposal. Beginning on the Georgia Tech campus, students ridiculed Griffin, burning several effigies of him before leaving the university's grounds. State police and police officers from Atlanta and three surrounding counties were summoned to quell the uprising. Proceeding to the state capitol, several students eluded state troopers and penetrated the building itself, overturning trash cans and smashing glass paneling. Leaving the capitol, demonstrators headed for the governor's mansion. As the crowd neared Griffin's home, the police regrouped, preventing any demonstrators from entering. By three-thirty in the morning, with its ardor finally tempered, the crowd began drifting away. At least three Georgia Tech students were arrested and formally charged at police headquarters, and many others were arrested and later released.

The next day, opposition to Griffin's proposal continued to surface. Students at Mercer University, Emory University, and the University of Georgia allied themselves with their Georgia Tech brethren. Tech alumni from across America sent telegrams to the governor, expressing their opposition to keeping their school from playing in the Sugar Bowl. The state's largest paper, the *Atlanta Journal,* editorialized against Griffin: "At a time when the state faces so many problems and decisions vastly more important, it is ridiculous that Georgia should be subjected to the teapot tempest stirred up by Governor Griffin's belated opposition . . . How can he expect this state to attract anything except ridicule when its chief executive so constantly seizes upon the slightest excuse to make political capital?"

Facing such concerted, unexpected objections, Griffin backed down and suggested a compromise to the board of regents. By a fourteen-to-one margin, the board voted on 4 December to accept the governor's new face-saving plan, approving Georgia Tech's Sugar Bowl appearance and permitting state colleges to continue playing games against integrated teams outside of Georgia, but barring schools from playing interracial contests inside state borders.

Griffin originally supported banning Georgia Tech from playing against the University of Pittsburgh because of his own racism and because he felt he needed to give a political payoff to segregationists who had voted for him and were eager for dramatic executive action bolstering Jim Crow. Georgia state representative Muggsy Smith, who helped police restore order on the night of 2 December, told the *Atlanta Journal* that Griffin and other politicians were using the integration issue for their own benefit, "just as a tool by which they can get elected. If [they] would keep their mouths shut, we could resolve this thing." In deciding to use the Sugar Bowl football game, a New Year's rite in New Orleans, as a galvanizing symbol in their fight against further integration, Griffin and his allies wildly miscalculated the response from students, alumni, and other opponents. Even some segregationists backed away from Griffin's proposal, distancing themselves from the governor when confronted with what was a startlingly vehement reaction.

Coincidentally, an interracial collegiate basketball game was played in Valdosta, Georgia, during the Sugar Bowl furor. Valdosta State College faced an integrated team from Moody Air Force Base. Those in Atlanta bent on barring Georgia Tech footballers from coming in contact with an African American player were too busy to notice that a similar affront to their racist attitudes was taking place just 230 miles away. Despite their best efforts, integration simply could not be stopped.

On 2 December, the morning before Georgia Tech students launched their Sugar Bowl revolt, the *Montgomery Advertiser* carried a small, unassuming item buried in the paper's police reports column: "A Montgomery Negro woman was arrested by city police last night for ignoring a bus driver who directed her to sit in the rear of the bus. The woman, Rosa Parks, 634 Cleveland Ave., was later released under $100 bond."

Within a day of Parks's arrest, black leaders seized upon this incident and began mobilizing citizens for a boycott of the city's buses. Ironically modeled on economic protests staged by White Citizens Councils against African American businesses, the Montgomery bus boycott was born. Black neighborhoods throughout Montgomery were blanketed with leaflets denouncing the treatment accorded Parks and decrying the continuing second-class treatment of African Americans. During an emotional meeting on 6 December, five thousand African Americans packed the Holt Street Baptist Church and enthusiastically voted to continue the boycott. They issued a resolution declaring that black citizens of Montgomery had been intimidated, coerced, and embarrassed while riding city buses and that they would endure this treatment no longer and would abstain from patronizing city buses until this treatment ended. The gathering heard the words of many compelling speakers, including the Reverend Dr. Martin Luther King Jr., pastor of the Dexter Avenue Baptist Church, who urged unity among the city's African Americans: "We must stick together and work together if we are to win and we will win in standing up for our rights as Americans."

As the year concluded, the Montgomery bus boycott remained in full force. A biracial committee was formed to work out a solution; none was forthcoming. With the new year's approach, this powerful example of African American collective action reflected how much had changed in Dixie. Black citizens united and steadfastly held their ground in protesting Jim Crow, demonstrating a solidarity that many whites did not expect. Indeed, this boycott exemplified how the cause of racial integration was moving forward. The Tuskegee Institute's second annual year-end report on the state of southern race relations expressed cautious optimism about what the future held for African Americans and Jim Crow. Although racial violence and murders continued and segregationists were doing their utmost to obstruct integration, there was tangible proof that change was coming. According to the report, "Recent court decisions established a climate of permissiveness in human relations within the framework of the clearly stated principle that segregation in public services on the basis of color or race is contrary to federal law . . . Hundreds of formerly segregated schools have been desegregated without serious tensions or conflicts."

While Tuskegee's report presaged future reform, events throughout the South demonstrated how hard fought racial victories were and would continue to be.

7 MAY

PINE BLUFF, Ark.—Honoring a [Cotton States League] ruling banning Negro players, Pine Bluff Business Manager Virgil Wooley last night kept three Negro players out of the Judges' game with Hot Springs. Wooley signed outfielder Charles Peppers, shortstop Russell Moseley and pitcher Charles Chapman in an effort to pep up his cellar dwelling team and to appeal to Negro fans for help at the gate. Shortly after he signed the Negroes, however, Cotton States League directors met at Greenville [Mississippi]. After the meeting, league umpires were instructed that Pine Bluff would forfeit any games in which the Negroes played.—*Arkansas Democrat*

11 JUNE

Negro fans have taken a concrete stand not to support the "Jim Crow Birds" until the front office hires Negro ball players capable of playing double A ball and eliminate segregation in seating facilities in Pelican Park. This is very important, for at last we are displaying unity on the local front in the fight for integration. This is the thing which has most frustrated the Pelican front office, for most whites are of the opinion that achieved unity among Negroes is an impossibility.—*Louisiana Weekly*

6 AUGUST

A Negro team which won the South Carolina Little League baseball championship by default because the other 55 white teams in the league withdrew, has been barred from playing in the regional meeting at Rome, Ga. . . . Touching off the mass withdrawals in South Carolina, was said to be the resignation of Daniel H. (Danny) Jones, the state Little League director, who issued a statement . . . "I am fully convinced that it is for the best interests of the people of our state to continue our way of life and customs on a separate but equal basis, and will do everything I can to preserve that way of life." But Robert F. Morrison, president of the Charleston Cannon Street YMCA, blasted Jones, saying that he was resigning after "reading several articles from Northern newspapers that implied the participation of a Negro Little League team in the tournament would be used as an opening wedge to abolish segregation in recreational facilities in South Carolina."—*Louisiana Weekly*

2 DECEMBER

JACKSON, Miss.—A Mississippi Citizens Council leader said . . . the state's traditional segregation will be threatened when Jones [County] Junior College plays Compton, Calif., Junior College, a team with Negroes, in the Junior Rose Bowl in Pasadena, California. Bill Simmons of Jackson, administrator of the Mississippi Association of Citizens Councils, issued a statement: "This is a typical example of how integration starts in small doses. We are sure the officials at Jones [County] Junior College will take whatever action in their best judgment will protect the vital interest of Mississippi."—*Atlanta Journal*

10 DECEMBER

The Sugar Bowl after twenty-one years dropped its color ban on the field . . . In 1941, Lou Montgomery, outstanding halfback, accompanied Boston College here for their New Year's outing with Tennessee but he did not play. The Sugar Bowl general manager concluded with a statement pertaining to seating arrangements . . . "Pittsburgh will sell its tickets on a non-segregated basis, but the rest of the stadium will be segregated."—*Louisiana Weekly*

8 | Louisiana's Sinful Ways: 1956

*The federal courts cannot coerce an unwilling people into
something they are determined not to do.*

—SENATOR WILLIAM RAINACH, CHAIRMAN OF
LOUISIANA'S JOINT LEGISLATIVE COMMITTEE ON
SEGREGATION QUOTED BY THE *Shreveport Times,*
17 JULY 1956

At the time of *Brown,* seventeen southern and border states maintained de jure segregation in their public schools. As Jim Crow's foes
hoped, the Supreme Court's ruling spurred school desegregation efforts in
several jurisdictions by 1956. Maryland, West Virginia, Delaware, Kentucky,
Missouri, Oklahoma, Texas, and the District of Columbia integrated their
public schools to at least some degree. However, Mississippi, Alabama,
Georgia, South Carolina, and Louisiana obstinately resisted attempts to
integrate their elementary and secondary educational institutions.

The year began on an optimistic note. African Americans in Louisiana
exulted when the Sugar Bowl's color line came crashing down on 2 January,
as the University of Pittsburgh's Bobby Grier took the field against
Georgia Tech. An integrated crowd of 80,175 watched Tech vanquish the
Panthers, 7–0. Thousands of black fans, more than had been seen at this
game in several years, helped fill the stands. Many had done their best to
avoid sitting in the Sugar Bowl's segregated area, writing to the University
of Pittsburgh weeks before the game in search of tickets in the university's
integrated seating sections. But events in Louisiana and other southern

states soon belied the sense of triumph that African Americans who attended the 1956 Sugar Bowl undoubtedly experienced. By summer, the Tuskegee Institute's optimistic year-end report on southern race relations in 1955 had faded into obscurity, quickly rendered moot by events on the ground across an ever more defiant white South.

Defeated in federal court, pro-segregation southerners in 1956 turned to state legislatures for succor and tangible support to save Jim Crow. Many southern lawmakers quickly responded to their white constituents' pleas, spending the year's legislative sessions passing laws intended to prolong segregation. These legislators, like their supporters, viewed as holy crusades their missions to erect bulwarks against various federal court integration orders directed at Dixie. Interposition, a tactic of segregationist state governments by which they used state laws to "interpose" themselves as protective barriers between their citizens and their federal government, came into its own in 1956.

State legislatures in Alabama and Louisiana exemplified this confrontational tone for the new year. In Alabama's capitol, four segregationist bills were introduced by legislators in the first week of January, including one authorizing county boards of education to fire schoolteachers who belonged to any organizations that advocated racial integration (e.g., the NAACP). On 7 January, Alabama's House of Representatives passed a resolution declaring that the Supreme Court's desegregation rulings were "null, void and of no effect" in that state. The resolution, similar to proposals being considered in other southern states to "nullify" high court mandates, was approved, 86–4.

Under a federal court order to integrate Louisiana's public colleges, and facing the possibility that the Archdiocese of New Orleans would integrate its parochial schools, Louisiana's elected representatives took action. More than a month before the start of the 1956 legislative session, state senator William Rainach announced he would introduce an interposition bill condemning *Brown* while also upholding Louisiana's putative right to maintain racially separate educational facilities. Alabama, Georgia, Mississippi, Virginia, and South Carolina had previously adopted their own interposition measures. Segregationists like Rainach and others throughout Dixie found inspiration in a pledge made on 11 March by more than eighty United States Senators and Representatives that they would exercise every "lawful means" to reverse Supreme Court decisions mandating integration:

> The Legislature of Louisiana does hereby solemnly declare the decision of the U.S. Supreme Court of May 17, 1954 . . . and any similar decisions that might be rendered in connection with the public school system, public parks and recreational facilities . . . to be in violation of the constitution of the United States and the State of Louisiana. We declare further, our firm intention to take all appropriate measures honorably and constitutionally available to us, to void this illegal encroachment upon the rights of the several states.

Rainach announced this interposition legislation with much flourish, declaring the bill would provide new ammunition in a battle against integration that he predicted would last twenty years. On 31 May, several other bills designed to maintain segregation in public buildings and terminate state aid to integrated schools were introduced in the Louisiana Senate and House of Representatives. These measures would

> Cut off free schoolbooks, school lunch funds, and other state aid to elementary and secondary schools ending racial segregation;
> Forbid state recognition of graduates from any desegregated elementary or secondary school;
> Require superintendents of public buildings to make sure separate facilities—sanitary, drinking, and seating—be provided for whites and Negroes in their buildings;
> Prohibit hotels or other lodging places and all public eating establishments from mixing the races.

The latter provision was proposed by the Joint Legislative Committee on Segregation, established in 1954 following *Brown,* after discovering—much to the surprise of many in a state already practicing such Jim Crow discrimination—that "there are no state laws that we can find which prevent mixing races in hotels and restaurants."

Governor Earl Long took office on 15 May as Louisiana's first three-term chief executive, after receiving substantial electoral support from black voters. Shortly after his inauguration, Long preached moderation in racial politics while assuring his conservative white supporters that he remained a firm believer in segregation. He pledged that "during my next four years, I'll handle the racial question in a way that should satisfy everybody." However, Long's performance during the first legislative session of his third term belied his assurances as he quickly abandoned the black Louisianans who helped elect him.

After little debate, the Senate and House unanimously passed Rainach's interposition measure by a combined vote of 119–0. This early legislative victory was greeted enthusiastically by segregationists, who were suddenly optimistic that they could prevail in their fight. To them, the Confederacy and its policies of racial separation and degradation were on the march anew. As the *Baton Rouge Morning Advocate* editorialized on 29 May, "Those who believe that there will be an uprising of sentiment in other parts of the country on the side of the South may be right, but they may as easily be disappointed. The South has a tremendous and difficult informational job to do. The segregation program now before the Louisiana Legislature is especially commendable because of its moderation and reason. It is designed to protect the traditions of the South from a disruptive attack."

Segregationists also turned to state courts to halt the spread of integration. In a backhanded acknowledgment of the NAACP's effectiveness, they filed state lawsuits seeking to ban the civil rights organization from operating within their jurisdictions. In Louisiana, for example, the state's supreme court unanimously upheld a lower court's order banning NAACP activities in the state. Ironically, segregationists had successfully invoked a 1924 law aimed at the Ku Klux Klan that required organizations to file annual membership lists with state authorities. Not wishing to subject its members to violent reprisals, the NAACP refused to divulge the names of members. Unsuccessfully relying on the freedom of association ostensibly guaranteed by the United States Constitution's First Amendment, the NAACP was declared to be an illegal organization in Louisiana and was ordered to shut down. An Alabama circuit court judge in Birmingham issued a similar order.

Besides legislative interposition, nullification, and conservative judicial activism, segregationists introduced other tactics to battle against desegregation. White Citizens Councils launched economic boycotts against African American businesses. Intimidation of black voters was used in many places to reduce the upward trend in the African American franchise. Louisiana White Citizens Councils, motivated by an increase in black voters from 8,000 to more than 160,000 in this state in less than ten years, mobilized to reverse what they saw as a troubling trend. Louisiana state senator Rainach, chairman of the state legislature's Joint Legislative Committee on Segregation, revealed in the 27 October *Birmingham World* how worried Jim Crow's protectors were about this issue when he said, "From the long range standpoint, our only hope in the segregation fight is to clear our rolls of all illegally qualified voters. I think this will spread all over the South." Racially motivated violence also continued to infect Dixie, with bombings, cross burnings, and assaults marking segregationists' increasing desperation and anger.

As the early months of 1956 unfolded, Alabama remained at the forefront of massive resistance to integration, in the state capital, in Birmingham, and across the state. Late at night on 31 January, four crosses were burned on the University of Alabama campus in Tuscaloosa to protest the registration of the school's first African American student, Autherine J. Lucy, breaking a 124-year color line. Four other crosses had been burned either on campus or elsewhere in Tuscaloosa just prior to the 31 January incident. Seeking to end prolonged litigation aimed at Lucy's admission to the University of Alabama, school officials gave her permission to register and attend classes. However, Lucy's admission was delayed when Alabama's board of trustees ordered school officials to deny her room and board in the women's dormitories, prompting her return to federal court.

On 10 April, Birmingham attracted unfavorable nationwide attention again when four white men were arrested after rushing onstage to assault Nat King Cole as he performed to an all-white audience. After knocking the performer to the floor, they were quickly arrested, along with two accomplices who were waiting in a car outside the theater. Their vehicle contained several weapons, including two rifles. In accord with Birmingham's racial strictures, integrated performances were illegal, requiring artists to entertain a white audience and then, if they desired, an African American one. Shortly after this incident, police revealed the discovery of a plot to attack Cole that involved more than one hundred white Alabama men. It was no coincidence that several Alabama White Citizens Councils had inaugurated a campaign against "Negro music" three days before the assault.

As segregationists were plotting their interposition strategy, Jim Crow's cause was dealt another serious blow by the nation's highest court on 23 April, when its nine justices unanimously banned segregated public transportation inside a state's borders. This decision came ten years after the Court struck down race separation on interstate buses. The Court's 23 April ruling, together with other recent court mandates and the ICC's 1955 decision, effectively declared segregation to be illegal in every conceivable form of public transportation.

In many places, however, the decision had remarkably little effect. Officials in Jackson, Mississippi; Macon; Memphis; Savannah; Shreveport; Baton Rouge; New Orleans; and elsewhere vowed that their systems and facilities would remain segregated. New Orleans's city attorney, Henry Curtis, even declared that the decision by the Supreme Court, the nation's ultimate legal authority, did not apply to Louisiana. State senator Rainach castigated the Supreme Court, calling the decision "an unconstitutional seizure of authority by nine unqualified men" in the *Shreveport Times*. Rainach vowed to introduce even more Jim Crow preservation bills than originally planned during the legislature's 1956 session. "We don't expect to lose ground," he inveighed, "we expect to gain." In contrast to this obstruction, other southern localities bent with the wind and abided by the Court's edict. Transit companies in the Virginia cities of Norfolk and Petersburg ended segregation on their buses and related facilities. Little Rock's buses also desegregated, without violent reaction.

The desegregation ruling also affected the Montgomery bus boycott. On the same day the high court acted, the Montgomery City Lines, through its main office in Chicago, announced its intention to abide by the decision. However, the situation remained unclear since the company's position directly contradicted the Montgomery City Commission's continued commitment to segregated transportation. Indeed, police commissioner Clyde Sellers informed bus drivers that any who permitted desegregation of their buses would be arrested. Facing such uncertainty, the Reverend Dr. Martin Luther King Jr. vowed to continue the boycott. After announcing their respective positions, all parties maintained a rough status quo and waited for a decision by a three-judge federal court panel in a lawsuit brought by four African American women against Montgomery's segregated bus system.

On 5 June, the panel voted 2–1 to abolish segregation on public carriers in Montgomery. City and state authorities promised an appeal to the Supreme Court, but the results were preordained. Having begun the process of change in 1954, the high court was not about to reverse course and uphold segregation in any form, especially after ordering the desegregation of intrastate public transportation in April. The boycott's ultimate success in Montgomery prompted similar efforts in other southern communities. In Tallahassee, for example, African Americans, who constituted 65 percent of city bus ridership, launched an effective embargo, prompting city officials to negotiate a "first come, first served" seating policy that was the hallmark of the Montgomery protest. Rudolph Reid, a nineteen-year-old African American, was arrested in Miami after he refused to move to the rear of a Miami Transit Company bus. "The bus driver asked me to move to the rear of the bus and I refused," said Reid to the *Montgomery Advertiser*. "He asked me if I could see all the seats in the rear of the bus and I said 'yes' but that I was happy where I was sitting."

By summer, it was clear that Jim Crow had suffered additional body blows. In response, segregationists turned up the heat. Dixie's increasingly hostile climate was readily apparent to southern civil rights leaders. Gus Courts, head of the NAACP's Belzoni, Mississippi, branch, was shot by unidentified whites who objected to his get-out-the-vote campaign for African Americans. Local White Citizens Councils launched an economic boycott of his business in a vain attempt to shut down the voting drive and to force his store to close. Segregationist determination to resist any semblance of integration is well reflected in this letter to the editor of the *Montgomery Advertiser*.

I am very much interested in the fight Montgomery is having to preserve segregation. It is a fight for every Southerner to preserve our white race that our grandfathers bequeathed to us. Fight in any and every way to prevent integration.

The ebb and flow of the struggle for de jure racial equality touched every corner of the South throughout 1955.

10 MARCH

PHOENIX, Ariz.—The Giants and the Indians, aware of the tense racial situation, have canceled their exhibition game on April 10 at Meridian, Miss. Both teams have Negro players. "Too close to Alabama," a spokesman for the New York club said today.—*New York Times*

21 APRIL

From all indications, the stay-on-policy concerning Negroes attending the New Orleans Pelicans' home baseball games is still in effect. For the Pels' opening game with the Mobile Bears last Friday night less than fifteen Negroes were present . . . Wouldn't it be nice if the Board members at City Park would start the ball rollin'—after all, the Supreme Court has ruled against segregation in Municipal Parks.—*Louisiana Weekly*

26 APRIL

The New Orleans Pelicans will not hire Negro players this season and that's final . . . Reliable Pelican sources here last week stated that the green light for hiring Negro players would not be set in motion this season . . . Last year, tan attendance at Pelican Stadium hit the cellar, the lowest in the club's history.—*Louisiana Weekly*

6 MAY

SHREVEPORT, La.—The Bossier Parish School Board has placed a ban on three national magazines—Time, Life and Look—because of what it calls their "distorted" view of the segregation issue . . . The resolution accused the three magazine[s] of "waging a systematic campaign to prejudice the American people against the south by presenting in their columns biased and distorted

views on the institution of segregation of races in our schools."
—*Birmingham World*

8 MAY

Louisiana State University . . . was denied a Supreme Court review
of a ruling that it could not refuse—on account of race or
color—to admit Negro Alexander P. Tureaud Jr. as a student.
[Louisiana's] appeal said: "The admission of Negro students to
the graduate and law schools of Louisiana State University has
resulted in major incidents such as the burning of crosses on the
campus, an attempt to organize and incite students against the
Negro students, rock throwing through the window of an apart-
ment on the campus occupied by a Negro student and his wife,
and the actual firing upon two Negro men students."—*Lake
Charles American Press*

8 JUNE

A news source discloses that in Danville, Va., recently, some sixty
percent of Negro fans rose and left the ballpark when they were
asked to move to their side of the rope in the third base bleachers.
—*Pittsburgh Courier*

18 AUGUST

HOUSTON, Tex.—For the first time in history, Negro and white
couples danced on the same floor here. Cause of the taboo-
breaking was Carl Perkins who appeared here with the rock 'n roll
show, Top Record Stars of 1956 . . . The cops were unable to
restrain or contain the delirious and screaming white teen-agers
. . . The crowd got so carried away that the police made the band
stop playing 30 minutes before the dance was to close. There were
no incidents and nobody was arrested.—*Pittsburgh Courier*

As baseball continued along the integration path, Jackie Robinson provided a racial report card on the game in taped interviews with the *Pittsburgh Courier* and the *Sporting News*. Robinson's opinions were published by
these papers in June 1956.

When we played in New Orleans during spring training the Negroes in the stands booed every time they announced anything about the New Orleans Pelicans. They booed so loud in fact, that the rest of the announcement might just as well not been made . . . they put some kind of unofficial boycott on the team and they are not going out to the ball park. At the same time, they are doing everything they can to make people realize that if they expect them to come out and see baseball, then they must give them somebody of color on the team. To me, it's good seeing the people working together trying to eliminate some of these problems. Too often, there are those of us who have the opportunity of doing something who say, "Well, I have reached a certain position and I'm not going to jeopardize that position." To me, that's wrong. It's something I never want my kids to accuse me of. I find in the South there are more and more people feeling the same way. After ten years of traveling in the South as a player, I have noticed many changes. Most of them have been for the better. However, there are certain areas in which there has been no change.

Evangeline League

Alexandria	Lake Charles
Baton Rouge	Monroe
Crowley	New Iberia
Lafayette	Thibodaux

Weeks before the start of the baseball season, recreation and parks leaders from eight Louisiana cities met to map out a Jim Crow strategy to present to their state representatives for legislative action in 1956. The group unveiled a three-point program calling for a constitutional amendment requiring state permission before lawsuits could be filed against recreation and park boards; laws giving the state exclusive power to maintain segregation in recreation facilities; and "complete segregation of the white and colored races in all recreational activities." In January, Norman David, vice-chairman of the East Baton Rouge Parish Recreation and Parks Commission, announced his commission's determination that African Americans would not be permitted to play baseball in Baton Rouge's Goldsby Park.

The Baton Rouge Rebels were one of eight franchises in the Evangeline League that had integrated without serious incident two years earlier. In reaching their decision, David and the commission acted in concert with many of their Deep South compatriots. They realized that permitting interracial athletics had been a grave mistake. They wanted to reverse baseball's integration and pretend as if nothing had evolved. The problem was that much had and was continuing to change; the South of 1956 was nothing like it had been when the decade began. When Jackie Robinson had played in Atlanta seven years earlier, Jim Crow's protectors had warned: Disturb one of segregation's dominoes, and the rest come tumbling down.

Undeterred by events in Baton Rouge, Lake Charles and Lafayette still planned to begin 1956 with blacks on their teams. Indeed, in a rare move of big-league racial enlightenment, the Chicago Cubs, Lafayette's major-league parent, made continued affiliation with Chicago conditional on their farm team's acceptance of African American ballplayers. Other league cities not only opposed Baton Rouge's restrictions but were also incredulous about why such a policy would be adopted now.

9 APRIL

Baton Rouge officials have succeeded in alienating a large percentage of the club's potential gate. One would suppose that a club that had such financial trouble a year ago would be attempting to create new fans instead of making certain that fans will stay away. I do not know the figures on the Negro population of Baton Rouge, but it is not likely that the Negroes will support the Baton Rouge club in any numbers this year . . . To say that no other club has a right to use Negro players and that Negroes have no right to be in the league is something else. Minor league law does not allow such a ban. To at[t]empt such a ban by subterfuge is attempting to hold back the clock, which has not been very profitable in the South since 1861.—*Lake Charles American Press*

The first test of Baton Rouge's color line came in late April when the Lake Charles Giants came to town for a weekend series. In a last-minute compromise, the Giants agreed not to play their three black players, Felipe Alou, Charles Weatherspoon, and Ralph Crosby, in exchange for the Rebels' benching their starting shortstop and center fielder. This agreement held Friday night, as Lake Charles, without its minority players, defeated Baton Rouge before 919 fans.

Saturday night was a different story. Lake Charles broke its deal with the Rebels by listing Ralph Crosby on the lineup card. Local officials ordered the game postponed, and Rebels president Bob Brazeale announced to six hundred disappointed, angry spectators that the recreation commission's segregation order had forced the cancellation. Evangeline League president Ray Mullins subsequently decreed that the game be forfeited to Lake Charles because of the Rebels' refusal to play a regularly scheduled league match. To avoid a similar result, Baton Rouge transferred a subsequent series against the Giants to Lafayette.

As time passed, sentiment against Baton Rouge's Jim Crow edict grew, with even the normally pro-segregation local paper editorializing against it on 3 May.

> The decision of the Recreation and Park Commission is understandable. Yet, it is not so easy to see why conditions should be different in Baton Rouge from conditions in other Louisiana cities where Negro players appear regularly without causing any comment. And in its road games even now, the local team competes against Negro players. The Rebels, we are afraid, are being forced to fight a losing battle against the rest of organized baseball . . . It is vain to expect that either the minor league or major league organizations will go along with a ban on Negro players. The best that could be hoped for in a showdown would be dissolution of the entire Evangeline League. —*Baton Rouge Morning Advocate*

Even Gene Nelson, chairman of the East Baton Rouge Parish Recreation and Park Commission, began to waver. In a memorandum, Nelson expressed the desire of many segregationists to have it both ways—to integrate professional baseball to keep the Rebels in town, with all the attendant economic benefits, without integrating other parts of society. He concluded that "colored baseball players in professional baseball is a part of baseball. If we must allow it, and I feel that we must, rather than see a vital part of the community fold, then we should make it clear there can be no integrated activities on our parks and playgrounds. We must not allow a change of policy in regard to the ball club to be used as a lever by integration leaders to move into other activities."

Days later, however, the Evangeline League solved its "racial crisis" the same way the Cotton States League did three years before. On 5 May, the league's five black players—Felipe Alou, Chuck Weatherspoon, Ralph Crosby, Sam Drake, and Manuel Trabous—were exiled from the circuit and Louisiana. All parties averred that the transfers had nothing to do with Baton Rouge's racial policy, claiming that the players were being either promoted to higher classifications or, in the case of Lake Charles's trio, demoted because they were not ready for the Class C Evangeline.

However, rumors of league pressure against Lake Charles and Lafayette to solve the racial issue quickly surfaced. Jack Schwarz, New York Giants assistant minor-league director, said he understood that the league had voted to expel the two franchises under a rule permitting action against "undesirable" members unless the black players were sent to teams outside the circuit. President Mullins and several team owners denied the behind-the-scenes machinations, but the *Baton Rouge Morning Advocate* confirmed Schwarz's account. "Two Sundays ago in [a] secret meeting, and for the first time they did keep a secret, and passed a law, regulation, or amendment to their constitution that any time a team was found 'undesirable,' it could be kicked out of the circuit. Supposedly the vote was 6–2 with Lake Charles and Lafayette voting against the measure. So the two clubs read the handwriting on the wall and Saturday disposed of their players."

Reaction from local African Americans was swift and unyielding. Before the black players were expelled from the Evangeline League, African Americans had been consistent supporters of the Giants, with average attendance of four hundred per game and a high of twelve hundred. After Alou, Weatherspoon, and Crosby were scattered across the minors, black attendance in Lake Charles dropped to less than a dozen per night. Several fans returned their season tickets to the Lake Charles box office.

When a Lake Charles Giants employee told an African American businessman that blacks were letting the team down by staying away from the ballpark, he fired back this retort reported in the *Louisiana Weekly:* "You let yourself down when you bowed to racial discrimination. We understand that certain whites do not want Negroes in the league. They have their wish. Now let them support the Lake Charles club."

Lafayette's attendance also plummeted, with black customers falling from an average of 200 to 16 per game. African Americans in this southern Louisiana city also planned a boycott in response to the exile of Lafayette's black players. For the season, nearly 27,000 fewer fans attended games in Lafayette than had the year before, despite the fact that the Cubs won the 1956 pennant. This franchise folded on 20 June 1957, after attracting an anemic total of 9,567 spectators to the ballpark midway through that season.

Within one month of the players' exile, the league dropped to seven members when the New Iberia franchise folded and Baton Rouge, faced with mounting red ink, announced it would also drop out of the Evangeline League if its finances did not improve. This circuit, with the Rebels still barely in the fold, staggered to the end of the 1956 season and operated for one more year before folding in 1958.

Felipe Alou was beginning his professional baseball career in the United States when he was sent to Lake Charles at the start of the 1956 season. Alou, who had not experienced the racial divisions of America's South while growing up in the Dominican Republic, was taken aback by the conditions he experienced in Louisiana and later in Florida, where he was sent after being banished from the Pelican State.

It was in Cocoa Beach that the twenty-one-year-old dispelled the notion that he was sent to the Class D Florida State League because his abilities did not measure up to the Evangeline's standards. Alou led his team to the pennant by winning the league batting title with a .380 average while hitting 21 home runs and driving in 99 runs. He tied a league mark by amassing two doubles, a triple, and a homer in one game and set a record by scoring on eight consecutive trips to the plate in another.

> My first year as a player, I was going to play in the Carolina League, but my visa was late by almost two months. Because of not having a visa to enter the United States on time for spring training, by the

time I got to Florida, the Danville [Carolina League] team had already left camp in Melbourne. Only the Lake Charles team was left. So they put me with that team. I practiced a couple of days with Lake Charles and left for Louisiana. That's how I wound up in the Evangeline League. I didn't know anything about racism when I went there, coming from the Dominican Republic. I was only in Florida for a couple of days, without having the slightest hint of any race differences. There was no preparation at all. My mother is a white lady, and my father is black, so to me, all that was normal.

It didn't take me very long to find out about racism in Louisiana. There were two other blacks on the team. They were American—[Ralph Crosby] was a shortstop from New York City, and Chuck Weatherspoon. I'll never forget them, because this was big stuff. We were put somewhere with a white family, of all things. We lived upstairs for whatever time we were there. I guess nobody knew, because we came back to the house late, after the games. We really didn't spend much time there. The few days I was there, they were very sweet. Obviously, I guess they had a mission to make us feel good.

We were told that there was something going on in the state. They told me I would have to leave. We had a player, Art Martinez, a Mexican American, who spoke a little Spanish. He told me what was going on, that I had to leave because they had passed a law about blacks not playing with whites. There was a trip to Baton Rouge where they didn't let me and the other two blacks onto the field. I remember the name of that team, the Baton Rouge Rebels. They put us in the bleachers with the black fans. I'll never forget—the bleachers for blacks was in left field. We had to take our uniforms off and go outside the stadium and come in, like we were fans.

I'm glad I didn't know any English, because I know there was some yelling at us from the stands. But I was no fool. I was a twenty-year-old college man from the Dominican Republic. I lived in Santo Domingo, a large city, before coming to the United

States. I was a city boy. I had traveled—to Mexico twice, to Venezuela, to Aruba. I didn't understand English, but I understood the situation.

All of a sudden I found myself where I had to go to sleep on the other side of the tracks. That's the way it used to be when I was with the Lake Charles team. After the white players went to the hotel, they took us to the black part of town. White people didn't have much confidence in having a relationship, being neighbors, with a black person, or having their daughter go out with a black man. There was a feeling of superiority, but it really wasn't racism. It was the way the establishment was working. There was a tradition of inferiority of blacks, going back to after the Civil War. I knew a bunch of people who were really not racists, but they didn't want to be seen with me in public. They knew I was just like anybody else. I wasn't going to steal or maim or kill. Except the color of my skin was different than theirs, and they didn't want to be seen with me. I'm talking about male and female.

There really was not much you could do. What were you going to do? Go home? Quit? I had a plan. I came to America to be a baseball player. I told my father that I left to be a baseball player. My dad did not have much confidence in that, because he didn't know baseball. He didn't know if I was a good player or not.

When they told me I had to leave Louisiana, it took me three days on a Greyhound bus to travel from Lake Charles to Cocoa, Florida. The bus stopped everywhere. When we stopped, I had to find the lines that said Colored People. By the time I found that line and got on the line, the bus was ready to depart. I never had a chance to eat. They gave me twelve dollars, meal money for three days. I arrived in Cocoa with ten-something dollars in my pocket. They used to have machines you could put ten cents or whatever in and you'd get some peanuts. That was my food for three days.

There were many times on that Greyhound bus that I changed my plans. I had a round-trip ticket, but many times I thought about taking that bus to Miami and going home. The man who signed me was Horacio Martinez, a shortstop in the Negro leagues. He was my baseball coach in college at the [Autonomous] University of Santo Domingo. He became a scout with the New York Giants. I was the first player he signed. I knew if I went back home, I would let Horacio Martinez down. I knew my dad and my mom were waiting for me to go back home. But I promised Mr. Martinez that I was going to be a good player—you know, his first player and everything. That's one of the reasons I stayed.

Every time we got to a city, the bus driver used to say we were in whatever city. I knew that by the time we got to Cocoa, he was going to tell me to get off. I got out of the bus in Cocoa at seven o'clock in the morning. There was nobody waiting. The Grey-hound station in Cocoa in 1956 was a bench. I thought about which way I was going to go. There was a beautiful black lady who was going to work early in the morning. I was sitting on the bench, and she came by. I guess she saw this man sitting in the middle of nowhere. She started talking and realized that I didn't know Eng-lish. With signs and a couple of words, I managed to let her know I was a ballplayer. She let me understand she knew a lady where some players were staying. She walked me to a house in the black part of town.

When we arrived, she woke the lady up. By now, it was eight o'clock in the morning. From what I understood, the Cocoa team had played in St. Petersburg the night before, and the players got back at five in the morning. The bus had a flat tire or something. The two players in her house were Puerto Rican guys—Julio Navarro, the father of [current major-league pitcher] Jaime Navarro, and a guy by the name of Hector Cruz from New York. These guys were considered white. Yet they were staying with a black lady. I sat on the porch of her house, and the lady didn't want to wake them up.

At noon, I was still waiting. I went to sleep and woke up, went to sleep and woke up. At noon, that girl that brought me there came back. She talked to the lady who owned the house, and she [the girl] took me to another house in the neighborhood. I'll never forget it was a Friday. She put me with that lady. I went to sleep at two o'clock in the afternoon, and nobody knew where I was. I didn't even know where the ballpark was. The lady I was put with didn't know anything about baseball, so I missed the game.

The two Puerto Rican guys found me the next day and took me to the ballpark. I stayed the rest of the year with that lady. She was a wonderful person. Her children were married and had left home. I became the best player on that team. They were so proud to have me there. It got to be good in Cocoa. If you hit a big home run late in the game to win it, they used to pass a hat [for fans to put money in and give to the player]. The stands were not integrated, but they used to pass the hat to everybody. I hit twenty-one home runs in the league that year. I must have hit twelve in Cocoa, all in late innings to win games. I always got enough money for everybody, for the black and the white kids.

When I got to Florida in 1956, I found it was more racist than Louisiana. It was in Florida that I started to understand English. When they got me out of Louisiana, I was told they would not let me in the ballpark. I was told, "You won't play," but I never understood what they were telling me. Everything was through an interpreter. But in Florida, after a couple of months, I started to understand. I was getting things myself, through my own understanding of the language.

I knew about Jackie Robinson. I knew what he had to go through. There was hope because of him. I was one of the first few Dominicans who came here to play ball. I always thought about Jackie Robinson. I had a wonderful manager in Florida, Buddy Kerr. He did a really great job with me and the other blacks on the team. He kept us away from trouble, not that we were getting in trouble. We were here to play baseball. He understood the racial situation. I hit .380 with Cocoa, and I have to give that man a lot of credit.

We didn't eat the best food. Our bus would stop in a parking lot, and the white players would go in and eat. When they came out, they would bring us food on the bus. One might say, "I'm going to bring Felipe a hamburger." They might not be what I wanted, but sometimes that was all they could get. There were two cities where the bus would stop, drop off the white players, and then drive off the parking lot and park it on the street because the restaurant owners didn't want blacks sitting on the bus in the parking lot. I swear to God.

There was a time when the bus was left there with the three of us, and within fifteen minutes, the police came. They were ready to arrest the three of us. The police wanted us to get outside the bus and walk. One of the players, Jim Miller from Miami, talked with one of the policemen. He then went inside the restaurant and came out with Buddy Kerr. He was also our bus driver. He drove the bus and parked us across the street until the other guys ate. That night, we didn't eat. That was in West Palm Beach. The name of the restaurant was the Vagabond. I wasn't going to tell you that, but I did.

I live here [in West Palm Beach]. My neighbors are white people and black people. The people love me. I've managed here ten years. You see how things change. We've come a long way. I've lived in this area now for thirty years, and I've never had any problems, race related or any kind, with the police, neighbors, the fans.

After his tension-filled introduction to professional baseball in the States, Felipe Alou went on to enjoy a stellar athletic career, including seventeen years as a player in the big leagues, where he became only the second Dominican player to reach the majors. On 15 September 1963, he and his younger brothers, Matty and Jesus, made history by appearing together in the same San Francisco Giants outfield. In 1992, Alou was appointed manager of the Montreal Expos. Entering the 1996 season, he had the second-best winning percentage among all active major-league managers.

No Mixed Sports Here

There is a lot of merit in the thought that we need to halt interracial activities in sports and other fields. There is a lot of public pressure being built up for

such measures and particularly there is growing resentment against integration in sports programs.
—LOUISIANA STATE SENATOR WILLIAM RAINACH, CHAIRMAN, JOINT LEGISLATIVE COMMITTEE ON SEGREGATION, QUOTED IN THE *Baton Rouge State Times,* 16 JUNE

By 11 June, both houses of Louisiana's legislature had unanimously passed several bills that, for example, eliminated compulsory attendance at any school forced by court order to integrate and guaranteed segregated waiting-room facilities for travelers. A slew of other similarly intentioned proposals were also introduced, including one banning television shows featuring white and black performers, which were considered "un-American" and "a conspiracy against the people of the South" by its sponsor, state senator Brenham Crothers.

The breadth of the segregationists' 1956 legislative agenda took many African Americans in Louisiana by surprise. Indeed, even legislators thought to be relatively friendly to black voters did not resist the segregationist tide that was sweeping over the statehouse. The overwhelming majority of these lawmakers abandoned their principles and bent to the prevailing political trend in Louisiana, lest they acquire such politically untenable labels as "accommodator," "carpet bagger," or "nigger lover." The *Louisiana Weekly*'s 9 June edition explained how troubling this segregationist tide was to black Louisianans. "The Negro citizens of this state are duly alarmed and concerned at the current outburst of vicious and repressive segregation legislation that is currently being passed in the Louisiana legislature. A mighty lot of goodwill and good race relations are being washed down the drain by the Louisiana legislature apparently trying to ape several defiant Southern states who have gone off on the deep end in this matter of refusing to abide by and comply with the law of the land as recently enunciated by the U.S. Supreme Court."

Although the bill banning interracial television was withdrawn because its proposed prohibition was considered unworkable rather than unacceptable, the Louisiana House did unanimously pass a bill to prohibit dancing, social functions, athletic training, entertainments, games, and sports or other contests involving blacks and whites. The penalty for violating this statute included fines ranging from $100 to $1,000 and imprisonment for anywhere from sixty days to one year. The bill included the following provisions:

> That all persons, firms and corporations are prohibited from sponsoring, arranging, participating in, or permitting on premises under their control any dancing, social functions, entertainments, athletic training, games, sports or contests and other such activities involving personal and social contacts in which the participants or contestants are members of the white and negro races. That at any entertainment or athletic contests, where the public is invited or may attend, the sponsors or those in control of the premises shall provide separate seating arrangements, and separate sanitary, drinking water and other facilities for members of the white and negro races, and to mark such separate accommodations and facilities with signs printed in bold letters. That white persons are prohibited from sitting in or using any part of seating arrangements and sanitary or other facilities set apart for members of the negro race.

It was no accident that this measure, known as the Sports Ban Bill, would affect the state's major athletic institutions: the Sugar Bowl; Louisiana State, Loyola, and Tulane Universities; the Shreveport Sports; and the Texas and Evangeline Leagues. The bill was intended to complement other segregationist legislation that had already passed. But it also sent a pointed, narrowly directed message to sports organizations that, despite their efforts to the contrary, segregation would remain the order of the day in Louisiana. Indeed, state representative Lawrence Gibbs, who sponsored the sports ban, stated that it was designed specifically to prevent and roll back integration in athletics.

This legislation was provoked by several previous cracks in Louisiana's wall of segregation on the state's athletic fields and baseball diamonds: Louisiana State University had recently rejected an attempt to prevent teams with black athletes from playing LSU in Louisiana; Loyola University had desegregated its athletic program and field house; on 2 January 1956, the University of Pittsburgh's Bobby Grier had desegregated the Sugar

Bowl in New Orleans; and Louisiana had experienced integrated professional baseball through its membership in the Texas and Evangeline Leagues. The ban would not only end integration in these contexts but also squelch the possibility, supported by some Louisianans, of scheduling 1957 spring training exhibition games in the state between major-league teams with black players while also preventing boxing matches between black and white fighters.

A *Los Angeles Times* article proclaiming that "baseball leads the way to an integrated America" bolstered the arguments of those urging a strong stand favoring segregation in sports. These southerners feared the continued influence of integrated athletics in moving society toward complete de jure desegregation. To them, the sports ban was symbolic of their larger fight against the Supreme Court, school integration, and more unwelcome changes in the region's racial caste system.

Indeed, the *Times* article galvanized those who were lobbying for passage of the sports ban. Aware of the *Times* piece, Dr. Emmett Irwin, former member of LSU's board of supervisors, who contended integration was a Communist plot, in an article in the *Shreveport Times* noted that YMCA workers were trying to "brainwash our children" and sell them on integration. "This bill will put the clincher on the question of segregation in this state." Shreveport's J. Stewart Slack, another former member of LSU's board, put the matter succinctly: "They want to integrate on the fields. The next step is the grandstands. The Legislature is the only one that can curb it."

As an LSU supervisor and a leader of Louisiana's White Citizens Councils, Slack championed the effort to ban teams with black athletes from visiting the university. LSU's board voted three times on this proposed ban, and three times it was defeated, failing by a 7–7 vote on Slack's final attempt before his term expired in June. Perhaps the strongest publicly recorded statement in favor of the sports ban was one by J. B. Easterly, president of the pro-segregation Southern Gentlemen's Organization. On June 26, he told a cheering crowd at the state capitol in Baton Rouge: "We want to go on living our own sinful way. We don't want to go to heaven because our mamas and papas are down below. We want to do this in a peaceful way, but we are going to stay segregated in Louisiana come hell or high water."

Despite opposition from Texas League president Dick Butler and the Sugar Bowl's sponsor, the Mid-Winter Sports Association—both lobbied against passage—the sports ban was unanimously approved by the Louisiana Senate on 5 July. A last-minute amendment exempting athletics and athletic training from the legislation was defeated, 30–2, leading to the unanimous vote in favor of the unadulterated sports ban.

However, the legislation's final version included one concession granted to the Texas League as a result of its lobbying efforts—an amendment changing the ban's effective date to 15 October, thereby delaying its implementation until after the end of the Texas League's current season. This was done so as not to interfere with the 1956 campaign's completion by preventing teams with black players from visiting Shreveport. In 1956, six of the eight Texas League franchises had black players on their rosters.

Once the sports ban legislation was sent to Louisiana governor Earl Long for action, Butler and the Sugar Bowl intensified their lobbying. Their earlier advocacy efforts had been somewhat muted because they misjudged the legislature's intentions. Ban opponents naively did not believe a bill with such far-reaching implications could pass. Scrambling to recover lost ground, these interests sent letters and telegrams to Long, pleading that a veto was necessary to prevent financial disaster from befalling the state's biggest showcase for college athletics and to prevent Shreveport from losing its Texas League franchise. They took out full-page advertisements designed to pressure the governor to veto the bill.

Earlier in the legislative session, Long had revealed his position on integration by signing four Jim Crow measures supported by Rainach. These included one maintaining segregated waiting rooms for interstate travelers, in open defiance of a United States Supreme Court decision. Given Long's support of this and similar measures, his signing the sports ban into law on 15 July should have surprised no one.

Nonetheless, the governor, in an effort to inoculate himself from criticism by the Sugar Bowl's sponsors, made a point of "seeking the views of the public" before acting on the legislation. By going through the motions of polling Louisianans about what course of action he should take, Long gave himself political cover for his inevitable decision to sign the bill. Long's call for public input and debate on the eve of his signing the bill was particularly ironic since there had been virtually no deliberation in the legislature during its consideration of the ban. The House held no public hearings, and the Senate convened only one, in its Judiciary Committee.

Long announced that although he had some doubts about parts of the bill, any blame for its consequences must be placed elsewhere. After all, the governor was merely acting as a responsible chief executive by fulfilling his (white) constituents' wishes. "The comments I've had over the state [have] run about four to one in favor of the bill," he claimed. "It looks like the majority of the people feel that way about it. In signing it, I'm going along with the majority that I've heard from."

Sugar Bowl sponsors mounted a second attempt to repeal the measure during a special legislative session in August. These interests enlisted the assistance of several New Orleans–area representatives, who had been educated about the bill's economic effects on their constituents should major universities refuse to participate in the annual football game. A proposal was introduced that would exempt New Orleans from the statewide interracial sports ban. The segregationists responded immediately, with state representative Wellborn Jack declaiming, "My children are not going to school with Negroes! I was brought up under this . . . and I make my motion under my way of life to table the entire matter."

But monetary concerns could not overcome segregationist fervor. Repeal efforts foundered as the House voted 64–15 to kill the exemption proposal.

Swift reaction followed the repeal's defeat. The Chicago Cubs transferred their minor-league spring training camp from Lafayette to Mesa, Arizona. The University of Wisconsin canceled its contract for a home-and-home football series with LSU. Three out of four invited universities, including Notre Dame, withdrew from participating in the annual December Sugar Bowl basketball tournament. The University of Pittsburgh announced it would not consider any future Sugar Bowl football invitations.

The new law also provoked a heated exchange between a New Orleans sports writer and Jackie Robinson. Bill Keefe, sports editor of the *New Orleans Times-Picayune,* wrote that the sports ban had received a push from the "insolence" of Robinson, who had committed the "sin," in the eyes of many whites, of integrating major-league baseball while also speaking out as a black man against segregation. In a column under the heading "Enemy of His Race," which appeared in the 18 July 1956 edition of the *Times-Picayune*, Keefe mirrored the attitude of many white southerners at that time: They could accept no interference from outsiders and African Americans in matters of local white custom and practice.

Gov. Long has signed the bill banning mixed athletic contests. The bill also calls for complete segregation in the stands at sporting events. It will greatly interfere with schedule making of Tulane and LSU and the selection of teams by the Sugar Bowl, but the stand of the people of Louisiana was forcefully presented by the legislators who voted 100 per cent for the new law. Public sentiment was overwhelmingly in favor of segregation in sports.

The National Association for the Advancement of Colored Peoples [*sic*] can thank—I was about to say the NAACP can thank Jackie Robinson, persistently insolent and antagonistic troublemaking Negro of the Brooklyn Dodgers. But the ones who should thank Robinson are all segregationists—all members of all White Citizens' Councils, Southern Gentleman organizations, and other groups pledged to fight integration. No 10 of the most rabid segregationists accomplished as much as Robinson did in widening the breach between the white people and Negroes . . .

He has been the most harmful influence the Negro race has suffered in the attempt to give the Negro nationwide recognition in the sports field, and the surprising part of it is that he wasn't muzzled long ago . . . Just recently Robinson authored a piece that gained wide circulation in which he abused the South for its fight for segregation. He said he wouldn't be satisfied until hotels in the South accepted Negroes just as they admitted whites. He said he isn't interested in these hotel owners that wish to protect their investments. Isn't that too bad? Perhaps Southern hotel owners will get together and decide to bankrupt themselves so Robinson will be satisfied. It will be surprising, though, if they do. Most of them think that opening of their inns to negroes would be just as

definite a step toward segregation as the present policy. Only difference would be that the handful of Negroes that would be
guests would not furnish revenue to keep going.

Sincere segregationists therefore should chip in and buy a
plaque to present Robinson for his yeoman work.

Robinson's impassioned answer of 23 July was published in several newspapers:

I am writing you, not as Jackie Robinson, but as one human being
to another. I cannot help, nor possibly alter what you think of me.
I speak to you only as an American who happens to be an American Negro and one who is proud of that heritage. We ask for
nothing special. We ask that we be permitted to live as you live,
and as our nation's constitution provides. We ask only, in sports,
that we be permitted to compete on an even basis and, if we are
not worthy, then the competition shall, per se, eliminate us. Certainly you, and the people of Louisiana, should be capable of
facing some competition.

Myself, and other Negroes in the majors, stop in hotels with
the rest of the club in towns like St. Louis and Cincinnati. These
hotels have not gone out of business. No investment has been
destroyed. The hotels are, I believe, prospering. And there has
been no unpleasantness. I wish you could see as I do, but I hold
little hope. I wish you could comprehend how unfair and un-
American it is for this accident of birth to make such a difference
to you. I assume you are of Irish extraction. I have been told that
as recently as fifty years ago, want ads in newspapers carried the
biased line, "Irish and Italians need not apply" in certain sections
of the country. This has been forgotten, or at least overcome. You
call me "insolent." I'll admit I have not been subservient but
would you use the same adjective to describe a white ballplayer—
say Ted Williams, who is more often than I, involved in controversial matters. Am I insolent, or am I merely insolent for a Negro
(who has courage enough to speak against injustices such as yours
and people like you)?

I am deeply regretful that Louisiana has taken this step backward. But, because your sports fans, and I believe there are many fine patrons among them, will be deprived of top attractions because of it . . . not for the Negro in Louisiana who will, because of your law, be deprived of the right of free and equal competition—but because of the damage it does to our country.

I am happy for you, that you were born white. It would have been extremely difficult for you had it been otherwise.

As the contretemps surrounding the ban subsided, attention turned to the 1957 Texas League season. With opening day's approach, the seeming contradiction of a league that permitted black ballplayers operating in a state where interracial athletics were illegal became clear. Louisiana, always a difficult place for African Americans, had become almost problematic from a racial perspective. Nineteen fifty-seven would not offer much to change this state's racially backward reputation.

9 | Small Towns, Big Cities: 1956–57

Sooner State League

Ardmore   Muskogee
Gainesville–Ponca City Paris
Lawton   Seminole
McAlester   Shawnee

If I had to go into little towns like Sanford, Florida, et cetera, it's a different ball game. I'd have felt quite uncomfortable because the relationship between the races was very intense. You had the diehards who didn't want to budge, regardless of the fact that things were opening up. In the larger cities, you found more tolerance between the races. As you get into the smaller towns, you saw less tolerance.

—ED CHARLES, 1997

Minor-league baseball in the South, as elsewhere, was played mostly in small or midsize cities and towns. These communities were often more racially stratified than large cities simply because there were smaller numbers of African Americans living in them. By contrast, in Atlanta, Miami, Dallas, Louisville, and other sizable southern metropolises, larger black populations generally translated into higher levels of acknowledgment and acceptance for those populations. However, a black ballplayer coming to a small southern community was something of an oddity, since towns-people often had relatively little experience dealing with minority peoples, especially African Americans. Such places were not safe harbors of toler-ance, and they could be found not only in the former Confederacy but also in states on the southern periphery, including Oklahoma. In small, off-the-beaten-track Oklahoma towns such as Ponca City, Ardmore, and Shawnee, integration controversies took place away from the glare of national attention.

Billy Leo Williams was eighteen years old in 1956. Just out of high school in Whistler, Alabama, near Mobile, hometown of Henry Aaron, he signed his first professional contract with the Chicago Cubs. Growing up in Alabama meant that Williams had lived with segregation. Each morning, he rode about six miles on a bus, passing several all-white schools along the way, until he and his fellow African American students reached their seg-regated destination, Mobile County Training School, from which future major leaguers Tommie Agee and Cleon Jones would later graduate. Despite its segregation, Mobile was still more tolerant than Birmingham, perhaps owing to the variety of people and customs that residents in this Gulf of Mexico seaport were exposed to.

Shortly after the rookie outfielder signed with Chicago, the Cubs gave him a bus ticket and instructions to report to Chicago's Class D farm club in Ponca City, Oklahoma, a community of about twenty thousand people near the Oklahoma-Kansas line. In terms of population, Ponca City placed in the middle of the Sooner State League. Lawton was the largest city in the league, with about sixty thousand people, and Seminole, in the central part of the state, southeast of Oklahoma City, was the smallest in the eight-team circuit, with about ten thousand residents. For Williams, who had never journeyed so far from home before, Oklahoma was an exotic location. It was there that he learned about the small-town version of racism.

Two days after I finished high school, I was on my way to Ponca City, Oklahoma. This is one of the first times that I had left home, being away from home over night. The ball club had an accident. They used to travel around in automobiles, and one hit an embankment. Lou Johnson got his ear taken off, and he had to be put in the hospital, so I completed the squad. I took the Greyhound bus for two and one-half days.

When I arrived in Ponca City, I didn't know where I was going. When I got off the bus, this one black gentleman came up to me—I think his name was Mr. White. He said, "I've got orders to pick you up." I didn't know who this guy was, and he started naming names in the Cubs organization, naming Buck O'Neil because I think Buck had called down there. He said, "I'm going to take you over to my house, where you're going to stay." At that time, I thought when you go off to play baseball, you live and be with the team. I didn't know the blacks go to a private home. It was surprising at first.

I went to the private home. Lou Johnson had been there, but he was gone. [Horace] "Chick" Greenwood, a guy from Chicago; Jim Gilmore, a pitcher; and Sammy Drake [were still there]. They accepted me. I enjoyed being there because we talked about baseball. We talked about a lot of things. They put me in the master bedroom, where the owners normally sleep. They slept in the living room. Every night, she'd cook us a big meal. We had a family atmosphere, playing baseball. But then you would venture off and try to go to a movie. You had to go in a separate area of town to watch a movie. They had this restaurant where I'd go. I didn't spend too much time in downtown Ponca City. I knew there was segregation. At the ballpark, you didn't see too many blacks watching us play. You saw a lot of Indians because a lot of Osage Indians lived in Ponca City, Oklahoma.

The next year, in '57, I went back to Ponca City, and I didn't have all these players around me. I was the only black guy on the baseball team. It was kind of awkward that year. I had to make friends with people in the area. I'll never forget a kid named Bobby Walton; he's in Oklahoma City now. He was around my age. I made friends with him, and we did a lot of things in that city.

When I would go to other towns, other small towns, I stayed at different black motels, which a lot of times were beat up. We didn't have private homes. They took me across the tracks to stay in separate hotels from the team. It was an awkward thing. What I didn't like is if a game was over about twelve o'clock, you'd get on the bus. I was the last one off the bus. You would be the last guy to get to bed that night, and they expected you to do good. You'd probably have to ride ten or fifteen miles in one direction, and then you'd go on the south side. I would still be on the bus. I tried to sleep fast because I was one of the main guys of the ball club. You ask yourself, "Why in the hell am I doing this?" But you see greater things from that time. You forget about that little picture here and think about playing major-league baseball.

In a lot of small towns with the population down, you don't have many blacks there. They weren't aware of too many blacks. When they saw a black coming in these small cities, they're not accustomed to that. The whites are a little afraid. They don't know how to accept them. They don't know what to say to them. They just don't know anything about them. A lot of times, when you don't know anything about something, you're a little frightened of it. In the big towns, because a lot of blacks are there, the white people are more aware. They probably have some kind of interaction with blacks, maybe in conversation. The small towns are more separate than the big cities because more people are needed to keep the big city going.

But playing in those small towns wasn't fun. You weren't making any money. You were staying at these old, beat-up hotels. Maybe the food wasn't what you'd like. You'd see the black/white signs. Everything was right in front of you. All of the towns, all of the ballparks, were segregated. I don't remember any little city where I could go to the hotel with the other ballplayers, where I could go to the restaurants. Everything wasn't rosy when you got there. You had to make your way or go home. In Mesa City, Arizona, Mr. Wrigley [owner of the Chicago Cubs] had to find a place for [future Baseball Hall of Famer] Ernie Banks. There were no places you could rent.

The few black people in these small towns realized I was the only black on the team. They saw me as a young black going through this game of baseball. They reached out to me. They wanted to do things for me. I remember in Paris, Texas, this one black guy came to the ballpark and saw me after the game. He said, "Whenever you come in the city and you need transportation, you can have the keys to my car." This happened wherever I went. When I would go to the hotels in the black part of town, the people would open up to me.

Every black that played the game of baseball, they saw the racial tension, saw the racial prejudice. You said to yourself, "How much more of this did Jackie Robinson take?" You hear the names, "black," "nigger." You hear people chanting from the stands. This happened in your city and other cities. At that time, you had to say, "I've got to go a little farther. Jackie took a lot, so I've got to do a little more. I just can't give up now." You had to take it if you wanted to play baseball.

In the minor leagues, most of the time, the black player was a good player. In order for you to be in professional baseball, you had to be good. You had the knockdowns. There would be four or five guys in the lineup ahead of you that the pitchers wouldn't hit. They've got to wait until you come up to the plate. You couldn't do anything about it, because you didn't have too many black pitchers on the mound. You had to take it. The black ballplayer was a good ballplayer, so they wanted to intimidate him.

There was a teammate of mine on the Ponca City Cubs. We were playing cards one day. It was something to do. You're making $250 a month, so it's not a big stake you're betting. This one guy was from Mississippi, probably never been around blacks in his life. As we were playing cards, he said, "How many cards you want,

Smokey?" It came out of nowhere. I hit him in the mouth. I don't like to get mad, but this brought out the anger in me. I knew where the guy was from. I wanted to stop it right away. The guy who owned the ball club disbanded the card playing after that. The guy I hit got released.

One night, we were playing the Ardmore Cardinals in Ponca City. I'm the only black player on the field. We get to the bottom of the ninth inning, and we have a runner on first and second. I hit a ball, and we scored the winning run.

There was this one black gentleman who was running the elevator at the hotel where the Cardinals were staying. I guess those guys were mad and pissed off after the game. They just hated everybody and everything. They got into an argument on the elevator. There were two or three guys who beat this guy up. He was hurt pretty bad. They kicked him in the groin. Through all of this, he said, "I'll get you guys tomorrow."

The next night, this one guy came to the ballpark and stood at the side of Ardmore's dugout. He asked where were the guys from the elevator the night before. One of them looked up, and he knew the guy looked angry. He knew what he had done. The ballplayer took off and started running. This guy took out his .38 and started shooting at this player. You could see the dust flying from the bullets. The center fielder jumped over the fence. The second baseman was trying to hide behind second base. I'm standing in left field. The manager got up, and I think he shot him in the side. They called the game. I hadn't seen anything like this before.

Since I was the only black player on the team, the ushers and policemen came and took me in the clubhouse. The club thought they were going to do something to me. I'm still a kid while this stuff was happening around me. The chamber of commerce wrote a letter to the Ponca City ball club guaranteeing my safety. That's the only reason I stayed around. That was a big racial thing that could have shot off down there. That guy had never been in any trouble. This guy is a preacher now. He told me, "You know,

Billy, you were the cause of that because they were mad they had lost the game."

Billy Williams started a professional baseball career in Oklahoma that would eventually span five decades. Williams played for the Chicago Cubs and Oakland Athletics for seventeen years in the big leagues, from 1960 to 1976. In 1987, he was inducted into the Baseball Hall of Fame. Today, he is a coach for the team that signed him to his first contract nearly forty years ago.

10 | The Sports Ban Takes the Field: 1957

Recently Sen. Leon Butts of Lumpkin Georgia said "When Negroes and Whites meet on the athletic fields on a basis of complete equality, it is only natural that this sense of equality is translated into the daily living of these people." That in a nutshell is what the bigots fear most—equality . . . They are willing to use every crooked trick in the book to block the equality of the Negro. Frankly there is no greater leverage in democracy than achievement in sports. Butts . . . and the rest of the diehards will soon be caught in the tidal wave of freedom which is slowly sweeping over them.

—*Louisiana Weekly,* 30 MARCH 1957

With 1957's dawn, the full effect of Louisiana's sports ban was experienced immediately. Most of the five hundred segregated seats set aside for blacks were empty on New Year's Day since only seventy-five African Americans bothered to attend the all-white Tennessee versus Baylor Sugar Bowl clash in New Orleans.

Given opposition to the sports ban from outside the South and the law's interracial athletic strictures, few if any northern colleges consented to play their Louisiana counterparts, either in the Pelican State or above the Mason-Dixon Line. Local tournament sponsors and Louisiana schools, particularly Louisiana State and Tulane, fearful of running afoul of the popular mood, shied away from integrated games, scheduling matches with and competing mainly against southern institutions with similar racial poli-

202

cies. The *Shreveport Times'* sports editor Jack Fiser editorialized in his 28 July column that "the law places no restrictions on interracial competition anywhere but inside the state. But athletic directors at the various state-operated institutions have been so eager to stay in step with the public mandate that they now avoid interracial competition ANYWHERE. LSU has steered clear of the various NCAA tournaments and the Gulf States Conference schools in most cases declined to enter NCAA or NAIA events."

In the Texas League, team owners fashioned a compromise to enable Shreveport to remain in the racially integrated loop. A league team traveling to Louisiana would be required to leave its nonwhite players behind in the team's home city since the circuit was unwilling to challenge the new law. To address the problem of integrated Texas League teams having fewer men available upon arrival in Louisiana, they would be allowed to carry nineteen players on their rosters while teams without nonwhite players could field only eighteen.

Only weeks before the first pitch of the new baseball season was thrown, Louisiana was roiled by yet another controversy that illustrated the difficulties now facing athletic competition in this state. In April, Ralph Dupas, a top lightweight boxer, was scheduled to fight against a white contender in New Orleans. However, the match was temporarily postponed in late March after Lucretia Gravolet, seventy-four, a childhood neighbor of Dupas's, claimed he was part African American and thus ineligible to fight a white opponent.

Affidavits alleging that Dupas was actually Ralph Duplessis, a black man, were furnished to the authorities. In proceedings before the Louisiana State Athletic Commission, the agency empowered to regulate boxing matches in the state, Dupas produced a variety of evidence to rebut Gravolet, including his grandfather's birth and burial certificates and birth documents from four siblings attesting to their Caucasian origins. Dupas's hearing before the commission grew testy, as this exchange between the two combatants illustrates:

GRAVOLET: You are a Negro. I know you are a Negro. Now put me in jail if you don't like it.
DUPAS: I'm white and don't know why I have to prove it.

The State Athletic Commission declined to rule on the boxer's racial lineage and reaffirmed his right to proceed with the scheduled bout. After a state court refused to intervene, Dupas fought and bested his opponent in a ten-round decision on 8 April 1957. Ruben Amaro, a Mexican citizen, played for the Texas League's Houston Buffaloes in 1956 and returned to them the following year. In spring training, he was aware of the Dupas affair and was informed, as were all nonwhite players in the Texas League, of accommodations aimed at ensuring compliance with Louisiana law: "They told me, 'Well, you're going to have two or three days off so you can go to Galveston.' When Houston went into Shreveport, they were either at the tail end or the beginning of a road trip. That's when I got to know Galveston. Those were my three days off."

The Louisiana sports ban was the latest indignity African Americans and other nonwhite ballplayers endured in order to continue their baseball careers while playing for minor-league teams in the South. Although the ban was indeed invidious, it was no worse in effect than other discriminatory laws on the books throughout the former Confederacy. Nonwhite players, already quite accustomed to different treatment because of their skin color, were well acquainted with being separated from their teammates when away from the ballpark. Not joining them in Shreveport was just one more indignity. But Louisiana's new law did have the ultimate effect of further distancing nonwhite players from the teammates they were already isolated from. Willie Tasby recalls, "I didn't know anything about it. Of course, it wouldn't have made any difference to me if I had. As far as I was concerned, it was already like that from the actions of everybody."

As 1957 progressed, segregationists across Dixie tried to emulate Louisiana's methods. Montgomery, Alabama, banned interracial sports in early April, preempting two scheduled exhibition matches between the Kansas City Athletics and the Birmingham Barons on 9 and 10 April. Kansas City had several black players. The Barons, unable to play integrated baseball in their hometown, were thwarted in their attempt to seek an alternative venue by journeying ninety miles south.

Georgia again stepped up to the plate in the state's third attempt to legislate against integrated athletics. In addition to the law that was defeated in 1955, a similar bill had been proposed but died aborning during the 1956 legislative session. This time, the state legislature seemed on course to pass its version of Louisiana's ban. On 13 February, the Georgia Senate approved state senator Leon Butts's interracial sports ban, 31–0, and sent it to the House of Representatives. One week earlier, the Georgia Senate had telegraphed its mood by passing a bill invalidating the Fourteenth and Fifteenth Amendments to the United States Constitution.

Butts championed his proposal because he believed that allowing whites and blacks to play sports together was dangerous. It gave African Americans "a sense of equality" that could be carried into other aspects of life, including work, schools, and social settings.

Opponents to the Georgia bill mobilized quickly. Nationwide condemnation of the Senate's action flooded into Georgia. The *New York Times* editorialized strongly against Butts's bill, deriding Georgia for its regressive ways: "If some of the white citizens of Georgia prefer 1857 to 1957 there is nothing we Yankees can do about it. We do assume, however, that those citizens of Georgia whose ancestors were held in servitude in 1857 would probably not like to go back to that date . . . Senator Leon Butts of Lumpkin said, and we quote, 'Anything that tends to break down the bulwarks of segregation must be forbidden by this General Assembly.' . . . It may well be that the winning candidate in 1860 was not Abraham Lincoln." High-powered interests lobbied the governor and legislature for the bill's defeat. Atlanta Crackers president Earl Mann met with Governor Griffin, warning of adverse consequences should the sports ban become law. Mann's meeting came shortly after Butts's bill was approved by the House of Representatives' State of the Republic Committee by a vote of 18–0. Mann was encouraged to call on Griffin by major-league baseball commissioner Ford Frick, minor-league commissioner George Trautman, and anxious major-league team owners. Four clubs—Baltimore, St. Louis, Cincinnati, and Milwaukee—operated spring training camps in Georgia, and others were affiliated with Georgia's four teams in the integrated South Atlantic League. Fearing passage of the sports ban, Pittsburgh had preemptively abandoned its spring site in Brunswick. All big-league teams would be forced to pull out of the state, and the Sally would likely fold, as the Georgia State League had, if teams were barred from employing black athletes. Ever the segregationist, Griffin was noncommittal with Mann about signing the bill if it passed. But he unambiguously revealed his inclinations at a 20 February press conference: "You ask me if I think Negroes and white people ought to play together, and I say no. It may knock out some organized baseball, but the people of Georgia have got to decide if they want a dollar or a principle."

As the legislature neared adjournment, the sports ban was easily the most watched and controversial bill yet remaining for legislative action. Sentiment seemed to be behind passage on 21 February as the House defeated a motion to postpone action on the bill. As debate unfolded, supporters spoke about what they believed to be segregation's religious and historical roots. Representative W. T. Bodenhamer had a spiritual rationale for his support: "I think this bill will help me serve my Master." Meanwhile, opponents chided their colleagues for advocating a far-reaching ban on racial interaction. They peppered segregationists with questions about the legislation's impact. For example, would the bill forbid "whites and negroes from working together in other fields or would it prohibit Negro entertainers appearing before whites as has been the custom in the south since pre–Civil War days?" With hours remaining in the 1957 legislative session, sports ban supporters seemed to have the votes they needed for passage. But in a surprising turnaround, opponents successfully derailed the bill through a series of deft parliamentary maneuvers and amendments.

After wading through untenable amendments making it "unlawful for white and colored people to maintain residences or be employed within the limits of the same town" and forbidding "any person, firm or corporation to employ or hire both white and colored people in the same business," the House of Representatives surrendered to the spirited opposition and adjourned at 5 P.M. Senator Butts and his allies were left dumbfounded, with Butts fulminating to the *Atlanta Journal,* "I think it's a shame the major league ball clubs and the NAACP have gotten control of the Georgia House." However, to assuage concerns that the General Assembly of Georgia could not "do right" by segregationists, both legislative chambers passed legislation calling for the impeachment of six United States Supreme Court justices. This measure, supported by the governor, passed by votes of 112–12 in the House and 37–11 in the Senate.

Several legislators in Georgia, unlike their counterparts in Louisiana, not only understood the ramifications of passing a sports ban but also had the courage not to run from their convictions. Their efforts held out the prospect that other aspects of massive resistance could be defeated. The Eastern League, a six-team Class A circuit with franchises in New York and Pennsylvania, had a wry response to the segregationist fervor that was sweeping through Georgia and Louisiana. Hoping to capitalize on southern disquiet and attract major-league teams to the Northeast, league president Thomas Richardson sent an open letter to the *Sporting News* in which he repeated the advertisement sent to all big-league farm directors: "Associated Press carries story of Georgian bill which would prohibit mixed sports competition. Wish to remind you that if circumstances present major problems for you, Eastern League ready, willing and capable of handling any operation seeking a new home . . . No segregation problem in the Eastern. We take them regardless of color, race or creed."

Richardson's ad must have had a favorable impact on its target audience. In 1958, the Eastern League split into two divisions and added two teams, reaching its desired number of eight member franchises.

In Louisiana, the sports law's effects were keenly felt in Shreveport. By summer, attendance was down 30 percent from the 1956 figure. Inspired by New Orleans's boycott, many African Americans in Shreveport hoped to make their own economic impact in northwest Louisiana, launching a local protest against the Texas League franchise and the state's interracial sports ban. Midway through the season, a loosely organized boycott also sprung up in Houston.

On 24 July, amid a disappointing season on the field and at the cash register, Shreveport Sports owner Bonneau Peters announced he would sell his franchise after the season. Peters's decision could be attributed to several factors, many of which confronted team owners throughout the country, such as the overall decline in minor-league attendance and the increasing economic difficulty of operating a franchise without major-league affiliation. When Peters made his announcement, the Sports was the Texas League's only independently operated team.

Although Peters denied it, Louisiana's sports ban undoubtedly had an impact as well. Like the New Orleans Pelicans, the Sports did not have the pecuniary strength to survive declines in white attendance coupled with the effects of an African American economic boycott. Shreveport's attendance dropped from 155,000 fans in 1953 to fewer than 90,000 in 1956, and then fell to 40,919 in 1957—the worst of any AA or AAA team. Such a decrease was too much for an already fiscally troubled franchise to endure. At the same time, the sports ban dashed any hopes the team harbored of securing a major-league affiliation. Many major-league organizations were not interested in operating an affiliated team in a state where interracial baseball was a criminal offense. The Milwaukee Braves even backed away from an affiliation with a proposed Texas League franchise in Austin because the Braves were unwilling to leave their black players behind while everyone else played in Louisiana.

Nineteen fifty-seven proved to be the final Texas League season for the Sports. The team folded after the campaign ended, when no legitimate buyers stepped forward to purchase the franchise. Although Texas League club owners throughout the league publicly sympathized with Peters, they must have been secretly relieved by the Sports' demise, for one simple reason: Come 1958, Louisiana's sports ban would no longer concern the Texas League.

In the end, Shreveport, with few options and little to offer major-league suitors, proved to be yet another victim of Louisiana's insidious racial policies.

Lorenzo Davis was a veteran in every sense of the word. He was thirty-nine years old when he played for Fort Worth in 1957. The son of a coal miner, Davis followed his father into the pits until an opportune strike ended his career there. Davis fled the mines after three months to accept a partial athletic scholarship to attend Alabama State University, where, with his father's help, he began to pursue his love of baseball.

Nicknamed Piper, after his eponymous hometown in Alabama, Davis began his professional career in 1942 with the Negro American League's Birmingham Black Barons and was with the team for nine seasons, batting more than .300 in six of them. During World War II, he also played basketball for the Harlem Globetrotters. Davis was so highly regarded as a baseball player that in 1946 he was considered by Branch Rickey as a possible candidate to break the major-league color line, only to be rejected because he was thought too old at twenty-nine. As the Black Barons' manager, Piper Davis introduced a talented seventeen-year-old Birmingham outfielder named Willie Mays to the rigors and joys of professional baseball in Mays's rookie season, 1948.

In 1950, Davis signed a contract with the Boston Red Sox, becoming the first African American player in that organization. While with the Oakland Oaks, of the Pacific Coast League, in 1952, Davis and teammate Ray Noble were in the middle of a bench-clearing brawl in San Francisco. After being hit in the head by a pitch, Davis soon repaid the offending hurler, scoring a run and sliding hard into the pitcher at home plate. As Davis and the pitcher uncoupled, both benches emptied and a free-for-all ensued, with Davis, Noble, and several white teammates knocking down more than an equal number of San Francisco Seals.

Following this incident, Davis and Noble received a threatening letter signed by several San Francisco fans, promising retribution. Oakland's baseball faithful responded immediately with their own missive to Davis and Noble, promising plenty of support in the stands when the Oakland Oaks journeyed across the bay again.

By 1957, Davis was almost numb to segregation's degrading effects. By the time he reached Fort Worth, Piper Davis was as well prepared as anyone for what the Texas League could dish out. As a member of the Fort Worth Cats, he used his experience with segregation to help other African American players adjust to the dual demands of baseball life for blacks in the Jim Crow South—coping with segregation and excelling on the diamond.

When you're in spring training, every player has to go before the man who tells you where you're going to play the next year and whatnot. Come my day to go in 1957, he say, "Come on in, Pipe. What we want you to do is help out with our young ballplayers in Fort Worth." So I go to Fort Worth. Being from Alabama, it didn't worry me, going to the Texas League.

To me, I was a senior at that particular time, in age and everything. I had played against whites in baseball and basketball and all that kind of stuff. It didn't worry me. Back then in Fort Worth, I was at the age to really understand everything about segregation.

I was born in segregation. I got an education when I played with the Harlem Globetrotters. You stayed in black hotels—like, you'd go to New York and stay in the black neighborhoods, just like in all the big cities. Chicago was the same way. But that was the team's hometown. I'd stay there with in-laws.

All the towns in the Texas League were the same—Dallas, Fort Worth, San Anton'. You were a nigger anywhere you went. I was called all kinds of names when I played. I've been called "black boy," "rastus," "coon," "snowball," "alligator bait." You know "nigger" was in there too. I can't tell you how many times I heard, "Stick one in that nigger's ear!" That was number one. There may have been seven or eight thousand folks in the ballpark, but you'd always hear the one who raised his voice, saying, "Stick one in that nigger's ear!" I ignored it. It didn't bother me, because I grew up in it. I grew up being called names. You stayed on one branch of the river, and the whites stayed on the other.

When the team went to Shreveport, I stayed in Fort Worth. I would join them after. It didn't bother me at all. It didn't matter how I felt. I was in segregation all the time, even ten years after Jackie Robinson. It lasted a long time. On each team I played with, I told other players how it was. In the Texas League, I told 'em, "You're gonna be called names. Just ignore them. Just don't think about it. You know you're going to stay in black homes or black hotels and stuff like that. Don't think about it. What you think about is hitting that pitcher and hitting that ball. That's the only thing." I helped three or four black players. They just listened to me. They were eager to play, like I was.

Two of the times when people called me names, I hit home runs. One was in the Texas League. The first was with Scranton [Pennsylvania]. That town was segregated just a little. Every town in the United States was segregated a little.

One game, I don't remember the town, when I came to bat, there was a guy in the stands who said, "Well, I'll be goddamned. Boston done got a nigger." I stepped back and I said to myself, "Lord, let me hit this ball for this peckerwood, please." And I hit me a home run. He was sitting right back there in the grandstand, in the box seats on the third base side next to the dugout. I circled the bases. After I touched home plate, I went over to him and said, "Take that!" One of the other fans close by said, "That's the way to go, Piper!" That was one of the highlights of my career.

After seventeen years in professional ball, Piper Davis retired in 1958. He died in 1997, at the age of 79. He never played in the major leagues. Elijah "Pumpsie" Green, whose promotion to the big leagues by the Boston Red Sox in 1959 made them the last team to integrate, grew up in California. One of his biggest baseball heroes was the man he beat to the majors, Piper Davis of the Oakland Oaks.

Ruben Amaro was born in Monterrey, Mexico. His father, a Cuban native and a baseball player himself, was black. Amaro's mother, a Mexican of Spanish descent, was fair skinned. Amaro first tasted segregation when his family lived in Cuba. There, Amaro discovered restricted neighborhoods and facilities, where an event would be held for blacks one month and Hispanic whites the next.

In 1956, Amaro was the twenty-year-old starting second baseman for the Houston Buffaloes. Although he was acquainted with racism, this was the first time in his life that its effects had been directed at him personally. After an emotionally wrenching 1956 season, Amaro contemplated quitting baseball. Following his second Texas League campaign, Ruben Amaro was painfully aware how racial discrimination also encompassed Latinos, particularly those with dark skin.

I came to Houston and the Texas League from Class C, the Arizona-Mexico League, where we had four teams in Mexico and four teams in the United States. The only place where we had some problems—in getting to the restaurant, getting served—was in El Paso, Texas. We didn't have any problems in Tucson, where we stayed in the best hotels. We didn't have any problems in Yuma, Arizona. Most of Arizona was okay, but Texas was tough. I had a glimpse of what it would be like in the Texas League because of El Paso. I had a tough time in that league.

But traveling in the Texas League was outstanding because we did all the traveling by train, and this was the best part of the league. The train was the most unique situation. This was where I had my only chance to be with my ball club and talk to my players because other than that, we were segregated [except at the ballpark]. I really had a chance to talk to my teammates, to Fred McCallister, Howie Nunn, Wally Shannon. This was the only place that wasn't segregated. We had a sleeper for the ball club. Off the train, in the cities on the road, I never stayed with the ball club. In places like Tulsa, Oklahoma, black players used to stay at the YMCA.

At the train stations, there were also problems. We weren't allowed to stay together. They had water fountains and bathrooms for blacks and whites. In the train stations, I remember Howie Nunn, Fred McCalister, trying to hide me when the team went to a restaurant. We would just come in, around seven-thirty in the morning, and we have to eat breakfast. Everybody on the team is sitting at tables. Nunn and McCalister whispered to me, "Come over here. They won't know you're here." This didn't work in Dallas. After they said, "No service," everybody on the team said, "We're not going to eat," and they all got up.

That happened three times, one time in Dallas, once in Austin, Texas, and one time in Fort Worth. It was always the same thing—trying to get something to eat with the rest of the team. The biggest problem in being restricted was in what I could and couldn't do with the ball club. I didn't have a job by myself. I was a member of a large group of people. But I couldn't stay with them or eat with them.

Benny Valenzuela, a Mexican ballplayer who was on the ball club, had fair skin. He had no problems going anyplace. I told Benny, "Don't stay with me." He wanted to, but the places I stayed were in the black communities of each town. Some were private homes. I said, "The restaurants, the ones that are open to blacks, are not very good. If you have good facilities on the other side of town, there's no reason to come with me." He ended up staying with me in Oklahoma City, Tulsa, and San Antonio. Other than those places where I had somebody with me, things were pretty tough.

On the field in '56, I remember Tulsa had a catcher named Lloyd Jenney. The entire game, he was all over me. You always get racial catcalls from the people in the stands. Even though black players could play in the Texas League, I don't think any ball club had more than one or two at any one time. You always heard the racial remarks from the players and the public, even in our ballpark in Houston.

During my career, I usually couldn't hear specific words that people would say from the stands. I could hear people applauding if you made a good play or people booing if you made an error. But I did hear specific words from a lot of players. Lloyd Jenney was a guy who was really an agitator. He played hard, and he always wanted to fight. Because he wanted to fight, he was always making remarks that were racial.

One of the things that my teammates always told me was, "Don't initiate any of the fights. Let us do the fighting so you aren't the culprit." My teammate Howie Nunn said he didn't want anyone to even look at me hard. If they did, he used to come out and say, "How about me?!" I like to talk. I don't like to fight, but I like to defend myself. Sometimes guys came in a little too hard at second base. Sometimes they made a smart remark. That might start something. We had about five free-for-alls in '56 and about seven in '57. Those were the way things were back then.

When we played Tulsa, I remember what Jenney said like it was today. He would say, "I'm going to knock your black ass all over the field." I guess that was a pretty good weapon to agitate people, and he said it so freakin' many times. Then you also heard things from other players. It was like this or more every time that we played those guys. The magnitude of this whole thing hit me so hard the first year. I remember going to the Mexican consulate in Houston, and they used to say, "Look, remember you're Mexican. If you have any problems, just call us." I had a great year in '56 [a .266 average, 2 home runs, and 64 runs batted in]. I made the All-

Star team. We won the Dixie Series. I was voted one of the Most Valuable Players on my ball club, all coming out of Class C. I was one of the youngest players also. When I went back to Mexico [after the season], I told my dad I'm going back to school and staying with my [nonbaseball] career. There's no way I'm going back to the Texas League. The general manager of the Houston Buffaloes talked to me three or four times after the season and kept sending me different contracts. I told him I'm not going back, I had a tough time, with no support from practically anybody.

The guy who convinced me to come back was my father, Santos. He said, "You know, for almost two years you fought me about letting you sign to play professional baseball. At that time, you told me that your goal was the big leagues. I didn't know that the Texas League was going to be your last stop in baseball." That got me. He told me that there was another stop in the organization called Rochester. "I don't believe it is as restrictive as Texas. Maybe you ought to be a better player and go to AAA." That really pushed me. I went back to Houston in '57.

In '57, [Houston outfielder] Alberto Baro and I tried to get into the movies one time in Fort Worth, Texas. The ticket taker asked me if I was Spanish. I said I'm Mexican. I bought the two tickets, we went in, and twenty minutes later, somebody came around looking for us. Baro had a lighter complexion than I did, but he had kinky hair. I could speak a little English. He could not. A big policeman came over and said, "You can't stay here, because of your friend." I said, "Why? I'm darker than he is." He said, "You're Mexican. There are some restrictions for people other than Mexicans."

In '57, I think Houston was really one of the first big cities to integrate without making a great big fuss. I recall very clearly in '56, the team had a Player of the Week award. They used to give the winner a gift certificate from a clothing store. If I went downtown and was hungry, there was just no place to eat. In '57, we had just won the Dixie Series, and I was the hero because I won the series with a home run. I was the Player of the Week. During the season,

I won several Player of the Week awards. I kept my certificates until the end of the year. I must have had about seven hundred dollars' worth. I went downtown.

Jaywalking was punished by fines then. In a hurry, I crossed in the middle of the block. A policeman, who was watching the World Series on TV, saw me, [came out of the store where he was watching the game], and yelled, "Come here!" He said he was going to write me a ticket and started to ask, "Who are you? Where do you live?" I'm a black man, standing there with big bags from the store, and with a policeman asking me questions. I told him who I was. He said, "Ruben Amaro! Good! For punishment, you're going to sit here and watch the last two innings of the ball game with me."

After the game he said, "Now, we can have a hot dog." I wondered where we could eat. "I've been here since '56, with money in my pockets, [and] there are places I can't eat," I said to him. We went to a Woolworth's store, and the cafeteria was open for everybody. I looked around, and the policeman told me they had been doing this without much publicity. Things were getting better, at least in Houston.

We won the Dixie Series both years, '56 and '57, and we played Atlanta. They didn't allow any integration there. I flew with the ball club to Atlanta, and that was it. I couldn't even come in the bus with the team. I had to take a "colored only" taxi to the Green Acres Motel, which was fortunately only thirteen or fourteen blocks from the ballpark. The rest of the ball club stayed somewhere else.

Howie Nunn was from the South [North Carolina]. Howie and myself were pretty good buddies. One time he said to me, "I like you." But with other black players, he was really derogative. I remember another teammate, Nelson Burbank, telling him, "The problem with you is you didn't give yourself a chance of knowing the other guys. How come you like Ruben? Ruben is no lighter than anybody else." It was true. But I was the only player Howie got to know. Many of the other players and other people took your race and put you in one category, without giving you a chance.

There's no question that when you have a chance to play with a big group of guys, contending, competing on the field, it's going to change your mode of thinking a little bit. The best example of that is Howie Nunn in his argument with Nelson. Before playing with me, he hadn't had a chance to be around black people. Now, he had a chance to converse and see what Ruben is like. Now, you're defining the character as somebody rather than saying, "I'm not going to get close to this guy, because he happens to be blue or green."

Amaro reached the big leagues for the first time in 1958, appearing in forty games with the St. Louis Cardinals. After a single season's absence, he returned to the majors in 1960 with the Philadelphia Phillies, where he stayed for ten seasons. Today, Ruben Amaro is a minor-league manager for the Chicago Cubs.

In 1957, the pace of desegregation quickened in some southern school districts as federal courts consistently ruled against segregation and efforts to impede Supreme Court mandates. Confronted with more and more changes, Jim Crow's defenders heightened the violence of their response. Police investigations in Montgomery linked January bombings to the Ku Klux Klan. The attacks were carried out by local Klan members in response to the integration of Montgomery's buses. The home of civil rights leader the Reverend Ralph Abernathy was bombed in the middle of the night as he and his family slept. Bombings and arson in African American neighborhoods also damaged homes in Chattanooga, the Birmingham suburb of Bessemer, and other southern communities.

In September 1957, Dixie was rocked by a series of violent episodes. On 9 September, an explosion destroyed Nashville's newly integrated Hattie Cotton Elementary School. No one was hurt, but this was the city's first brush with racially motivated violence. Police held five men in connection with the bombing. After detaining them and searching their car, which was decorated with the initials KKK, the police discovered a weighted club with the Klan's initials carved into its handle and wire used in setting off explosives. Elsewhere in the city, police escorted African American children through picket lines of angry segregationists so they could safely reach their new elementary school. Immediately after they entered the building, several white parents berated the police and then withdrew their own children from the school. At Birmingham's all-white Phillips High School, students were evacuated after a bomb threat. One day earlier, the Reverend Fred Shuttlesworth had been beaten by extreme integration opponents while he tried to enroll four African American girls at the school. After being told that city police would not allow the four students to enroll on 9 September, a bruised and battered Shuttlesworth did not return to Phillips that day.

While violent resistance to integration was being perpetrated in several locales, no instance of massive resistance focused the world's attention more in 1957 than events that were transpiring in Little Rock, Arkansas. In one of the most significant events in civil rights history, Arkansas governor Orval Faubus called out the National Guard to block the implementation of school desegregation orders issued by the federal courts. The bigotry and regressive intransigence exhibited by Faubus and his white supporters during the standoff indelibly branded Little Rock as one of the South's most racially intolerant communities.

On 2 September, Faubus declared a state of emergency and called out the Arkansas National Guard to "preserve peace and order." Faubus was relying on the armed might at his disposal to defy the federal judge in Little Rock who ordered that there be no interference in desegregating Little Rock's Central High School. The next day, some three hundred troops took up positions outside the school, blocking its entrances to implement their governor's commands. Intimidated by this show of force, the local school board requested that the African American students who were being barred from assuming their legal places in school remain home and not attempt to enter the school building. Faubus referred to the Little Rock situation as a "southwide test" of federal authority over state laws. "We have state laws opposing integration in school districts where it is violently opposed by the people in that district," Faubus told the *Arkansas Democrat*. "If the time comes when the people of Little Rock will accept integration, then that is the time to let the Negroes into the white schools." Asked if he thought Little Rock would ever accept school integration, he answered, "Not this year."

On 4 September, nine African Americans were turned back from Central High by national guardsmen. As fifteen-year-old Elizabeth Echford approached one entrance, she had to walk through a crowd of jeering white bystanders who spat obscenities at her: "Go home nigger, you will never get into this school. We don't want you here." After surviving this gauntlet, she was turned away at the schoolhouse door by armed guardsmen. When one officer was asked by a civil rights leader if he was carrying out the governor's orders, he matter-of-factly replied, "That's right."

The atmosphere around the school remained tense as the troops' ongoing presence signaled Faubus's continued defiance of federal law. After he ordered the National Guard away from Central High on 20 September, the federal government in Washington finally intervened. On 24 September, President Eisenhower took the historic step of putting the Arkansas National Guard under federal command and at the same time prepared to send the United States Army to Little Rock. Events unfolded quickly after Eisenhower decisively stepped into the conflict following nearly three weeks of relative caution and inaction. The next day, twelve hundred paratroopers from the army's 101st Airborne Division flew into Arkansas's capital from Fort Campbell, Kentucky. In a scene vaguely reminiscent of the Union occupation of southern communities during the Civil War, nine African American students, escorted by twenty-two federal troops, entered Central High School at 9:22 A.M. while an army helicopter circled protectively overhead. A group of protesting white students stood nearby and chanted, "'Two, four, six, eight, we ain't gonna integrate.'" They represented the only demonstration against their school's integration. The building itself was surrounded by upwards of three hundred soldiers. No incidents inside the school were reported as the twenty-two federal troops escorted the students from class to class throughout the day.

Troops kept nonstudents behind barricades and away from the school. Those who refused to obey orders to disperse were given no quarter. One recalcitrant man was bayoneted in the arm, and at least two other resisters were struck in the face with rifle butts. The professionalism of the paratroopers contrasted with the laissez-faire attitudes of the state guardsmen, who were unwilling to disperse demonstrators before Eisenhower federalized them. Little Rock police officers, outmanned and outgunned by Faubus's militia, were ill equipped to carry out the federal court's orders before the 101st Airborne arrived.

As events in Birmingham, Nashville, Montgomery, and Little Rock made clear in 1957, ardent segregationists were not about to surrender quietly. Their campaign of massive resistance and terror would continue even as court rulings and the deployment of federal military power made their efforts increasingly resemble the "lost cause" of the last century.

20 MARCH

One of the first segregation disputes reported on Shreveport's trolley system occurred yesterday when two Negroes refused to heed a driver's request to move to the rear of the bus. Approximately 30 other Negro passengers, many of them school children, booed and yelled insulting remarks to [bus driver] J.B. Rich . . . When the driver requested the two Negroes to "please move to the back of the bus," the Negroes refused to do so, declaring, "We paid our fare and can sit wherever we please."—*Shreveport Times*

18 APRIL

DURHAM—A delegation of Negroes refused segregated seating for a Carolina League game . . . and announced they will fight for equal seating rights in the municipally owned ballpark . . . According to [N. B.] White, a leader in Negro civic affairs here, "more than 150 Negro citizens" attempted to buy tickets to the opening game of the season [Durham's first with black players] between the Durham Bulls and Greensboro Patriots . . . They were told, White said, that they would have to enter the park through a segregated entrance and sit in a segregated section of the stands.—*Raleigh News and Observer*

1 JUNE

Annually, Colored customers [at New Orleans's Pelican Park] totaled between 40,000 and 50,000 depending on the success of the club. Last year's total paid attendance was 3,400 . . . Feeling that unity among Negroes was an impossibility, Negro fans were completely ignored from the outset . . . The Pelican brass felt almost certain that . . . Negro Fans would support [the] Pelicans. It was sort of take-for-granted, like: "Well, they use to come out under [Jim Crow] conditions . . ." The Pelicans forgot that times have changed and so had the trend.—*Louisiana Weekly*

With team fortunes rapidly dwindling, New Orleans mayor Chep Morrison desperately tried to save the Pelicans and keep them in the city. Civic leaders and team executives launched a campaign to raise money for a new stadium. The Pelicans explored several money saving suggestions, such as finishing the season on the road at the expense of the Southern Association. Although the Pelicans had lost $130,000 since African Americans began their local baseball boycott in 1955, team ownership and *Times-Picayune* sports editor Bill Keefe could not fully conceive of the impossible: that black fans, through their collective action, had brought the Pelicans to the brink of financial collapse. New Orleans Pelicans General manager Vince Rizzo, however, did acknowledge reality when he grudgingly conceded, "Give me the 40,000 Negro fans we lost last year and we're out of trouble."

Minor-league attendance was down across the country in 1957. However, this cannot be used exclusively to explain New Orleans's economic bind. To do so ignores the local boycott's impact. Suffering from a drop in white patronage, the Pelicans, like virtually any other southern team, could scarcely withstand the nearly total loss of revenue from black fans as well. Rather than face this discomfiting racial truth, Keefe hewed to an accepted, comfortable line, using his column in the *Times-Picayune* to blame the attendance decrease on such easy-to-understand excuses as "television, air-conditioning . . . lack of close acquaintance with most of the players, inadequate parking facilities . . . too many pleasures like Pontchartrain Beach and boating on the lake." By August, average attendance at Pelicans games fell to under 1,000. The last-place Pelicans finished the season with the second-worst overall (67,287) and average (874) attendance of any AAA or AA franchise.

Nineteen fifty-seven was one of the most confrontational years in the post-*Brown* era. Events across the region revealed how much more needed to be done in the struggle for equal rights.

13 SEPTEMBER

EASTON, Md.—A Negro father of two children attending a formerly all white elementary school found a homemade bomb of 10 sticks of dynamite on his front lawn . . . Protests to integration of elementary schools in Talbot County have been made by a white citizens' association . . . Talbot County opened its first three grades to integration last year and expanded it to the fourth grade this year.—*Birmingham News*

19 OCTOBER

Gladness turned to sadness . . . when little Barbara Ann Remo, 12-year-old golden voice soprano, originally scheduled to sing with the New Orleans Symphony Orchestra in New Orleans was regretfully informed that she would not be permitted to perform in January at Booker T. Washington High School on a statewide network because of the law . . . that bans interracial activities. Thus Barbara, seventh grade pupil at McKinley Junior-Senior High School, became another person that has been denied an opportunity to display God given talent.—*Louisiana Weekly*

5 NOVEMBER

FARMVILLE, Va.—The center of the resistance to school integration in Virginia and perhaps in the entire South seems to lie here in Prince Edward County. Its school system was one of the five directly concerned in the Supreme Court's integration decision of 1954, and Virginians are preparing to do battle on the county level . . . Prince Edward County is prepared to switch from a public school system to private schools the moment the courts set a deadline for integration.—*Birmingham News*

7 NOVEMBER

BIRMINGHAM, Ala.—A young Ku Klux Klansman was convicted and sentenced to 20 years in prison today for the Klan castration of a Negro handyman last Labor Day night . . . The Circuit Court jury was closeted only 45 minutes in deliberating over testimony in the trial of Bart A. Floyd . . . Floyd was identified as the Klansman who cut Judge Edward Aaron in the Klan lair at Clarksville while four other Klansmen looked on.—*Birmingham News*

18 DECEMBER

The Colorado State College Board of Athletic Control . . . canceled three basketball games in Louisiana . . . Dr. Arthur Reynolds, president of the Athletic Board, said earlier . . . the team would leave Negro guard Ollie Bell behind when the team left for Louisiana . . . Thomas Girault of Denver, President of the CSC board of Trustees, said: "If we agreed to go ahead and play the games, it would also mean a forfeiture of principle. I would favor a ban on all games where discrimination is in effect."—*Birmingham World*

Segregationists were unyielding in their resistance, often writing rapid, passionate letters to their local paper:

What the people now fear . . . is forced integration. The ultimate outcome of course would be miscegenation. The fathers and mothers of this country place the welfare of their offspring ahead of everything else. They try to bring their children up as their equals or if possible to give them a little more elevation than themselves. What encouragement have the parents to advance their offspring when they are forced into mongrelization, a race of people God didn't make or He would have made the race Himself?—in the *Shreveport Times*

The Bible is strongly opposed to integration. To anyone who loves Negroes, I advised him to get on the north side of the Mason-Dixon Line and dwell there forever. If state rights mean anything, . . . if peace, quietude and harmony among our two races mean anything, then Governor Faubus ought to be backed by the people of our State, and those who are here interfering, those who again are trying to reconstruct us after abysmal failure some 80 years ago, ought to get out of our state and permit us to continue the advancement of our colored friends as we have throughout their freedom.—in the *Arkansas Gazette*

As 1957 drew to a close, the *Birmingham World*'s Marion Jackson examined what Louisiana state senator William Rainach, Georgia state senator Leon Butts, and other segregationists had wrought in their fervent drive to cleanse the South's athletic fields of racial integration. In his 18 December column, Jackson's conclusions did not leave much room for optimism as the new year approached.

Acrimonious and outspoken segregationists who have been making inflammatory and irresponsible statements to advance their political fortunes might well analyze the staggering blows that athletic competition has taken in the South. State laws and city ordinances forbidding mixed sports events have resulted in several minor leagues folding, turned once major bowl games into sectional spectacles, limited intercollegiate scheduling and made subpar competitors of athletes confined behind the cotton curtain. New Year's Day will see only the Rose, Orange and Prairie View bowls with mixed squads. Lilywhite bowls are the Sugar, Cotton and Tangerine. Except for Rice-Navy in the Cotton Bowl, Ohio State-Oregon in the Rose Bowl, and Oklahoma-Duke in the Orange Bowl, the post-season tussles are sectional showcases. Not a single Big 10, Eastern or West Coast team (most with integrated personnel) will appear in Dixie bowls.

In Louisiana, the Evangeline League is dead, and the franchise of the Shreveport Sports is up for sale. Barnstorming baseball [teams] during their spring safaris have had to bypass such jim-crow bastions as Louisiana and Mississippi and diehard segregation cities [such] as Birmingham and Montgomery, Ala. . . . The evil scars of segregation are showing throughout the structure of sports in the Deep South. They have virtually doomed minor league and small town baseball, black-balled top flight basketball competition and decreed only synthetic track meets. The void imposed upon dark skinned American competitors by the hate peddlers have imposed sanctions upon whites which resulted in severe curbs on their freedoms.

. . . Barriers which limit the Negro's right to unfettered play merely pinpoint Booker T. Washington's emphatic declaration that you can't keep a man in a ditch without staying down there with him.

11 | Closing Out the 1950s: 1958–59

This Court must hold with the plaintiff that, as to athletic contests, Act 579 of 1956 is unconstitutional on its face in that separation of Negroes and whites based solely on their being Negroes and whites is a violation of the Equal Protection Clause of the Fourteenth Amendment of the Constitution of the United States.

—JUDGE JOHN MINOR WISDOM, *Dorsey v. State Athletic Commission,* 28 NOVEMBER 1958

They may upset, ban and prohibit any form of segregation in Louisiana, but no action can change our firm convictions.

—LOUISIANA STATE REPRESENTATIVE LAWRENCE GIBBS, QUOTED IN THE *New Orleans Times-Picayune,* 29 NOVEMBER 1958

The end of southern minor-league baseball's most turbulent decade left Dixie far different from the place it had been ten years earlier. By 1959, most cities, towns, and leagues had integrated their teams, with the notable exception of the Southern Association. In that same year, twelve seasons after Jackie Robinson's Brooklyn debut, the Boston Red Sox, the major leagues' last holdout against integration, finally put an African American ballplayer on the field.

The effects of white and black men's playing America's national pastime together in southern ballparks was difficult to gauge at the time. But the region and its people had been transformed nonetheless. Baseball integration forced southerners, whether consciously or not, to reexamine racial attitudes. With increasing numbers of black ballplayers coming south and competing with whites, the tired stereotype of African American inferiority began to fall away. For the first time in southern history, blacks and whites were working together as genuine equals, except, of course, in Birmingham and the Southern Association.

With the 1958 baseball campaign headed into the postseason play-offs, these two retrograde baseball outposts again drew unflattering attention to themselves. The Birmingham Barons, Southern Association champions, were set to face either Austin or Corpus Christi, of the Texas League, in the Dixie Series. However, both of these Texas teams featured black players, who were barred from playing in Birmingham by that city's sports ordinance. The stage was set for the next conflict in this corner of minor-league baseball. Responding to a telegram from minor-league commissioner George Trautman, Birmingham mayor James Morgan said that the sports ordinance could not be suspended pending completion of the Dixie Series.

The Corpus Christi Giants earned a place in the Dixie Series as Texas League champions by overcoming a three-run eighth-inning deficit in the deciding game to defeat Austin, 5–4. The comeback was highlighted by Bo Bossard's three-run homer. Ironically, Bossard, one of the African Americans at the center of the Georgia State League's racial controversy in 1954, was one of Corpus Christi's three black players.

However, Corpus Christi owner E. J. Humphries quickly deserted Bossard and the other black ballplayers who had helped get him to the Dixie Series. He proposed substituting whites for the team's three African Americans, but Trautman refused him permission to do so. As he told the *Sporting News,* "No provision of any professional baseball rule bars a man from appearing in a game because of his race, color, or creed. There is, therefore, no reason under baseball rules why the Negro players could not participate in the games at Birmingham. Because of this, I will not approve any agreements for substitution solely to enable the playing of a white player for a Negro."

Nonetheless, Humphries was determined to preserve the Dixie

Series—and the lucrative ticket sales that came with it—at all costs, even at the price of betraying his own players. Two of the Giants' African Americans athletes remained in Texas while Corpus Christi visited Birmingham. A third player, placed on the disabled list, was ineligible for the entire series. Unable to overturn Trautman's edict, Corpus Christi was left with only sixteen available players for the games in Birmingham while the Barons had their regular complement of nineteen.

The Barons won four of six games to capture the southern championship. However, diversions such as college football and the major leagues' World Series helped keep attendance in Birmingham down. An unprecedented day-night doubleheader to close out the series attracted fewer than twenty-three hundred fans to the Barons' Rickwood Field, a paltry turnout that served as a measure of retribution for the injustices thrust upon the Giants' African American players by the owners of both teams and by Birmingham's political establishment.

Judicial victories in 1958 and 1959 further presaged the future of southern race relations. De jure segregation lurched toward extinction as various southern communities took steps to comply with court orders while federal courts across the South invalidated scores of segregationist measures passed in reaction to *Brown*. By the end of January 1958, thirty-nine southern cities, including Daytona Beach, Hot Springs, Miami, Tampa, Nashville, Norfolk, Richmond, and Greensboro, North Carolina, had desegregated their bus systems. Only three cities—New Orleans, Montgomery, and Columbia, South Carolina—had desegregated their buses in direct response to federal court orders; the rest had acted without similar judicial directives.

Judges also dealt three setbacks to Jim Crow's defenders in Louisiana. On 14 February 1958, the United States Court of Appeals for the Fifth Circuit affirmed a lower court's command that public schools in New Orleans integrate; rejected Louisiana State University's attempt to prevent African Americans from attending state universities in the Pelican State; and affirmed a trial court's ruling that New Orleans could not keep blacks out of its public parks.

But perhaps the biggest blow to segregationists came on 28 November, when a federal three-judge panel declared Louisiana's sports ban to be unconstitutional. The ruling came in a case brought by Joe Dorsey, a boxer who had been barred from participating in mixed fights because of his race. The court unanimously rejected the state's attempts to justify the sports ban, noting the law was a "clear challenge" to the Supreme Court's *Brown* decision and its progeny. The court's disdain for the sports ban and the ease with which it swept the law aside sent a clear signal that similar measures, passed by southern legislatures since 1954 with much bravado, would likely meet the same fate when examined by federal judges from Texas to Washington, D.C.

The *Dorsey* decision ended legislative efforts in Louisiana to block integrated athletics. State officials subsequently appealed the district court's ruling to the United States Supreme Court, which declined to intervene in May 1959. After 28 November, state senator Rainach and other bitter segregationists could do nothing but bemoan unwelcome intrusions into the southern way of life while waxing nostalgic about a time that would never come again. As the *New Orleans Times-Picayune* reported on 29 November, "Segregated athletics have been preserved for many years by custom rather than by law in Louisiana. The interracial athletic bill was designed to give legal status to this custom. The custom still remains with or without the law. The law has worked effectively because the people generally approved the provisions incorporated in the bill. Regardless of what a federal court might or might not do now or later, the operation of the act since 1956 has shown the people of the state [expect] to keep their athletic contests segregated."

On 29 September 1959, Montgomery's two-year-old ordinance forbidding integrated public recreational facilities was summarily declared unconstitutional by United States District Judge Frank Johnson after a forty-minute hearing. The judge ruled that if the parks, which had been shut down to prevent African Americans from using them, reopened, they must be available for all to use. Despite the court's unequivocal decision, the city commissioners and their elected successors all vowed to keep municipal parks and facilities closed indefinitely in order to avoid the specter of racial mixing.

Although legal realities held out little promise of success for Jim Crow's defenders, many stubbornly maintained their fight against racial integration nonetheless. The 1950s ended with new legislative targets and efforts. In several southern states, attention turned to beaches and public parks, the next battlefields in the segregation conflict. As was Dixie's pattern, many communities resisted integration despite federal court orders mandating integrated recreational facilities. In St. Petersburg, City Manager Russ Windom closed the all-white municipal beach on 5 June after eight African Americans swam there. At the time, fourteen African Americans seeking to play golf at the city-owned golf course in Charleston, South Carolina, were turned away. Predictably, as had happened dozens of times over the preceding four years, such municipal disobedience resulted in federal lawsuits seeking to force compliance with previous Supreme Court edicts. The result, judicial orders ratifying the high court's decisions and mandating integration, had become similarly commonplace in Dixie.

Violence continued to be the weapon of choice for white extremists. In Poplarville, Mississippi, FBI agents investigated the 25 April lynching of M. C. Parker, an African American arrested and charged with raping a white woman. Early on a Saturday morning, he was dragged from his cell by several masked men, who beat and bloodied him with sticks, a broom handle, and a garbage can. Many southern communities also continued their schizophrenic pattern of resisting, complying, and then resisting again, few more obdurately than Little Rock. Arkansas's capital was the scene of renewed conflict over school desegregation. Police in riot gear roamed the city's streets after the school board building and mayor's office were dynamited.

Political defiance, massive resistance, and violence continued to plague the South, but progress toward integration was clearly being made, in and out of federal courtrooms. More school systems desegregated their classrooms. Front Royal and Charlottesville, Virginia, public schools admitted their first African American students. Just one year before, white parents in Front Royal had boycotted Warren County High School. In 1959, this school admitted twenty-one African Americans without conflict. Four blacks entered Miami's Orchard Villa school, making it the scene of Florida's first integrated classrooms.

28 SEPTEMBER 1958

LITTLE ROCK, Ark.—Final returns from all 31 precincts . . . in Saturday's special integration election showed: For integration of public schools, 7,565; against integration of public schools, 19,470. Gov. Orval E. Faubus said such a verdict would enable him to turn the all white high schools into private institutions and reopen them with no Negro students . . . He assured [voters] that his plan to operate the schools on a private and segregated basis is wholly legal—that they do not have to comply with U.S. Supreme Court rulings.—*Louisiana Weekly*

20 DECEMBER

Only seventy-five segregated seats were allocated for Negro football fans for the [twenty-sixth] annual Sugar Bowl classic, January 1 between the National football champions, Louisiana State, and Clemson . . . [Claude] Simons, [president of the Mid-Winter Sports Association, sponsor of the Sugar Bowl], stated that in the past, hundreds of seats were allocated for Negro patrons, but during the past two Sugar Bowl games, the demand for tickets have [*sic*] never exceeded 50, therefore the section was reduced to 75 seats for the 1959 Sugar Bowl game. Consensus of opinion is that Negro attendance dropped to rock bottom because of the Louisiana mixed sports ban.—*Louisiana Weekly*

28 MARCH 1959

RICHMOND, Va.—Two Negro high school bands have withdrawn from a parade welcoming home Richmond's professional baseball team in a parent-inspired protest against bleacher seats for Negro fans. Roy Puckett, administrative assistant to the city school superintendent, confirmed today that the bands of Maggie Walker and Armstrong High Schools had dropped out of the parade April 8 because of objections of the Negro students' parents . . . They object . . . to the seating of Negro fans in outfield bleacher seats. —*New York Times*

4 APRIL

Out in Houston, Texas, Negro baseball fans are protesting the conditions at Busch Stadium, the home of the Houston Buffalo baseball team. The reason for the protest is that Busch Stadium has one entrance at the front for whites and another at the back of the stadium for Negro patrons. According to the Buffalos' [*sic*] general manager, H. B. Richardson, the policy concerning White and Negro patrons at Busch stadium this season will be the same as in the past . . . Because of this, Houston baseball fans are "hot under the collar."—*Louisiana Weekly*

23 APRIL

Many Southerners feel that Dixie states must band together in common cause, and that we must try harder to sell our viewpoint to the rest of the nation. Our "sales pitch" must be based not on racial issues but on the fact that local government can best handle local problems. It becomes increasingly clear that the federal courts have made up their minds to change Southern customs and force unwelcome changes.—*Jackson Clarion-Ledger*

Gov. John Patterson of Alabama . . . denounced the Civil Rights Commission for recommending the use of federal registrars in areas where Negroes are deprived of the right to vote . . . Of the six commission members, only former Gov. John S. Battle of Virginia dissented . . . Two other Southerners, former Gov. Doyle E. Carlton of Florida and Vice Chairman Robert G. Storey, joined in the recommendations.—*Montgomery Advertiser*

A Montgomery restaurant owner who employs three Negro men as waiters received a letter from the local Ku Klux Klan . . . advising him to remove either the Negro employees or the Confederate flag from its place . . . [The letter said] "the Confederate flag is the symbol of white Christian integrity and certainly has no place in your cafe under the conditions in which you prefer to utilize new Negro waiters."—*Montgomery Advertiser*

When the 1959 baseball season began, Billy Williams was entering his fourth year of professional ball. After finishing 1958 on a high note, batting .304 for Burlington, Iowa, of the racially placid Three I League, the twenty-one-year-old Alabaman found himself headed south again, this time to San Antonio. In the Texas League, Williams encountered the same barriers he had lived with three years earlier in Ponca City, Oklahoma. Beaten down by Jim Crow life and tired of being expected to excel at baseball despite such difficult conditions, Williams rebelled. Like many African American players of his generation, Billy Williams walked away from the game. He suddenly found his dream of reaching the big leagues in serious jeopardy.

> I strayed away from the goal of playing in the major leagues. I just got tired of the racial stuff, of being the last one to get home, of going to private homes. I decided I didn't need this anymore. I'm the biggest guy on the ball club. I'm hitting home runs. I'm driving in runs, and yet, I'm treated like I'm nobody. I think this is what every black ballplayer saw when he played. I took off and went to Alabama.
>
> I left the ball club and went to Mobile. I talked to my brother. He was having a lot of fun, and I'm not having any, riding up and down the highway on this damn bus. I stayed home a week. Because I was leading the club in hitting, they sent Buck O'Neil down to get me. I came back, but I just wanted to get away, maybe for a while, maybe forever. I wasn't thinking at the time about the major leagues. I just wanted to get out of this game of baseball. I don't need this. I could go home and have a good time. But you've got to have that focus, that someday, the way I'm going, I might play in the major leagues. That and Buck O'Neil brought me back. He oversaw a lot of blacks in the Cubs organization.

Near the end of the 1958 season, Willie Tasby was promoted to the majors for the first time in his career. He appeared in eighteen games for the Baltimore Orioles, batting .200. The next year, a stellar spring training earned the twenty-six-year-old outfielder a place on the opening-day roster. He headed north with the Orioles from Florida to Baltimore.

Tasby's joy at getting a chance to spend an entire season in the majors was tempered by what he found when he reached Baltimore. Much to his dismay, the Orioles rookie encountered segregation almost as pernicious as what he had experienced in minor-league outposts such as Hagerstown and Shreveport. Finally at the pinnacle of his career, Willie Tasby found himself in a city below the Mason-Dixon Line in 1959.

In those years, you would barnstorm your way up from Florida to your hometown, six or seven days before the season starts, because you have to go to all these banquets. The Kiwanis club was giving us a dinner in a Baltimore hotel. I was a rookie. I had a sensational spring training. I didn't go to the banquet, because I'm still bitter from the minor leagues.

The next day, we were opening the season. I was sitting in front of my locker, and Luman Harris, the third base coach, said, "The manager wants to see you." I went in there, with I guess a devastating frown on my face, and Paul Richards said, "Come in, son. Sit down."

He said, "Everybody asked me where the man who wants to be our center fielder was last night." I said, "I tell you what, skipper. I was thinking that if I hadn't been Willie Tasby of the Orioles and wanted to bring my wife to this hotel to eat, they probably would have thrown me out of there. I let my imagination run away with me, and I didn't come." He said, "Okay. That's good enough for me. Let's go out and kick their ass." That's all he said.

Manny Mota was nineteen when he journeyed from the Dominican Republic to Florida to begin his professional baseball career in 1957. The San Francisco Giants assigned their rookie outfielder to Michigan City, Indiana, of the Midwest League, where he was paired with Matty Alou, a fellow Dominican and younger brother of Felipe, who had made the same journey one year earlier. Since Mota found himself in a part of the country that was mostly integrated, his transition to life in the United States was markedly easier than it would have been had he played in the South.

However, his rookie year was not free of racial incidents. On one road trip, Michigan City played a series in Lafayette, Indiana. With time before a game one afternoon, Mota and Alou ventured into a restaurant around lunchtime. They sat down at a table and waited for someone to take their orders. Time passed, and no one approached them. Finally, another customer went up to the confused and hungry ballplayers, who spoke little English, and explained in Spanish that their wait was fruitless. "You guys are wasting your time," she told them. "They are not going to serve you here. You guys had better go." Heeding her advice, Mota and Alou found someplace else to eat. Unaccustomed to such treatment in the Dominican Republic, Mota and Alou learned much about discrimination that summer in the Midwest League, experiencing several similar incidents before the 1957 campaign ended. Mota's first baseball season in America prepared him for 1958, when he spent the year in the Carolina League, with the Danville Giants, seven years after Percy Miller had broken the color line in this southside Virginia city.

Like so many other nonwhite ballplayers in the 1950s, Manny Mota was picking up where Miller and his fellow line breakers left off. By simply playing baseball with whites, by enduring and overcoming racism, he was proving a point in 1958. Just as an earlier generation of ballplayers had paved the way for him, so too would Manny Mota take up the challenge and help ease the way for the next class of blacks to play the game down south.

> My goal was to play baseball; I wasn't going to let anything stop me from playing in the major leagues. I knew I had to go through a lot of sacrifice. I had to get used to the situation in this country in 1957.
>
> But '58 was worse. I went to the South to play in Danville, Virginia. At least in '57 you could ride the bus as a human, everybody together, no matter the color of your skin. You couldn't do that in Danville. What really hurt my feelings was seeing black people sitting in different places than white people. To me, I didn't think that was fair. It wasn't right. But I couldn't change the system. I was there to do a job—to play baseball. By the same token, I had some feelings. I felt the same way those people felt, but they had been discriminated against longer than I had. I felt bad.
>
> I was surprised. We don't have that color problem in the Dominican Republic. That was different. I felt bad about how they treated colored people here. It's a different culture in this country, people talking about people by the color of their skin. I heard stories about how things were, but you have to see it to really believe that's what happens.

The front office and the manager treated us very well. Our manager was Bobby Hofman. He talked to us in spring training about what to look for, what to expect. He told us, "Don't let those things bother you."

The first time I rode the bus, I tried to sit in front. The bus driver told me, "You can't sit in front." I had to get used to things like this, knowing where to sit and where not to sit. Black people were treated differently everyplace. But if you played well and did your job, you ignored those kinds of things. You can hear [racial epithets] because you never heard that before, and you keep that in the back of your mind. You can't block [them] out, because you have feelings. I felt sorry for those people. I called those people ignorant. When they said things about your family, that was personal. You feel like going over and throwing the guy against the wall. But you have to control yourself. If you pay attention to them and let them know that bothers you, it's going to be worse.

You can't forget what they say, but you have to do your job. I concentrated. When I was at the plate, I just thought about hitting the ball. When I was in the field, I just thought about catching the ball. But I suffered and suffered a lot with the other people who were being discriminated against.

In some places, fans threw garbage, they threw coins, they threw bananas. That's not fair. You have enough problems hitting a guy throwing ninety miles an hour. Now you have to deal with this fan calling you names, calling your family names, too. They were idiots, ignorants.

What are you going to do? At the time, I felt the humiliation, the embarrassment of that particular moment. That was bad! But life goes on. You can't let those things stop you from making it to the major leagues. Those things stay with you for the rest of your life. I tried to look at those things in a positive way. They motivated me even more to try harder, try to prove what minorities as a group can do.

I got a lot of respect for Jackie Robinson and the early black players. They made it possible for us to play. We made it possible for the people coming behind us.

After Danville, Mota spent four more seasons in the minors, including one year, 1960, and part of another, 1962, in the Texas League with Harlingen, Texas, and El Paso. After playing forty-two games for San Francisco in 1962, he was promoted again in 1963 to the majors, where he remained for the next twenty years. When his playing career ended in 1982, Mota had established himself as the most prolific pinch hitter in big-league history, with 150 career hits. He also amassed a .304 lifetime batting average. Today, Manny Mota is a coach for the Los Angeles Dodgers.

12 | Walls Collapse: The 1960s

So you say go back to Africa? Well, I've got news for you. I didn't come from Africa. My ancestors did and they came because they were forced. This America belongs to me, too. My brothers, brothers-in-law and cousins have fought for this land and here we will stay and here we will have equality and peace.

—LETTER TO THE EDITOR OF THE *Richmond Times-Dispatch,* 13 SEPTEMBER 1963

Although great strides had been made in integrating the southern minor leagues by 1960, there was still work to be done. The Southern Association stubbornly continued to resist reform, holding out as the nation's only Jim Crow professional baseball league. Not coincidentally, many of the association's members, most notably Birmingham, Memphis, and Little Rock, were also on the front lines in the larger battle to eradicate segregation throughout society. These implacable cities, which had resisted the presence of African American minor-league ballplayers since 1947, remained intractably opposed to any integration in their communities.

The 1960s witnessed the great tragedies and triumphs of the civil rights movement: The march from Selma to Montgomery, Alabama; the 15 September 1963 bombing of Birmingham's Sixteenth Street Baptist Church, which killed four African American girls; and the passage of the Civil Rights Acts of 1964 and the 1965 Voting Rights Act all represented milestones in the fight for equal rights during this decade. By New Year's Day 1970, Jim Crow, just barely breathing, was on the losing side of the white South's effort to preserve its tradition of racial inequality.

The 1960 baseball season presaged the role southern minor-league baseball would continue to play in eliminating segregation throughout the decade. After five years of protests and boycotts by African Americans, the fiscally troubled New Orleans Pelicans folded on 15 March 1960. *Louisiana Weekly* sports editor Jim Hall, who championed the crusade against the team's Jim Crow policy, was gleeful about African Americans' crucial role in the Pelicans' demise. On 2 April, he wrote:

> There was jovial feeling among the tan fans, for this corner listed the apparent total lack of fan interest as one of the prime causes of the Birds' death . . . The solid support of the fans not to attend any of the home games, began to hurt the club at the gate. In the past, it had been the Negro patrons' attendance which had kept the Birds in a healthy financial state.
>
> But without their support at the turnstile, along with other financial problems, [and] no major league working agreement, the Birds began staggering on the ropes . . . The Negro fans did not mourn the loss of the team, for there was no sympathy for the team which had slapped them in the face with segregation.

Once the United States Supreme Court declined to overturn the 1958 *Dorsey* court decision, declaring Louisiana's interracial sports ban unconstitutional, there were no longer any legal barriers to staging major-league baseball exhibitions in the state. Reversing its ban against integrated games from New Orleans, that city's Recreation and Parks Board approved two games between the Boston Red Sox and the Cleveland Indians for 9 and 10 April. Reaction to this decision was immediate. African American leaders called for fans to attend if facilities at City Park Stadium were integrated. The Southern Louisiana White Citizens Council, objecting to the prospect of five black major leaguers playing with whites in its own backyard, called for a boycott of the game.

Unlike the winning protest that contributed to the end of organized baseball in New Orleans, this one was a dismal failure. More than twenty-one thousand fans attended the exhibition games. With the integration of City Park Stadium, African Americans came to watch baseball in numbers unseen at New Orleans games since the Pelicans boycott began in 1955. Nearly sixty-four hundred black patrons sat in the grandstand alongside white fans and participated in something remarkable for this city—an integrated sporting event. With no racial incidents reported at the ballpark during the two-game set, the White Citizens Council's boycott call was resoundingly rejected. Change was in the air. Such protests were exposed for what they were—pleas to maintain a bygone age that was slipping irretrievably away.

The Southern Association's loss of New Orleans was more significant for its symbolic impact than for any actual damage caused by the departure of the league's economically weakest member. At a time when the association's financial health was steadily declining, the Pelicans' departure resembled flight from a sinking ship. Memphis, a league member since 1902, was forced to abandon the association in 1960, after its ballpark burned down. That city remained without minor-league baseball until 1968. The Atlanta Crackers, one of the association's cornerstone franchises, announced that they would drop out of the league after 1961. Looking to position the city as the South's leading sports market—with an eye toward attracting a major-league sports franchise—Atlanta's leaders understood the necessity of distancing themselves from the Southern Association's Jim Crow policies. By bolting from the Southern Association, Georgia's largest metropolis was signaling its readiness to assume a place among America's leading cities.

The Crackers, who unsuccessfully attempted to break the loop's color line in 1954, were eager to be free of the racial straitjacket imposed by the Southern Association. Atlanta sought and was granted entry into the integrated Class AAA International League for the 1962 campaign, a season distinguished by the presence of several black Crackers. The city's forward thinking was rewarded in 1964 when ground was broken for the construction of a baseball stadium, future home of the Atlanta Braves, who in 1966 became the first major-league sports team based in the Old South.

While the Crackers separated themselves from the Southern Association, developments in the league's most racially polarized city suggested the end of sports segregation there as well. On 18 August 1961, a federal judge in Birmingham ruled that the city's interracial sports ordinance was "unconstitutional on its face." Judge H. H. Grooms permanently enjoined city officials from discriminating against African Americans at municipal recreation facilities. In a subsequent ruling, Judge Grooms imposed a 15 January 1962 deadline for the city to end segregation of its parks.

With Birmingham's sports ordinance now apparently dead, the Southern Association could conceivably welcome African American ballplayers and try to reverse a steady decline in attendance. But Birmingham's segregationists would not surrender quietly. Public Safety Commissioner Bull Connor, Mayor Arthur Hanes, and others railed against the ruling. The city appealed Judge Grooms's orders while insisting that the ordinance would still be enforced. It was as if Jim Crow's defenders, seeing their cherished tradition of legally mandated race separation disappearing, decided to make one final effort to stave off the result many suspected was inevitable.

Mayor Hanes, claiming a popular mandate to keep Birmingham segregated, announced the closing of all city recreational facilities on 16 January 1962. If the parks were closed, he and the city commission reasoned, they could not be integrated, regardless of court rulings precluding similar closings in other southern communities. Hanes declared that integrated parks would be the first step toward desegregating the entire city and "submitting to the will of the minority." His defiance was heartily endorsed by Commissioners Connor and J. T. Waggoner. Invoking language similar to words used by Confederates one hundred years earlier, Hanes claimed the mantle of states' rights in defying federal authority and invoked the dread specter of Communism, using both as battle cries in Birmingham's latest effort to resist desegregation.

The *Birmingham News* printed an open letter from Mayor Hanes in which he said,

> We'll have more trouble and create a worse image if those parks are open . . . The real issue isn't integration. The main thing is the overriding principle of people's rights to determine something for themselves. It is the idea of the Communists to destroy every tra-

dition and symbol that this country has ever stood for. I feel that men should progress by their own ability and gain by their own effort and not by the passage of laws. If [Negroes] merit acceptance, it will be given naturally, just as night follows day. I will never negotiate with Communist Negroes, Negro radical groups . . . They have nothing to negotiate with. Their attitude seems to be "What's ours is ours and what's yours we'll negotiate for." I don't subscribe to that theory and therefore will not negotiate with them. The Negroes in Birmingham have been treated with kindness, generosity and warmth.

Birmingham's latest attempt to turn back the clock proved fruitless, for the city's appeals were ultimately denied. The day that this city would no longer be a bastion of de jure segregation loomed closer than ever before.

The Southern Association, however, did not take advantage of the opportunity to end its color barrier, and it continued to suffer at the gate. Total league attendance in 1961 dropped to 526,120, a 15 percent reduction, with six of eight franchises suffering losses at the turnstiles. On top of the league's attendance woes, there were rumblings from the big leagues that if the loop did not abolish its color line in 1962, the Southern Association would no longer be sent players to fill team rosters. By 1961, most big-league organizations were no longer willing to conspire with segregationists committed to keeping the circuit segregated. With financial tensions and pressure from the majors for reform, something had to give.

Desperate because of mounting financial losses, teams tentatively began to explore the possibility of adding black players. In September, the Nashville Vols' board of directors, facing a deficit in excess of $57,000, approved the use of black athletes in 1962.

But by November it was clear that the Southern Association would not be the same in forthcoming seasons. On 28 November, the Birmingham Barons, a charter member of the Southern Association since 1901, went out of business. Before announcing his decision, Barons owner Albert Belcher spoke with Mayor Hanes about the status of the sports ordinance in light of Grooms's decisions. After being told the law remained in effect, Belcher informed his fellow league owners that Birmingham's continued presence in the association was impossible. Without the ability to add black players and attract larger numbers of African American fans to increase team revenues, Belcher believed that continued operation of the Barons was financially untenable. Belcher found himself with no option but to fold his club. He knew that other team owners intended to use black players in 1962, whether or not Birmingham's ordinance was removed from the statute books. With city government declaring its intention to ignore Judge Grooms's orders, Belcher fled the teetering Southern Association. Within days of the Barons' announcement, Shreveport and Mobile followed the Birmingham franchise out of the Southern Association, leaving the league with only four teams.

League officials frantically tried to save the Southern, futilely proposing a merger with the South Atlantic League. But the Southern Association was doomed. On 24 January, the league suspended operations, ending sixty-one years in minor-league baseball. While the circuit faced problems common throughout the minor leagues, the Southern Association essentially committed suicide, with its segregation policy as the instrument of its destruction.

Marion Jackson, sports editor of the *Atlanta Daily World,* wrote a baseball obituary for the association. In his 25 April column, Jackson opined on the causes of the league's collapse. He noted that some of the South's most racially recalcitrant cities also happened to be members of the segregated Southern Association. Such a situation was far from coincidental.

> Only the cities of the South that conditioned themselves for a change in folkways have baseball . . . Gone with the wind is the old Southern Association which could not embrace democracy and died in the changing social tides that are so much today in ferment . . . It is strange to note that baseball died first in those cities that conducted the most extensive experiments in riots, defiance and intolerance against the U.S. Supreme Court and the powers of the Federal government. The names of the cities where baseball has fled have been emblazoned on the front pages of the nation's newspapers as political hold-the-liners fought school integration, interstate travel rights, and human rights in general. This passing

parade includes Little Rock, New Orleans, Birmingham, Chattanooga, Memphis, Nashville, and Mobile. The "Little Rocks" are known throughout the civilized world . . . The helmet-wearing soldiers arriving in Little Rock . . . immediately conjure up in one's mind the passions that have not only gripped a nation but entrapped and destroyed baseball . . . When the May 17, 1954 U.S. Supreme Court decision on public schools came many enlightened students of government saw a new era projected in which the old mores, myths, and stereotypes of race would have to be discarded. Thinking public officials recognized that no matter how much [whites disagreed] with the High Court, its decree was the law of the land. It is perhaps the most unfortunate part of the dilemma that faced organized baseball in the South . . . The finger that had so long plugged the dikes of deceit, denial and discrimination was now as tired and weary as all other props of subterfuge. As Martin Luther King Jr., puts it, "segregation is dead and we're just waiting for the funeral arrangements." . . . Baseball will survive only as long as it is the true American game with all the embodiments of the Constitution and the Bill of Rights, meaning the equality of man without regards to race, creed or color.

In contrast to the regrets and recriminations accompanying the Southern Association's demise, the 1962 season would be a memorable one for baseball fans in Atlanta. As the Crackers embarked on their initial International League campaign, the team roster featured two African Americans, Johnny Lewis and John Glenn. But unlike Nat Peeples a baseball generation earlier, these men were in Atlanta to stay. Their presence enlivened Atlanta's African American community, sparking fresh enthusiasm for the newly integrated Crackers, according to the 26 April 1962 *Atlanta Daily World*:

Seeing Glenn and Lewis riding down Peachtree [Street] with their team, was an exhilarating experience. As I saw them, there was a flashback to [the] visit of the Brooklyn Dodgers in 1947, when a record crowd flooded Ponce de Leon Park. Other major league clubs—the old New York Giants, Cleveland Indians, Cincinnati

Red Legs, Chicago White Sox, etc. followed the Dodgers here. A fine racial climate always greeted these teams despite fears and cynicism spread by the gloom spreaders . . . Atlanta ball fans scorned the Southern Association turnstiles, wanting no part of restrictive competition. Yet when the real thing came along . . . Atlantans showed that the cosmopolitan atmosphere which had greeted desegregation in downtown lunch counters and public schools—could be extended with the same cordiality to baseball. This attitude was quite a shock to the standpatters, status quo set and the we ain't ready crowd.

Jim Crow was also showing signs of weakness in Arkansas. On 17 April 1963, Arkansas governor Orval Faubus and seven hundred African Americans attended the first desegregated baseball game in Little Rock as the Travelers defeated the Rochester Red Wings in Little Rock's International League debut. Integration of the grandstand coincided with the arrival of the Travelers' left fielder, Richie Allen, the first African American in team history.

Although integration of the Arkansas Travelers was a significant event in this state, the appearance of a solitary African American player did not sweep away the city's racial ugliness. Allen spent a difficult year in Little Rock, where he was the target of epithets from the same people who had undoubtedly supported Faubus's vitriolic resistance to the integration of the capital's Central High School six years earlier.

Willie Tasby, who played with the International League's Jacksonville team in 1963, recalled his conversations with Allen during that season in Little Rock:

> When I went to Cleveland in '63, I got hit in the eye. My bat slipped out of my hand, hit the net, bounced back, and hit me in the eye. They sent me to Jacksonville for rehabilitation. In that particular year, Richie Allen was at Little Rock, by himself. He hit thirty-something home runs there, but those people would call him all kinds of names, and he was playing for their team. That was the worst thing I ever saw.
>
> Richie hung out with us and came over to where we stayed.

We sat around all night playing cards just so he wouldn't be lonesome. He was there by himself. In that town, black people didn't support the team. He was all alone, no fans, nobody. They treated him like a dog down there. They'd call him the *n* word and yell, "What are ya gonna do this time?" He'd knock the hell out of the ball.

He wouldn't say a word but he talked to us. I said, "Richie, hang in there. You can't stay here. They can't keep you here." He said, "I hope not." When he came to the big leagues, he became an eccentric. He did what he wanted to do because he was a hell of a ballplayer. Anybody who knew him knew why he was different, because of what he took to get there. When he established himself, he did exactly what he wanted. He would tell us, "The sons of bitches owe me. They owe me more than they ever are going to pay me." I knew what he meant.

During his year in Little Rock, Allen took his anger out on the ball, batting .289 and leading the International League with 33 home runs and 97 runs batted in. In 1964, Allen was promoted to the Philadelphia Phillies and took the big leagues by storm, batting .318 en route to his selection as National League Rookie of the Year.

On 11 September 1963, the Virginia Supreme Court invalidated segregated seating in the state's publicly owned ballparks. Although the United States Supreme Court had previously ordered the integration of public recreational facilities, a similar decision by Virginia's highest tribunal had a singular local significance. The Virginia high court's ruling, arguably taken more seriously among Virginia segregationists than a high court edict from Washington, D.C., effectively ended any further attempts to resist federal mandates concerning integrated parks. In a unanimous opinion, the Virginia court ratified applicable United States Supreme Court decisions holding that racial restrictions in parks and playgrounds were unconstitutional.

As other places began to accept change grudgingly, Birmingham continued to lead the nation in mindless defiance. The city lapsed into an unprecedented period of racial violence and hate, culminating in the 15 September 1963 bombing of the Sixteenth Street Baptist Church. A bomb was thrown at the church from a passing car, killing four children—Cynthia Wesley, Carole Robertson, Addie Mae Collins, and Denise McNair—and injuring fifteen other African Americans. The attack was the forty-first bombing in Birmingham since 1947.

Enraged, Birmingham's African Americans took to the streets, venting their anger and sadness about a tragedy that represented the last straw for the vast majority of local blacks. Within an hour of the bombing, several whites were hospitalized after being struck by bricks hurled by African Americans. Demonstrations and protests blanketed much of the downtown area. As Birmingham lapsed deeper into a paroxysm of violence, rocks and other objects were thrown at passing cars and at people of both races, gunshots retorted across the city, and dozens of injuries were reported. Blazes set during the night kept firefighters busy. A bomb was thrown atop a black family's home, and a church meeting featuring Martin Luther King Jr. had to be canceled following a telephoned bomb threat. The conflagration reached its peak when two black teenagers were shot and killed by members of the city's all-white police force. Tensions and emotions continued to run high as national guardsmen and state troopers took up position to try to impose an uneasy peace on city streets.

This tragedy marked the most agonizing chapter in Birmingham's history. The grief, rage, and frustration unleashed as a result of the murders of four African American girls proved to be a turning point for this city, as reflected by this 16 September report in the *Birmingham News:* "And Birmingham prayed. Prayed for forgiveness on this the city's blackest day. Blacker even than the days of the cholera plague shortly after Birmingham's birth, when hundreds fell. For this day of wrath and warning followed a day of murder, murder most black, most reprehensible, most sickening. Four innocent children lay dead, mangled by 10 sticks of dynamite . . . Men, women and children paused a minute to pray."

Exhausted after years of racial division, Birmingham began charting a course toward moderation, with the 1964 baseball season providing a highly visible symbol of change for citizens eager to move away from confrontation. By 1964, the integration of southern baseball was complete. That year marked the return of a reconstituted Southern League to the minor-league firmament. Freed from its predecessor's racial restrictions, this circuit featured a host of black ballplayers. Birmingham was back in minor-league baseball, but the old rules had changed. Four men—Birmingham-area native Stanley Jones, Santiago Rosario, Luis Rodriguez, and Bert Campaneris—became the first nonwhites to play integrated minor-league baseball in the Magic City.

To mark the occasion, Jim Crow restrictions were eliminated at Rickwood Field. For the first time, Birmingham's black community felt part of America's national pastime. The presence of integrated baseball in this city, prostrate after years of strife, also represented one of Birmingham's first, awkward attempts to move beyond its racist past and chart a new course for its citizens, free from the discrimination and violence begotten by Jim Crow. Baseball integration here symbolized that times had indeed changed.

29 APRIL 1964

Organized baseball fled this coal, steel and industrial center two years ago under the pressure of crescending [*sic*] racial conflict. The demise of the Great American Game trumpeted the death knell of the Southern Association which died because of its refusal to accept Negro competitors . . . What a difference two years make. Since baseball fled here, Birmingham has been heralded in infamy through out the world as a symbol of police brutality, murder, bombings, arson, hate mobs, discrimination and prejudice . . . Rickwood seating is integrated. No incidents . . . Friendly exchange is frequent between Negro and white fans who sit side by side. Integrated fans sit beside each other or behind each other in the grandstands. Mixed lines can be seen leading to concession stands for food and refreshments . . . Acceptance of the Negro players by the front office . . . has been indoctrinated into the fans, press, radio and TV, as well as the general public.—*Birmingham World*

From the moment Percy Miller stepped onto the diamond in Danville, Virginia, thirteen years earlier, the South had witnessed moments of tragedy and triumph both on and off the baseball field. From a tradition of segregated teams, the South had moved, voluntarily or not, to a time when baseball in Dixie was completely integrated. By 1964, many hotels and restaurants that had previously been closed to African Americans were now open to all, thanks to court decisions and the legally coercive power of the federal government. Segregated seating in ballparks also began disappearing into the mists of history.

Now that the war to integrate southern minor-league baseball had been won, attention could shift to the more difficult task of having African Americans accepted for who they were without regard to skin color. Although they had won the right to play baseball throughout Dixie, blacks still faced strains of racism that laws and court rulings could not cure. These men discovered a painful truth in the early '60s: that some people are incapable of reform.

HANK PETERS

In 1961, I was farm director for the Kansas City A's. Charlie Finley had bought the ball club. We would train our minor-league players all along the Florida Gulf Coast. We had some in Fort Walton Beach and some in Panama City. Charlie said, "Where do the players stay?" I said, "We have them in boardinghouses." We had to have separate places for the black players. "That's not right," he said. Charlie was a southerner, too. He was from Birmingham, Alabama. I said, "I'm sorry, Charlie, but you're not going to find anyplace in those towns down there to accept the black players and let them live in the same building as the white players."

The next year, we were successful in moving our spring training over to Daytona Beach, Florida, where we had our own barracks building and cafeteria so that the black and white players could live together. You almost had to create your own facility if you were going to truly integrate your players. It didn't make a lot of sense for them to play together out on the field, share clubhouse facilities with each other, but when they left that clubhouse, one turned to the right, the other turned to the left. These facilities weren't built to speed up the integration of blacks and whites. That was one of the big benefits, of course, but there were also a lot of benefits in having all your teams train together in one location, where you had greater control and better facilities for everyone, black or white. There were a lot of clubs by that time who had started to build these central spring training camps.

MANNY MOTA

The Carolina League was tough, but the Texas League was even tougher. How would you feel if you're going into a restaurant, you're talking to your manager, and he says, "Okay, I spoke to the owner of the restaurant, and everybody is going to eat as a team." The light-skinned guys go in first. Then, when it comes to be your time to go in, how will you feel, seeing the owner meet you with a shotgun at the entrance to the restaurant? That was in the Texas League in 1962.

ED NAPOLEON

In Asheville in '63, the black ballplayers had to stay in a residential area other than at the hotel where we were. We'd get on the bus to go to the ballpark at the hotel. We'd go down to the neighborhood where the black players were staying. They were waiting for us, and they'd get on the team bus. We'd reverse it coming back. In '64, everybody stayed together in the hotels. From then on, it was like it is now.

Ed Napoleon has witnessed much change in the South over the past forty years. From his rookie season with Dothan, Alabama, of the segregated Georgia-Florida League, in 1956, he moved on to a largely integrated Asheville, North Carolina, as well as other towns throughout North Carolina and Virginia, where he played from 1964 to 1970. Now in his fifth decade in professional baseball, Napoleon is currently a coach with the Texas Rangers.

Don Buford grew up far away from segregation, in California, but his minor-league experiences were similar to Ed Napoleon's. At the University of Southern California, he played on the school's 1958 NCAA championship baseball team and was an All-Pacific Conference football player.

After signing a contract with the Chicago White Sox, Buford was assigned to Lincoln, Nebraska, of the Three I League, in 1960. He was the team's only African American. In this Midwestern community, he absorbed his first lesson in segregation. Shocked to learn he was barred from something as simple as going to a movie theater because of his race, the young outfielder spoke with the team's general manager, imploring him to speak with the theater owner so Buford could relax and watch a movie in his free time.

Management eventually allowed Buford to patronize the theater—as long as he sat in the last two rows of seats. Later, his career took a southward turn, and he found himself playing in the South Atlantic League in Charleston, South Carolina (1961), and in Savannah (1962). Buford discovered that although progress had been made in hotels and restaurants, the attitudes and sensibilities of many whites lagged far behind.

When I first moved to the Sally League, the situation there was very difficult. We had no place to stay. We had Deacon Jones, who's the advance scout with the Orioles now, myself, and another gentleman from the South who was used to it. For Deacon, who's from Ithaca, New York, and myself, from the West Coast, it was a new territory, a new experience totally. When we got there, there was no lodging for us. Mr. Ackerman, who owned the club at that time, rented a house and furnished it for us. We had an old jalopy car that we shared to take us back and forth to the stadium.

At one of the hotels in Savannah in my second year in the Sally League, where the All-Star Game was, they said blacks could not even attend the All-Star functions at the hotel, because the hotel was segregated. We said if we and our wives can't attend the functions, we're not going to play in the All-Star Game. It was that simple. They eventually let us into the All-Star luncheon.

We were aware of the civil rights movement. We'd go into towns and read about it, hear about it. We'd hear about people getting kicked out of places, people being kicked off the bus. One time, we stopped between Savannah and Macon, Georgia, at a bus depot which was a Greyhound bus station. We could buy food and go right out, but we weren't supposed to sit at the tables. I happened to be on the bus at the time Deacon went in. He bought something with the team. The other guys sat down, and he was talking to them, sitting at the table. The guy from behind the counter pulled out a double-barreled shotgun and pointed it at him. He said, "You get this nigger out of here or I'll blow his brains away." One of our other teammates ran out to grab me and said, "Somebody's pointing a shotgun at Deacon," so I ran in. I grabbed Deacon and said, "Let's go!" I pulled him out of the place. I never went back in there. We never even stopped there again.

We'd go from Knoxville, Tennessee, to Jacksonville, Florida. Instead of stopping in a large city, where we might be able to get something to eat, the bus would stop at a restaurant in a small town somewhere, and you can't go inside. For you to get something to eat, someone would have to bring out something, or they wanted you to sit in the kitchen. Hell, there's no way I was going to sit in the kitchen. I'd eat anywhere else, I don't care how demeaning it is. You're out there trying to play baseball, and you can't even get a decent meal in order to have nourishment to go out and play. That was a disadvantage as well.

In Macon, they used to have megaphones at third base, behind home plate, and at first base. Any black coming to the plate, and they'd start chanting. The guy behind home plate would say, "Hit the nigger in the head." When you get on base, they'd say, "Watch out. That nigger's gonna steal." That was their tone, their approach to how they wanted to see a game. If they were intimidating, I'm sure they felt that. If you made a great play, they'd say, "Say 'Hey, Willie Mays,' nigger." But for us playing, the emotional part of it was you'd have tears in your eyes from those kinds of things being said. Many times, we'd have great games just from being totally determined to hit the ball hard, get base hits, play hard to win, to not only beat that team, but beat that whole city. That's a rousing concept, to go out and kick some butt in that situation. You didn't want to be a loser in that situation. On the field, there was no such thing as segregation when you're playing a sport. You're out there in battle with the opposition. You're out there to win. You're playing as a team and as a unit. I think there was a contribution, what we were doing, to breaking up some of the segregated areas. Some of the hotels that we went into had never let minorities in. I think they opened the door because we were a baseball team. We were saying, "Hey, if we [the black players] can't stay there, nobody stays there." I think that happened on a few occasions. I think the hotels realized that was a lot of money. Three days of our staying there, that's pretty good money. You're talking twenty-five, thirty rooms. This happened, I think, all throughout the Sally League, in just about every city we played. In some cities, of course, like in Macon, we stayed out in a black-owned motel. Charlotte opened up eventually. We used to stay in a tourist house. By the time we were finishing there, the hotels opened up.

You always felt you had to do better to get the same opportunity. In some areas, you had a lot of minorities coming out to the game mainly because they heard about you being a pretty good ballplayer. They came out, and if you played well, they were pulling for you. They'd cheer and yell for you. It was great. They were segregated, sitting out in the outfield bleachers. The outhouse was out there for them. They couldn't use the other facilities. Those were the kinds of things you had to face in '61, '62.

Don Buford reached the majors with the Chicago White Sox in 1963, beginning a ten-year playing career that included his best seasons, with the Baltimore Orioles. As an Oriole, he played in three World Series (1969–71), winning in 1970. Buford compiled a .264 lifetime batting average, and he led the American League with 99 runs scored in 1971, the year he was named to the All-Star team. After retiring as a player, Buford served as a major-league coach with the Orioles and the San Francisco Giants. Today, as Baltimore's assistant minor league director, Don Buford is one of the few African Americans holding front office positions in baseball.

In 1962, Billy Williams visited Houston with the Chicago Cubs to play the expansion Colt .45's. Just as Don Buford did in the Sally League, Williams found segregation, both at the ballpark and at the hotel. However, times had changed since Williams's tenure in Ponca City, Oklahoma, five years earlier. Now major leaguers, Williams and other African Americans had the stature and clout to push back hard when confronted anew by Jim Crow.

> When I went down to Houston as a AAA player [in 1960], our dugout was on the first base side. My wife came to Houston in June. Lou Johnson's wife was down there, too. They made a little segregated area for them behind the dugout, behind a screen, while the other wives sat behind home plate. They protected our wives with a chicken wire fence.
>
> In '62, when Houston became a major-league city, we went to this motel by the ballpark. As we checked in, the traveling secretary said, "You guys can stay here, but you can't eat in the dining room of the hotel." I told him, "Why don't you take us and put us in a black hotel, where we would be free to roam around and do things that everyone else can do?" I think I put a little pressure on him. He went back to the manager and said we could eat in the dining room. So we ate in the dining room. This started something, so that blacks could go down to the restaurant and eat. [Because of] the team concept, seeing blacks and whites together, knowing they could get along, you had to wonder, "Why can't everybody else do the same thing and accept people for who they are and not look at their skin color?"

Clarence "Cito" Gaston spent five years playing in the minor leagues, from 1964 to 1968. During that time, he made stops in several southern locales, from large cities such as Richmond and Shreveport to smaller communities including Greenville, South Carolina. Like Don Buford, Manny Mota, and other black athletes, he experienced enough discrimination and racism in the South of the '60s to last a lifetime.

> I started 1964 in Binghamton, New York, and I had a cracked bone in my shin. They probably sent me down to [Greenville] South Carolina for the warmth of the weather. Our manager was named Bill Steinecke, who was a real nice man. He took good care of us. We used to go to Lexington, North Carolina. There would

be a big fat guy who would sit behind the dugout. He would always ask Steinecke, "Where'd you get those three monkeys?" They called us bad words all the time. But we hung in there, and that's all you could do.

Greenville, South Carolina, was pretty tough on us. There was myself and another kid named Samuel and Jose Cruz. One was from Puerto Rico, one from the Dominican Republic, and myself. We were called a lot of names in a lot of different places. They called us "monkeys" and everything else in Greenville and other places. There were times we weren't able to get off the bus to get anything to eat. But it was the verbal abuse we had to take that was the worst. The one thing that got me through it was that my mom always told me, "It's better to walk away sometimes than to go out and do something about it, because you're outnumbered anyway."

The Western Carolina League was the worst. I think they were still heavily segregated at the time. Ballpark seating was segregated. You certainly didn't see any mixed marriages or anything like that. I played left field, and I had an awful year. There was a hill in left field, and this guy would stand there, a big farmer with coveralls on, with a little kid who came right up below his waist. He used to scream at me all the time. He'd call me names. He'd start off with the *n* word and he'd say, "Gaston, you can't hit, you can't run, you can't throw," and he'd use the *n* word and go holler. He was on me every night, but I never turned around and looked at him.

It started before then, in spring training in Waycross, Georgia. When we went downtown, the bus would drop us off on the corner, and the white players went downtown, and we went to the black neighborhood. We were actually segregated as far as where we lived. But we all ate together. The Braves were a really good organization. They tried their best not to put too many guys in situations where they had to play in the South in bad cities.

Playing in the South was quite an experience. It's something that I don't think people have an idea about. That's why I have so much respect for Jackie Robinson as far as being a strong person, to endure what he had to go through. It must have been amazing on and off the field because I'm pretty sure guys were throwing at him all the time, I'm pretty sure he wasn't getting balls and strikes called properly.

I played in Austin, in the Texas League. There was one place in Amarillo, a bus station, where we would eat. You could only go eat in the back. But we stayed in all the same hotels, and we ate in most of the same restaurants. In Leesburg, in the Florida State League, there was one place across from the ballpark where we couldn't eat.

I carried myself in a manner where they'd see I wasn't a troublemaker. They could see I could play on a team and mix with other players. I would say I had a role in integrating society. I'd have to think so. As a manager, I must have given them [whites] a message that I could do that, too, without being conscious of doing that, by going out and just being myself. My mom always taught me to treat others the way you wanted to be treated, no matter what color you are. She never taught me to hate the color of anyone.

Ever since I was like five years old, I said to myself that I was going to be a baseball player. You can do anything you want to do if you want to do it bad enough. I live by this right now. I know I had a lot to overcome. I know I had to put [the racial insults] on the side and try not to listen to it and not worry about whether they were going to treat me as well as they were going to treat the other guy. If I show them I can play, then they're going to keep me around. Someone will end up liking you and giving you a chance.

What upsets me is with a lot of those restaurants in the South that I couldn't go into. My uncles, a good friend of mine, and my father fought in [World War II]. The people they fought against could probably go in quicker than I could. That upsets me. Otherwise, I don't hold a grudge on anybody. I treat people the way I like to be treated. It gets a little better, but it gets better slowly. It was not easy at times to keep your mouth shut, but that was all you could do. I just played a small role, and I was happy to do it. It's something I'm glad I was part of.

After reaching the majors to stay in 1969, Gaston went on to enjoy an eleven-year playing career in the big leagues, with the San Diego Padres and the Atlanta Braves. Cito Gaston spent nine years (1989–97) as manager of the Toronto Blue Jays, whom he led to World Series championships in 1992 and 1993, the first such titles won by an African American manager.

13 | Baseball and Civil Rights

The whites that were in the southern states were not used to seeing black and white people playing together. It was a shock for most people to see this. A lot of people were still not prepared to accept it. But it had to be done. Not only from a baseball standpoint. It had to be done for hotels, restaurants, for everything. Baseball was certainly instrumental in starting it. As much as people talk about what the civil rights workers did by marching in the streets, we did some things in baseball. We proved that given the opportunity, we could do the same things as anybody else could do. I'm very proud of what we accomplished. I'm very proud of what we went through.

—HENRY AARON, 1997

The 1950s marked a time of reform and resistance in the former Confederacy. Seminal civil rights events such as the Montgomery bus boycott and the *Brown v. Board of Education* decision signaled the revolutionary change that lay ahead for white and black southerners. Integration, with all its inherent promise and risk, was approaching, whether or not segregationists were ready to accept it.

Helping to lay the groundwork for such an ostensibly open society were young black men scattered throughout the South, in places like Danville, Virginia; Savannah, Georgia; Hot Springs, Arkansas; Lake Charles, Louisiana; Dallas, Texas; and Tulsa, Oklahoma. Not ministers or conventional civil rights activists, they were teenage or twenty-something baseball players. Their primary purpose for spending summers in these disparate southern communities was to burnish their skills and advance their careers, but they nonetheless played prominent roles in another, larger drama.

These men were among the earliest foot soldiers in the long struggle for equal rights. Before bus boycotts, protest marches, and KKK terror became front-page news, cities and towns were getting their first taste of desegregation in decidedly unrevolutionary settings—ballparks. It was on these stages that blacks and whites caught their first significant glimpses of equality between the races. Although southerners had seen African American entertainers, such as musicians, performing together, integrated baseball was strikingly different. Here, black and white were side by side on the field, playing as teammates, seemingly as equals. This was an extraordinary sight in a region almost uniformly segregated by race.

That baseball was the catalyst of such change was especially significant. In the 1950s, the game had the sports spotlight nearly all to itself. No other major-league sport came close to having its impact, exposure, and fan loyalty. Indeed, with minor-league teams located in hundreds of cities and towns across the nation, baseball could boast of touching the lives of millions of Americans in ways basketball or football teams could only dream about. All this gave baseball a unique power to touch hundreds of communities and influence events and attitudes across the nation.

The appearance of blacks on southern baseball diamonds sent powerful tides of empowerment through African American communities. When a black player could win a game with a home run and compete alongside the best white professionals, it became harder to accept or rationalize what had become as entrenched in the South as Spanish moss—the perception that blacks were inferior to whites. Despite segregation, despite being told through words and deeds that they were not as intelligent or talented as whites, African Americans now had powerful, objectively undeniable evidence that this old myth simply was not true.

For the first time, in Greenville, Mississippi; Durham, North Carolina; Newport News, Virginia; and elsewhere, African Americans united and agitated for change, demanding integrated ballpark accommodations. After seeing black players on neighboring teams, they clamored for African American players for their own local franchises. More often than not, these demands were satisfied, as increasing numbers of teams integrated and ballpark seating and other facilities opened up. In many places, this progress was made long before federal courts began systematically attacking segregation.

Southern racists were right about one thing: If Henry Aaron, Ed Charles, Percy Miller, Felipe Alou, and many others could work, compete, commiserate, and celebrate alongside white teammates, it was possible that such egalitarianism could be extended to other parts of society. This idea, previously scoffed at as mere fantasy, was harder to dismiss when blacks were besting whites in the world of athletic competition, where all that mattered was how well you could run, throw, and hit a ball.

Southern baseball integration helped soften racial prejudices, hardened by decades of segregation. Although they were not often acknowledged as participants in the war against segregation, the black men who appeared in the southern minor leagues from 1950 to 1964 nonetheless were combatants in this struggle. They overcame vile insults and degrading living conditions and gave blacks and whites a glimpse at what life could be like in a desegregated society.

ED CHARLES

There were a lot of social events involving the team that the larger community was involved in that began to open doors to us in the South. In Jacksonville, you began to integrate other areas because of your association with the baseball team. They might say, "We want you to go to this function or this charity event." But these areas had been closed before. You had a chance to interact with whites in various fields. It gave us a chance to know each other better. Once you get to know someone, you're not going to feel as threatened. You probably tend to be more compassionate toward that person. You reach a higher level of a relationship when you interact together.

There was one incident in Knoxville I'll never forget. There was this old southern gentleman. He was calling me everything. Everything that came out of his mouth was derogatory. You could hear him all over the ballpark. His voice just carried. He stayed on me throughout the game. He was slinging some mud at me. It just seemed, for some reason, that I had one of the best games that I can recall. You name it, I did it. Leaving the dugout to get to the clubhouse, we had to go under the stands. After the game, I was going through this gate to get to the clubhouse, and there was this old southern gentleman standing there. All kinds of thoughts went through my mind. I've got to pass by him. What's going to happen?

I made up my mind to ignore him and go on about my business. As I neared him, he stuck out his hand to shake mine. He said, "My God, nigger. You're one hell of a ballplayer." I just looked at him, shook my head, and kept going. But in his own way, he wanted to acknowledge my abilities. In his eyes, as he was raised from day one, blacks are inferior. This was the way you were supposed to treat blacks. This was the way you were supposed to refer to blacks. He had been taught all that. But he showed me something—that he was large enough, in his own ignorant way, to acknowledge what I did.

I could see that this was something that was ingrained in people. He was a victim of segregation, of the Jim Crow system, just as much as I was. That was a good example of what happens when people are brought together and get to know each other. Had baseball not provided that forum for him to see me on that particular Sunday, God knows if he would have ever made any move toward accepting blacks. Any forum that brings people together can lift the cloud of ignorance from all of us.

DON BUFORD

I think sports played a big part in desegregating a lot of areas, in a lot of hotels and in a lot of community type situations. Baseball [was] influential because you had a lot more teams, a lot more players, than the other sports. Baseball had to be very significant and influential in the desegregation of the segregated areas. I think that happened because you never really saw a baseball player get into any real difficulty. There were some situations, because we all faced them. We got harassed by the police officers, harassed by somebody else. I don't think you ever heard of anyone having a death or anything like that related to baseball.

In Savannah, Georgia, I'd take time for the kids. We'd sign autographs, give them balls and that kind of stuff. I'll never forget, there was this one youngster that came in and asked for an autograph. I wrote his name out, said best wishes, signed my name and et cetera. It just so happened, a few nights later, I found out the kid's the son of a police officer. The officer came up to me and said, "You know, I'll never forget you for what you did for my kid." It was very meaningful to him. He said, "You're human. You're nice people." To me, that was a tremendous feeling. That's everlasting. I think that was an influence, and hopefully that was happening a lot, not only with myself but with other players.

JOE DURHAM

Once the teams became integrated in the different leagues, there was the possibility of [widespread] integration someday. But it was hard to make changes. Some people didn't want to make changes. People said, "Well, we've got the [black players] in. There are enough black motels, hotels, in these areas to house these people and restaurants to feed them." Most teams traveled by their own bus, so you didn't have to worry about segregation on your bus. But sooner or later, they would have to get around to integrating the restaurants, hotels, because times had changed.

We were pioneers, that's for sure. There are a lot of things you'd like to [change] and hope the guys who come behind you follow instead of coming in with a hot head, because if you do, you're in trouble. Just go out and do your job. Forget about everything else except just remember one thing. The people up in the stands have paid their way in. If they want to be ignorant enough to call you all kinds of names, let them do so. You can't let that sort of thing get close to you. If it does, you can just wipe out the season, because every town you go into will be practically the same thing. You have to do your job.

Sometimes doing your job under some of these conditions can be kind of horrible, but that's part of the job. It was, in those days. But you've got to remember that people suffered long before you did. There were some tough times. Somebody would take all your freedom and you can't do anything. They'd put you on a boat, cross the seas, and you'd have nothing to do. Times can't be as bad as your great-great-great-grandparents had them. You have to think, "You've got to give a better effort, withstanding all the things people could throw at you."

BILLY WILLIAMS

You didn't associate with whites, and they didn't associate with you. Growing up in Mississippi or something, whites weren't around blacks. They didn't go to school together. Every time we started to play football against each other, you'd hear the police sirens, and they'd stop us. As kids, you didn't mind doing it, until they tell you, "You're a segregated community and we're going to keep you segregated."

When you can see black and white ballplayers on the field, it really helped the racial situation. When you can look out and see the team play together and win and see guys from different places enjoying themselves, it lets society know that, "Hey, if they can do that, why can't we?" It was just a matter of getting to know that person. You get to know that individual, know where he's coming from, know the type of person he is. You're not shy or afraid of that person. You get to know him."

During the 1960s, Julian Bond dedicated himself to fighting for equal rights for African Americans in the South. As a student at Morehouse College in 1960, Bond cofounded the Committee on Appeal for Human Rights, the student organization that helped achieve integration of Atlanta's movie theaters, lunch counters, and municipal parks.

Bond later became the communications director of the Student Non-violent Coordinating Committee, heading SNCC's publicity department and working on voter registration drives in rural Georgia, Mississippi, Alabama, and Arkansas. In 1965, he was elected to the Georgia House of

Representatives, which voted not to seat Bond because of his opposition to the Vietnam War.

Julian Bond won two more elections but was again denied his place in the legislature. In December 1966, the United States Supreme Court ordered the Georgia House to allow Bond to assume his position in the legislature, ruling that his colleagues' decision not to seat him was unconstitutional. In 1974, he was elected to the Georgia Senate. When he left the Senate in January 1987, Julian Bond had been elected to public office more times than any other black Georgian in history. Since leaving public service, Julian Bond has remained active in the causes he championed in the 1960s. Today he is a Distinguished Scholar in residence at American University and a faculty member in the Department of History at the University of Virginia. In 1998, Bond was elected chairman of the NAACP.

Jackie Robinson showed white America that here's a black guy who can compete in what had been a white sport. He could do all the things that the sport demands, and he could do them at an excellent level. He was quiet, reserved, and he took all kinds of abuse and kept on coming. To black Americans, it confirmed what we always believed—given an opportunity, we could compete. He became a hero. For white Americans, it dispelled long-held beliefs. It was the important event of its time.

As far as black minor leaguers in the South, I would say they had the same effect. Here's a guy doing something no one like him had ever done before. The result would be the same as with Jackie Robinson. Blacks would say, "We knew we could do it—hitting the ball, catching the ball, running around the diamond. He's doing what we knew we could do all along, and this is just confirmation." For whites, some of them might have said, "He's okay. He's our guy. He's on our team, making a contribution. Maybe I've been wrong about some things. I'm not going to change overnight, be instantly transformed into an integrationist. Maybe I should rethink some things." It is undeniable that these prominent black athletes do so much to temper attitudes. They don't eradicate them; they don't make them disappear; but they do temper them. The athletes played an enormous role in breaking down barriers.

I remember when black players [Johnny Lewis and John Glenn] came to the Atlanta Crackers [in 1962]. They became little miniheros in some circles. This guy [Glenn] was invited to parties, and I met him two or three times. Black Atlanta welcomed him. Black people thought this guy was like a little Jackie Robinson. I can remember being awed by him, being awed by his putting up with whatever he had to do, this and his skill.

When I was seventeen or eighteen, in Atlanta, I can remember people pointing out heroes. They'd say, "There's the president of the NAACP. That's Reverend Smith, who filed a lawsuit against this or that." In the everyday world, these people achieved some kind of heroic proportion. These athletes are operating in this larger, public sphere where whites see them, too. They're performing in an arena where it's merit, merit, merit; that's all there is to it. You can either do it or you can't. They're daily showing white people that we can do it. That's just awfully confirming, uplifting, and thrilling. Even though I wasn't a fan, you couldn't escape hearing about it. The black press was trumpeting these things. It was a tremendous psychic boost that was more than just symbolic.

These guys embodied the race in their own ways, in their own parts. If they did well, they lifted the race. But a lot of these men weren't really race men. They were just athletes. They weren't activists in any kind of way. They didn't have to be. By what they did, they became activists, champions of the race, just by hitting and catching the ball. They're not political figures in the sense that they're doing anything except what they do for a living.

Sports generally, and baseball particularly because it was *the* sport, had a role to play in integrating society. People developing relationships with their teams and their players—it's so basic that you have to know that someone is being affected by what they see being played out on this field before them. They've invested so much in it. If they're white, and something new comes into the equation, and they make an adjustment to it without saying "I'm never coming to another game," and stay and cheer, they're affected by that. Blacks who have been not coming or who have been coming and are relegated to the corner of the grandstand, are affected too. Those who are not there are going to read about it, follow it at some distance, are also affected by it. Human beings are affected by these things.

Born in Montgomery, Alabama, Paul Delaney was much more interested in major-league baseball than in the minor leagues. He felt alienated from his local, all-white team, the Montgomery Rebels, whose very name evoked thoughts of slavery, the Civil War, and Jim Crow. Delaney maintained his distance from the Rebels until he left Montgomery in 1950 to attend Ohio State University. It was only when Dixie's minor-league teams began integrating that Paul Delaney felt, as many other southern blacks did, that America's game was finally living up to its billing as the national pastime.

He returned to the south in 1958, when he went to work for the *Atlanta Daily World,* starting a journalism career that has spanned four decades. Delaney has worked as a reporter for the *Dayton Daily News*, the *Washington Star,* and the *New York Times*. After joining the *Times* in 1969, he became an editor on the paper's national desk. He eventually assumed the position of senior editor in newsroom administration.

Delaney left the *New York Times* in 1992 to assume the position of Journalism Department chairman at the University of Alabama. After a five-year tenure in academia, Paul Delaney returned to journalism, becoming editorial page editor for *Our World News* in 1996.

My first introduction to baseball was radio. Jackie Robinson, naturally, piqued my interest. I fell in love with the Dodgers. Then, I read about the local team, the Montgomery Rebels, in the local paper all the time. I didn't fall in love with the team. I didn't like the name, the Rebels. I didn't like the fact that it was all white. The stands were segregated. It was a complete turnoff.

Looking back, I think there was a feeling of alienation from baseball, of bitterness, especially living in a place where segregation was rigidly enforced, where whites put blacks in their place and kept them there. All of that is tied into my rejection of local baseball. It's tied in with segregation, to the harshness of white rule. My feelings about anything local were influenced by this kind of thing.

I don't ever recall cheering for the Montgomery Rebels. Probably, I cheered for the opponents. I didn't react to home runs by the Montgomery Rebels. I didn't react to any winning ceremonies after the game. I didn't participate. I didn't rejoice. My experience was muted by the local social problems.

Before I left Montgomery in 1950, I had never experienced integration. I had very little contact with whites. If I had stayed in Montgomery through the integration of baseball, this would have changed my feelings about Montgomery. The experience would have been comparable to Jackie Robinson's entry into baseball. If the Rebels had integrated earlier, I would have become much more of a Rebels fan and a fan of baseball. I would have gone to the ballpark enthusiastically.

[African American] men and boys who fancied themselves becoming great stars could not dream that in Montgomery. The fantasies were based on players—Jackie Robinson, Larry Doby—who were far away. They were up north. To a little boy growing up in Montgomery and fantasizing about becoming a star, I could not do that locally. You didn't even think about becoming a ballplayer. When integration came, it planted the seed. That was an extremely powerful symbol.

Baseball integration gave some hope that this rigidity [segregation] was going to change. When I left in 1950, I had no hope. I thought this place would never change. These white folks will never give it up. If baseball had integrated earlier, I would have seen a crack in the wall. I would have been more optimistic and would have had a more positive feeling about Montgomery and the prospects of integrating society. If they integrate sports, they can integrate other things.

The hard-liners knew that any opening would be the end of segregation. They knew that if they let up on baseball, what would be next? Schools, public accommodations—where would it end? I would rate baseball integration very highly. If that had not happened, the rest would have been delayed. Baseball integration softened the South. Even rigid segregationists had to think, "Here are some baseball players, some folks whom I didn't think could think and execute on the baseball field. And they're doing it." Maybe they weren't convinced of equality, but somewhere in the back of their minds, there would be the thought that these guys are doing well, these guys can play, sometimes even better than whites. It might not change their minds that we're not all equal, but it has to have some effect on their psyche, just raising some doubt in their mind. Happening in the early '50s, maybe there was this unconscious influence that baseball had on even unsuspecting, rigid segregationists. We opened the door a crack, and the Supreme Court decision in '54 opened it more. It was validation of the fears of many southern whites.

Think what would have happened if southern teams and southern cities had Branch Rickeys. They would have been influential. Imagine the influence they would have had in the Southern Association—for example, in Tennessee, from Chattanooga all the way over to Memphis. It's possible they could have softened their cities to the extent that the resistance which eventually occurred might not have been as great. It would have gotten people mentally ready for social integration. But in most cities, people gave in to the primal instincts of racism and became losers.

Born the son of sharecroppers in Troy, Alabama, John Lewis eventually became one of the leaders of the civil rights movement. In 1961, he was a Freedom Rider, riding southern buses to protest continued segregation of bus terminals. Three years later, he was named chairman of the Student Nonviolent Coordinating Committee, a post he held through 1966. He was one of the planners as well as a keynote speaker for the historic March on Washington in August 1963. In 1964, Lewis coordinated SNCC efforts in Mississippi to organize voter registration drives in that state's Freedom Summer.

In one of the watershed events of the civil rights era, John Lewis led 525 marchers across the Edmund Pettus Bridge in Selma, Alabama, on 7 March 1965 in an effort to secure voting rights for African Americans. They were met and attacked by Alabama state troopers in a violent clash that came to be known as Bloody Sunday. This march helped shame Congress into passing the Voting Rights Act of 1965.

John Lewis was elected to the United States Congress in 1986. He continues to serve today as the representative of Georgia's Fifth Congressional District.

While growing up in the South, John Lewis was a baseball fan. Like many young African Americans of his time, he closely followed the achievements of Jackie Robinson and other black major leaguers. As an African American southerner, Lewis was also acutely aware of black minor leaguers who desegregated teams throughout the South. He recalls how much their presence and accomplishments meant to him, other southern blacks of the 1950s and 1960s, and the struggle for civil rights.

> When I was growing up in the rural South in the '40s and '50s, I was very much a baseball fan. I played a little softball with cousins and schoolmates. I can remember very well—I was seven years old in 1947—when Jackie Robinson was accepted by the Brooklyn Dodgers. We followed the drama of baseball. In those early years, we couldn't afford a television. We listened to the radio. We were glued to the radio to follow Jackie Robinson and, after him, the other black baseball players who broke down segregation in baseball.
>
> I was not aware so much of the names of certain players, but I had heard of the teams. All of our news for the most part came from the radio and the local newspaper, the *Montgomery Advertiser*. I knew of the team in Birmingham. I knew of the Crackers in Atlanta. I knew of the team in Nashville and in other places throughout the South.
>
> For the great majority of blacks in the South, the act of a black man, whether it was Jackie Robinson or others, and later, black men playing in the segregated South, created a great sense of

pride. You heard over and over again, "Did you see what that black man did?" "Did you hear, did you read what that black player did?" It was a black man who struck someone out, who hit a home run, who stole the base. It was seeing black people in positions that people had never seen them before. It created a sense of pride and, especially for blacks in the South, a great sense of hope and optimism, that if people can play baseball together in the segregated South, then, just maybe, we can desegregate other areas of American life.

Baseball did create the climate, the environment, and set the stage for other walls to come tumbling down. It helped to free and liberate the minds and attitudes of many people in the South and throughout the country. It said to the white South that black players could play baseball and be successful. If they could play baseball, they could do other things. If we can accept a guy hitting the ball, running the bases, and being successful at it, then we can accept people in other areas. You see people out there hollering and supporting their team and the player just happened to be black. People accepted that.

Baseball paved the way for what came on a few years later—the Montgomery bus boycott, the sit-ins, the Freedom Rides, and then you had the Supreme Court decision in 1954. You had all these things coming together in less than a decade, from the late '40s to the late '50s. It was a great feeling, hearing about the accomplishments of some of these individuals. In 1954, I was fourteen years old at the time of the Supreme Court decision. You had people involved in sports, and you had the decision. A few months later, you had the Montgomery bus boycott, a whirlwind of change all around. You knew something was happening.

The black baseball players, in a real sense, were making a contribution. They were playing a role. They were not necessarily boycotting buses or walking a picket line, sitting in at a lunch counter, or going on a Freedom Ride, but what they did in a very quiet and dignified manner on the field was just as powerful, just as significant. It's not just having an impact on the larger society but also with their fellow players. It created a sense of community, a sense of family. Many of us years later came to believe that if people can play and get along on the field as a family, as a team, just maybe we can do it off the field. People saw what they did, and it carried over into the larger community.

It was impossible to separate baseball from the larger community. It was part of the larger society. You couldn't say, "We're going to integrate a baseball team and have black players," and just sort of hold it there. In a sense, the genie was out of the bottle. We had to go forward.

Baseball played a significant role in helping to open up American society. Baseball was like an actor in a big drama. Different organizations, institutions, individuals, had a role to play. Baseball played that role very well. Long before the sit-ins, the Freedom Rides, the Montgomery bus boycott, you had black and white men playing the game of baseball, very visible. It was America's pastime. People identified with it. It was this game of baseball that pulled people together. It didn't matter if you were black or white, young or old, rich or poor. If you believed in a particular player or team, you got up there and hollered. It was my team playing.

Whether it was the political climate or the lack of enlightened political and business leadership, and to some degree the social climate, some communities resisted the integration of baseball. Those cities, like Birmingham, paid a price. Birmingham paid a heavy price. Little Rock paid a heavy price. Atlanta tried to follow the path of least resistance. Birmingham, years ago, during the '50s, was in competition with Atlanta. Atlanta just surpassed it and went on.

It carried over into the larger community. Places that came on board and didn't resist baseball integration, or resisted in a very moderate way, had the same experience with their larger society. It was true in Atlanta and in other places in the South. There, you had a different type of leadership when it came to desegregating baseball, schools, lunch counters, or restaurants.

When the height of the civil rights movement came along,

baseball had conditioned and had made people much readier to buy into this idea of an integrated society, an interracial community of what Dr. King would call "the beloved community," an open society. Baseball was a unifier. Maybe one day we will be able to measure the contribution that baseball made toward desegregation of the South. It helped to open and liberate people from stereotypes and attitudes. It broke down walls. It ended those feelings that somehow people could not be together. It had a profound effect on southerners. It was more than race relations. It was just pure human relations.

11 JULY 1953

One Negro fan expressed the attitude of others when he said: "They call these segregated seats for us, 'separate but equal.' That's the same story they give us about everything in the South that is operated on a segregated basis. They are separate, but certainly not equal . . . The day is over when they can take our money and shove us aside in some hovel. We are glad there is a Negro player in the Carolina League. But we aren't so glad that we're going to flock to the ball parks and accept segregation. We'll continue to sit home until the situation is changed."—*Pittsburgh Courier*

Bibliography

Newspapers

Arkansas Democrat

Arkansas Gazette

Atlanta Daily World

Atlanta Journal

Baltimore Afro-American

Baton Rouge Morning Advocate

Baton Rouge State Times

Birmingham News

Birmingham Post-Herald

Birmingham World

Daily Oklahoman

Dallas Express

Dallas Morning News

Danville Bee

Danville Register

Durham Morning Herald

Durham News and Observer

Florida Times-Union

Greenville Delta Democrat Times

Hot Springs Sentinel-Record

Houston Post

Jackson Clarion-Ledger

Lake Charles American Press

Knoxville Journal

Los Angeles Times

Louisiana Weekly

Louisville Courier-Journal

Memphis Commercial Appeal

Memphis Press Scimitar

Meridian Star

Mobile Press Register

Montgomery Advertiser

Nashville Banner

Natchez Democrat

New Orleans Times-Picayune

New York Times

Norfolk Journal and Guide

Norfolk Virginian Pilot

Palm Beach Post

Pittsburgh Courier

Raleigh News and Observer

Richmond Times-Dispatch

St. Petersburg Times

San Antonio Express

Savannah Morning News

Shreveport Times

Spartanburg Herald

Spartanburg Journal

Sporting News

The State

Tampa Tribune

Tulsa Daily World

Books

Aaron, Hank, with Lonnie Wheeler. *I Had a Hammer: The Hank Aaron Story*. New York: HarperCollins, 1991.

Adelson, Bruce, et al. *The Minor League Baseball Book*. New York: Macmillan USA, 1995.

Branch, Taylor. *Parting the Waters: America in the King Years, 1954–1963*. New York: Simon and Schuster, 1988.

Carter, Craig, ed. *Daguerreotypes*, 8th ed. St Louis, MO: The Sporting News, 1990.

Clark, Dick, and Larry Lester, eds. *The Negro Leagues Book*. Cleveland, OH: The Society for American Baseball Research, 1994.

Dolson, Frank. *Beating the Bushes: Life in the Minor Leagues*. South Bend, IN: Icarus Press, 1982.

Filchia, Peter, *Professional Baseball Franchises: From the Abbeville Athletics to the Zanesville Indians*. New York: Facts on File, 1993.

Johnson, Lloyd, and Miles Wolff, eds. *The Encyclopedia of Minor League Baseball*. Durham, NC: Baseball America, Inc., 1993.

Karst, Gene, and Martin J. Jones, eds. *Who's Who in Professional Baseball*. New Rochelle, NY: Arlington House, 1973.

McCarthy, Kevin M. *Baseball in Florida*. Sarasota, FL: Pineapple Press, 1996.

Moffi, Larry, and Jonathan Kronstadt. *Crossing the Line: Black Major Leaguers, 1947–1959*. Iowa City: University of Iowa Press, 1994.

O'Neal, Bill. *The Southern League: Baseball in Dixie, 1885–1994*. Austin, TX: Eakin Press, 1994.

Riley, James A. *The Biographical Encyclopedia of the Negro Baseball Leagues*. New York: Carroll & Graf Publishers, 1994.

Sumner, James L. *Separating the Men from the Boys: The First Half-Century of the Carolina League*. Winston-Salem, NC: John F. Blair Publisher, 1994.

Thorn, John, and Pete Palmer, eds. *Total Baseball,* 3rd ed. New York: HarperCollins, 1993.

Tygiel, Jules. *Baseball's Great Experiment: Jackie Robinson and His Legacy.* New York: Oxford University Press, 1983.

Articles

Bisher, Furman. "What about the Negro Athlete in the South?" *Sport* (May 1956).

———. "The Sports Revolution in the South." *Sport* (September 1964).

Bowman, Larry. "Breaking Barriers: David Hoskins and Integration of the Texas League." *Legacies* 3, no. 1 (spring 1991).

Collections

Department of Archives and Manuscripts, Linn-Henley Research Library, Birmingham Public Library, Birmingham, Ala.: Papers of Mayor James W. Morgan; Papers of Mayor Arthur J. Hanes; Papers of T. Eugene "Bull" Connor.

National Archives: Court file in the case of James C. Tugerson v. Al Haraway, et al., United States District Court for the Western District of Arkansas, Hot Springs Division, Civil Action No. 558.